DEMOCRACY AND ASSOCIATION

Contents

Tables

Acknowledgments _____

THIS BOOK originated with a paper presented to the Critical Theory Roundtable at Saint Louis University in September 1997. The paper was overly long and dense, and it became obvious that it was not, in fact, a paper but rather an outline for a book. Nonetheless, I persisted in presenting the paper in successive formats at Columbia University, the American Political Science Association meetings, and the Georgetown University Conference on Civil Society and Governance in the United States. I am indebted to those who suffered the paper and kindly offered the many suggestions and criticisms that guided development of the book. They include Mark Brown, Josep Colomer, Lisa Disch, Michael Foley, Nannette Funk, Carol Gould, Virginia Hodgkinson, Josh Mitchell, Robert Putnam, Steve Salkever, Graham Smith, Ric Uslaner, Iris Marion Young, and Ross Zucker. I am especially indebted to Clyde Wilcox, Jon Van Til, Nancy Rosenblum, and Stuart White, each of whom read the entire manuscript. Clyde offered numerous insights from the perspective of religious associations, one of his many areas of expertise. Jon provided invaluable suggestions and examples from the perspective of sociological theory as well as from the burgeoning field of "third sector" research. Nancy and Stuart both provided exceptionally knowledgable, insightful, and extensive comments, suggestions, and criticisms. Jane Mansbridge and Joe Fletcher bear some of the responsibility for the gestures the book makes toward social science. By example, both convinced me that it is possible, desirable, important, and interesting to craft political theory so that it might meet social science halfway. Those who have offered their time and conversation are in large part responsible for whatever strengths this book has, although I remain liable for the many weaknesses that remain. The Graduate School of Georgetown University provided a research fellowship for the 1998 fall semester that enabled me to expand the paper into a book. I am grateful to Gerry Mara, associate dean of the Graduate School, for his encouragement and support. The Ford Foundation Project on Civil Society and Governance in the United States, under the direction of Virginia Hodgkinson, provided summer funding that allowed me to refine some of the ideas in this book as they relate to the Ford Foundation initiative. Ann Wald, former editor-in-chief at Princeton University Press, provided advice even before the book was written, and then guided the manuscript through review and revision. Ian Malcom, editor at Princeton University Press, has seen through production with diligence and good judgment. Cindy Crumrine copyedited the manuscript with care and competence. Mark Mitchell prepared the index with competence and speed. My daughters, Hannah and Victoria, are responsible for alerting me to the thicket of associations that surrounds the Arlington Public Schools. Last but not least, I have depended upon the love, indulgence, friendship, and support of my wife, Janet E. Joy, daughters, and father, Charles E. Warren.

Arlington, Virginia
September 1999

DEMOCRACY AND ASSOCIATION

One

Introduction

WITHIN democratic theory a remarkable consensus is emerging around Tocqueville's view that the virtues and viability of a democracy depend on the robustness of its associational life. The consensus is rooted in a renewed appreciation for the limits of states and markets as means for making collective decisions and organizing collective actions. Associations promise other ways of getting things done, from supporting pubic spheres and providing representation to cultivating the virtues of citizens and providing alternative forms of governance. When institutions are properly designed, according to the consensus, associations provide the social substance of liberal-democratic procedures, underwrite the very possibility of markets, and provide means of resistance and alternatives when states or markets fail. Moreover, when associational life is multifaceted and cuts across identities, communities, geographies, and other potential cleavages, it provides a dense social infrastructure enabling pluralistic societies to attain a vibrant creativity and diversity within a context of multiple but governable conflicts.[1] A robust associational life may enable more democracy in more domains of life, while forming and deepening the capacities and dispositions of democratic citizenship. Finally, for those committed to political equality, associations promise the means for voice for those disfavored by existing distributions of power and money.[2]

There are, of course, many other reasons to value associational life. Most if not all of the goods related to sociability, intimacy, socialization, and freedom have associative dimensions and conditions. My interest in associational life here, however, is somewhat more narrowly focused on its democratic effects. I use the term *effects* because associations formed for a variety of goods and purposes may serve democratic goods and purposes as well. To be sure, there are often trade-offs between democratic and other kinds of goods. The extent to which freedom and democracy trade off, for example, is a staple of liberal political thought. But there are many cases in which a single purpose produces a variety of effects that, although different, do not trade off against one another, as when a nonpolitical association develops skills of organization that can be put to political use in other venues. And sometimes the trade-offs among associational effects are internal to democracy, a problem that has gone almost unremarked in the literature. The solidarity required for effective political voice and representation, for example, may work to dampen dissent and deliberation within the association, and thus limit members' experiences of dealing with conflict by deliberative means.

Given the current state of democratic theory, however, it is virtually impossible to relate these democratic hopes and expectations to the kinds of associational life we have or might have in the future. Associational life may be moving to the center of many democratic theories today, but there has been relatively little theoretical work that specifies

- *what* we should expect associations to do for democracies or
- *why* we should expect associations to carry out these democratic functions.

This book is a modest attempt to think about and theorize these two questions.

The most important reasons to attend to the associational terrain of democracy have less to do with democratic theory, however, than with social and political changes that are surpassing its conceptual capacities. Our received democratic theories were crafted during an era in which the nation-state was consolidating and had become the primary locus of nonmarket collective action. Under these circumstances, the business of doing democratic theory was relatively simple—at least compared to what it has become. Democratic theorists could focus on questions of representation, inclusion, distributions of state and state-sanctioned powers, and the characters of citizens. These traditional issues in democratic theory are hardly obsolete. Strong constitutional states are necessary to robust democracies, remaining central agents in achieving distributive justice, enforcing rights, providing security, and carrying out many other functions necessary to democracy. But they are now less encompassing of politics and collective action: the locus, domain, and nature of politics is changing, becoming more extensive and many times more complex.[3] The era of the nation-state is not gone. But the forces and capacities distinctive of the state are increasingly overlaid by numerous other forces and contingencies, so much so that the terrain of politics is no longer focused solely by state-centered institutions, organizations, and movements. Nor, with changing modes of production, technology, and communication, is the landscape of economic interests as it was even a few decades ago. Combine these changes with an increase in identity politics and other postmodern features of political culture, and we can see that we are now faced with the very generic problem of rethinking the nature and location of collective action.[4]

The new prominence of associations—and the need for a democratic theory of association—needs to be understood broadly within this context, which involves four distinct although interrelated features. In different ways, each pushes the question of association to the foreground.

Globalization

Numerous forces are now pushing toward interdependencies among nation-states, including the development of global markets in finances, capital investment, labor, manufacturing, and services. There is an absolute increase in the numbers of immigrants and refugees flowing across borders. Environmental degradation likewise flows across borders, in many cases producing global effects. Global security alliances are in flux, as state-based actors such as NATO seek to redefine their missions in the aftermath of the Cold War. At the same time, new forms of communication are enabling new global publics, especially in the areas of human rights and environmental issues. There are new global associations as well as new transnational political regimes such as the European Union (EU) and the North American Free Trade Agreement (NAFTA) labor and environmental riders. Each such development means that states lose some of their control over their resources and populations, a condition that can limit the extent to which democratic self-rule can be achieved through the state. But these same developments can weaken the powers of predatory states, while opening new, global venues of democracy.[5]

Differentiation

Late-modern societies reproduce themselves through differentiated systems and sectors, each with its own distinct logics, purposes, criteria, and inertia. At the highest level of abstraction, states are differentiated from markets, with states attending to matters of social order through law and administration and markets organizing production and consumption via the medium of money. States and markets are in turn differentiated from systems of social reproduction located in families, schools, religious institutions, and other social groups. Late-modern societies likewise involve specialized systems for the reproduction of knowledge and culture located in universities, sheltered government research programs, and institutions devoted to arts and culture. More generally, differentiation enhances capacities for segmented collective action, not only owing to the advantages of specialization, but because distinct sectors develop their own norms and criteria. Markets respond to effective demand, art responds to aesthetic criteria, states work within the domain of positive law and administrative law, science develops factual claims, families cultivate primary socialization and intimacy, and so on. At the same time, differentiation tends to politicize society in ways that constrain these enhanced capacities. In differentiated societies, states do not control the resources necessary to the reproduction of society. Ironically, perhaps a measure of the success of liberal-democratic constitutionalism is the extent to which capacities for collective action migrate into society. But these same developments shift political conflict into society in ways that exceed the capacities of state institutions to mediate. In addition, differentiation fuels coordination difficulties—not just because of the lack of agents with capacities to coordinate, but also because the criteria embedded within sectors are often incommensurable. For example, socialization within families often conflicts with demands of the market; art for art's sake can conflict with moral socialization; market-driven demands for technology can conflict with pure science; and ethics of duty cultivated by religious and secular moral codes can conflict with the instrumental reasoning typical of markets and government bureaucracies. Differentiation thus increases sectoral capacities for collective action, while also increasing the zones of political conflict and undermining political responsibility. The state's control over coercive resources makes it a key player—maybe even the *ultimate* player[6]—but it increasingly lacks capacities to respond to political conflict, let alone engage in global planning.

Complexity

While increasing differentiation increases capacities, it also increases the complexity of collective actions. As Ulrich Beck has argued, the era in which collective actions could be conceived on the *modern* model—the application of rationally developed and monitored plans to deal with social problems—is over. Large-scale collective actions within complex environments produce unintended consequences, which in turn politicize their environments in reactive ways. Owing to the unanticipated side effects of engineering-based models of social change (for example, the costs of monoculture and pesticides in food production, dysfunctional neighborhoods resulting from planned urban renewal, birth defects caused by new medicines, and stockpiled nuclear wastes), there is a broadly based public skepticism about large-scale planning—what in a similar spirit James Scott refers to as the unmasked pretensions of "high modernity."[7] We have, in Beck's terms, entered into an era of risk avoidance.[8] In a "risk society," collective actions are accompanied by political calculations that distribute risk according to the constituencies that are mobilized by any given plan. Risk consciousness tends to focus on complexity and contingency, increasing the potential political opposition to any given collective action. As Claus Offe puts it, "The larger the horizon of 'actually' possible options becomes, the more difficult grows the problem of establishing reflexive countertendencies which would make reasonably sure that one's own action remains compatible with the 'essential' premises of the other affected spheres of action."[9] This "absence of concern for consequences" is crisis inducing and erodes tolerance for modernization processes.[10] In Beck's terms, political institutions have become subject to an increasing "congestion": mobilization around distributions of risk produces an "involuntary deceleration" of the political capacities of governments as "various groups and levels of decision-making . . . mobilize the legal means of the state against one another."[11]

Pluralization and Reflexivity

These developments are intertwined with changing patterns of individuation. Owing to their differentiation, complexity, and fluidity, modern societies array multiple biographical choices before individuals. As with other developments, this one is paradoxical as well. On the one hand, individuals are subject to the late-modern condition of choice. Choice cannot, as it were, be refused, nor can the responsibility that accompanies choice. And yet, paradoxically, individuals' capacities to be responsible for the consequences of their choices are diminished by the complex and fluid contexts within which they are made. Add to this the fact that choices and risks are unequally distributed, and we can see how protean, postmodern personalities can coexist with closed, fundamentalist personalities, produced by slightly different locations and experiences within the same kind of society.[12] Identity politics is, in part, the result of the kind of society that raises—indeed, forces—the question Who am I? and in the process induces individuals to discover and think about how their social locations interact with their race, ethnicity, gender, age, religion, profession, regional attachment, and lifestyle. Insofar as this pluralism of identities is not merely a matter of interesting difference, it is the result of raised consciousness of differential distributions of risks—injustices, if you will. The political consequences are ambiguous. On the one hand, the increased reflexivity provoked by these circumstances provides the space for ethical growth in politics.[13] Only reflexively conscious individuals can ask the political questions (as Max Weber put them) What should we do? and How should we live? In this sense, politics permeates individuation as never before, as feminists noted two decades ago with the slogan "the personal is political." On the other hand, the persistence of choice can also make the temptations of fundamentalist identities more irresistible, which in turn can produce a politics within which little reciprocity or compromise is possible.[14]

Paradoxically, then, late-modern societies cultivate capacities for self-rule at the same time that they dislocate the institutions through which these capacities might be realized. As Claus Offe notes in commenting on the changing fortunes of parties, legislatures, and other familiar political actors, "What turns out to be surprisingly and essentially contested is the answer to the question 'who is in charge?' "[15] I am not going to argue here that associations in general provide new locuses of political agency—or that by extension they provide, in general, new locations and meanings for democracy. No such generalization could be meaningful in today's environment, given the extensive diversity of associational forms, and given the fact that their capacities are quite different from those of states and markets. Rather, the question of associational life provides a more modest take on democratic possibilities: it provides an opening to the domain of questions we need to ask if we are to grasp the potentials and dangers of the changing terrain of democracy.[16] The question Who is in charge? will begin to make sense only if disaggregated. The topic of association is a key trajectory of disaggregation, one that will allow us to put reasonably precise questions about whether and how these new patterns of politicization might admit of democratic possibilities.

The relationship between democracy and association stands out from a normative perspective as well. Associational life is distinctive as a linkage between the normative and conflictual dimensions of politics—a linkage that has always defined the heart and soul of democracy. If we resist for the moment limiting what counts as an "association" (say, by speaking only of secondary associations, voluntary associations, and the like), we can see that questions about associational life return us to those defining features of politics that enable democracy. The concept of association evokes the possibilities of collective action, but in a way that retains social (as opposed to legal/bureaucratic or market) modes of mediation among people, through language, norms, shared purposes, and agreements. The concept of association thus connects the normative questions that define politics—What should we do? and How should we live?—to the social and linguistic media that enable these questions to be asked, discussed, and decided. In this sense, as John Dewey appreciated, democracy is closer to associational life in spirit and ethos than it is to any other means of organization.[17] States, for example, can embody these definitive questions only encumbered by its systematic functions and their legal-administrative modes of organization—although they can use their resources to structure associative venues within which these questions might live. Markets displace such questions: there is no "we" in a market, and therefore no structural possibility of collective self-rule, but only an aggregate of individual preferences and firms responding to these preferences—although democracy can often live within such market-oriented organizations. Insofar as democracy evokes the ideal of collective self-rule; insofar as self-rule evokes decision making with the possibility of normative content; insofar as democracy evokes the collective consideration of future purposes, democracy regenerates itself through its *associative* medium, however necessary state and market modes of organization. Of course, there is nothing new about these ideas in themselves: liberal constitutionalism has always been based on the premise that states must structure associative venues for political judgment—parliaments, for example. What is new, rather, is the possibility that democracy might, via its associative media, expand within and beyond its current state-centered venues. The resurgence of the interest in associations across the ideological spectrum draws on this generic democratic idea.

Given the current state of democratic theory, however, it is virtually impossible to relate even these generic democratic hopes and expectations to the kinds of associational life we have or might have in the future. No doubt our suspicions should be aroused by the breadth of the current consensus about the democratic contributions of associations. Of course, an authentic consensus would be a remarkable achievement. But it is difficult to gauge the extent of consensus, owing to numerous conceptual and normative differences, not least about the meanings of "democracy," but also about what constitutes an association and its virtues, what the domain of associational life entails, and—perhaps most importantly— what the nature of the society is within which these associative relations are conceived.

Thus Michael Sandel, Robert Bellah, and other civic republicans have emphasized the impact of associations on the civic virtues.[18] Influenced by civic republicanism, Robert Putnam's important *Making Democracy Work* argued that in Italy successful democratic governance and associational life are interdependent. Putnam's work has spurred a wave of debates and focused an increasing amount of empirical work on the nature and effects of associational life in amassing "social capital"—the dispositions of reciprocity and trust that enable collective actions.[19] Nancy Rosenblum's *Membership and Morals*—the first careful theoretical account of associational life—details the multiple ways in which the diverse landscape of association contributes to pluralistic democracy through multiple effects upon character.[20] The work on political culture within the American pluralist tradition represented most prominently by Gabriel Almond and Sidney Verba, *The Civic Culture*, has not only regained its stature, but has combined with a normative emphasis upon democratic participation in an impressive survey by Verba, Schlozman, and Brady, *Voice and Equality: Civic Voluntarism in American Politics*.[21] Liberals have rediscovered associational life as well. John Rawls's hopes for the moral effects of association expressed in *A Theory of Justice* have gained rare mention until recently.[22] In addition, there has been renewed attention within the field of constitutional law to the fact that the U.S. Constitution does not explicitly protect freedom of association—a fact that sits uneasily with the liberal view that freedom of association is an intrinsic value.[23]

In a different vein, critical theorists who favor radical democracy, such as Jürgen Habermas, Jean Cohen and Andrew Arato, Claus Offe, Ulrich Preuss, and Ulrich Beck, have emphasized the ways in which liberal rights—traditionally understood as protections from the state—may also be understood as constituting a society within which associations can develop distinctive means of collective judgment and action. Associations can provide the social infrastructure of robust democracy by enabling direct self-governance, providing venues for participating in public conversations and opinions, and securing influence over states and markets.[24] Finally, there is an emerging school of "associative democrats"—most prominently Paul Hirst, Joshua Cohen, and Joel Rogers—who see associations as means of unburdening the state and revitalizing smaller-scale, functionally delineated arenas of democratic decision making.[25] In most cases, growing interest in associations tracks the rediscovery of the political weight of civil society—a sectoral rubric I shall explain but do not use here for reasons elaborated in chapter 3.

Moreover, the sheer complexity of the associational landscape provides ample opportunity for selective exemplifications of associative virtues. The *Nonprofit Almanac* lists 576,133 tax-exempt organizations, excluding religious organizations, as of 1995. These associations are distributed over virtually every social need, identity, and function, and represent 645 identifiable kinds.[26] Add to this count religious associations, groups that lack tax-exempt status owing to their political purposes, the numerous groups that simply lack a tax status because they lack income (neighborhood watch groups, sporting and other social groups), as well as various semilegal and criminal associations. Even more expansively, Robert Wuthnow reports that over 3 million small, informal support groups exist in the United States, covering virtually every conceivable social need.[27] Broader conceptions of association provide an even more extensive picture: counting workplaces as modes of association, for example, would add many millions more.

If the sheer diversity of associational landscape should give us pause about the difficulties of theorizing, recent commentators have not let it pass unnoticed that there seem to be no obvious generalizable ways in which associations enhance democracy. Indeed, many kinds of associations do not seem good for democracy at all, as Amy Gutmann rightly emphasizes when she suggests that the contemporary enthusiasm for associations is even irresponsible given our relative lack of knowledge about the associational terrain.[28] Wherever associations have capacities for collective action, they also possess the potential to convert their control over one resource into another, as firms may do when they control social investment, urban design, the lives of their employees, and even public policy through their power of exit.[29] Jon Van Til calculates that 77.5 percent of nonprofit expenditures and 64 percent of nonprofit employment are within associations that act much like for-profit organizations in that they pursue economic interests within competitive markets.[30] These include hospitals, private schools and universities, organizations providing social services under government contract, business and professional associations, unions, and fee-based arts groups. Business associations in particular can use their unparalleled capacities to accumulate money to undermine the powers of deliberation and voting, the two key means of democratic influence. Hate groups damage deliberation through their combined racism and secretiveness, even when they do not bypass politics through violence. Some kinds of associations transform pluralism into parochialism, as do fundamentalist religious sects when they breed intolerance that carries over into political life. Nancy Rosenblum notes that freedom of association and social mobility "are vast engines of social cliques. They generate groups that labor to preserve their social restrictiveness and pretended distinction, and to claim deference from others. Above all, there is the American penchant for secret societies and the groups formed in reaction, to combat their 'conspiracies'—the Masonic fraternity, for example, and the rabid associations, also secretive, organized to counter Masonic power."[31]

From the point of view of democracy, then, it seems that there are associations and then there are associations. Perhaps it was for good reason that Madison was suspicious of factions, and Rousseau outlawed secondary associations in *The Social Contract* altogether as incompatible with the common good! At a minimum, one might be forgiven for wondering, as does Rosenblum, whether it might be meaningless to generalize about the democratic effects of associational life at all.

I am convinced that we can generalize. But to do so we shall need to move beyond the abstractions that too often dominate the debates and make the right kinds of distinctions—distinctions that capture the diversity of associational goods, powers, and structural locations, and then compare these with the many different kinds of democratic functions associations might serve. After discussing background conceptual and methodological issues in chapters 2 (the literature) and 3 (the concept of association), in chapter 4 I delineate the many democratic effects associational life might potentially have. These I consider under three broad classes of effects: *developmental* effects on individuals; effects in constituting *public spheres* of political judgment; and effects that underwrite *democratic institutions* such as representation. The point of distinguishing these effects is threefold. First, the differences among democratic theories today tend to register in different views of what the functions of associations ought to be. Second, once the functions are detailed, it is clear that a democracy requires all of them. Differences among democratic theories are, from the perspective of associational life, differences in the mix and weight of their functions, both manifest and latent. The meanings of "democracy" are now plural—not just because the term is contested, but because the venues of politics are increasingly plural while decreasingly contained by formal political institutions. Third, distinguishing these functions makes it clear that not every kind of association can perform every kind of function. To the contrary, there are trade-offs: associations that are able to perform one kind of function may, for that very reason, be unable to perform another. A robust democracy will require, at the very least, a pluralism of different effects related in aggregate as if it were an associational ecology with numerous niches and specializations—an ideal I denote with the metaphor of a "democratic ecology of associations."

The reasons for trade-offs among the democratic effects of associations become clear in chapter 5, the theoretical core of the book. Here I develop three sets of distinctions that have an impact on democratic potentials of associations. First, whether an association is *voluntary* or *nonvoluntary* is important for how conflict is handled within associations, and hence whether politics is internalized or externalized. These differences affect what I refer to as the *developmental* effects of associations on individuals' political capacities, knowledge, civic orientations, and other dispositions relevant to forming democratic citizens. Second, the *constitutive media* of association—whether it is primarily embedded within or oriented toward social resources (such as solidarity, friendship, or identity), power, or money—make crucial differences in the capabilities of an association (for collective action, resistance, representation, and the like) as well as the structural pressures that come to bear on its capabilities. In addition, differences in media affect the kinds of dangers associations may potentially pose for democracy. A corollary distinction has to do with whether an association is *vested* in its medium of reproduction or not—a distinction that indicates associational resources as well as whether or not it seeks change through opposition. Third, the *purposes* or *constitutive goods* of an association make a difference for democratic effects. Some kinds of goods (for example, the public good of community development) require collective action, and so will foster coalition building. Other kinds of goods (for example, individual material goods sought by wage-oriented unions) lend themselves to bargaining and compromise. The identity goods that hold together lifestyle or religious associations tend toward public displays aimed at recognition. And still other kinds of goods (the status good of private schooling, for example) are difficult to achieve in democratic settings, and will tend to be pursued in nondemocratic ways.[32]

In chapter 6, I suggest that when these distinctions are combined, we have the beginnings of a theory of association within democratic theory. Together, these distinctions cut across one another to show that associations with different kinds of attributes speak to democratic functions in highly diverse ways. Here I develop a set of typologies designed to distinguish associational kinds according to differences in their democratic effects. Finally, in chapter 7, I suggest that democracies require a mix of different kinds of associations to carry out the diverse and complementary tasks that, together, enable democratic responses to political conflict—a democratic ecology of associational life. Fostering and maintaining a democratic society depends upon protecting, adjusting, empowering, and regulating associational life to achieve an optimal mix of democratic effects.

The analyses I provide in this book are not empirical claims. They are nothing more than theoretical elaborations of questions, and I do not intend them as anything more. What I provide, in the end, is a relatively modest piece of middle-level theorizing—without empirical evidence or analysis—devoted solely to the question of what we might expect of associations based on their structural locations and their purposes, if only we know what our expectations are. The analysis is not simple, and I shall be the first to admit that detailing the complex, plural, and ambiguous terrain of associational life in terms of democratic effects has its tedious aspects. Knowledge can bear a certain amount of tedium; what it cannot bear is pointless tedium. While ultimately the reader will be the judge, my own view is that conceptualizing the terrain of associational life is now one of the most important tasks for those democrats who, like myself, believe that democracy can still be expanded and deepened.

I do have hopes for this analysis that go well beyond what I am able to accomplish here. Within democratic theory, I should like to contribute to reviving the radical core of the democratic idea—the idea of collective self-governance. I am impressed with the possibility that even today democracy might be rethought and even radicalized within the vast array of participatory spaces that large-scale, complex, and differentiated societies now offer combined with the multiple means of making collective decisions that now exist.

In characterizing my aims in this way I do not intend to be sectarian. Depending upon how my analysis is read, it may also contribute to liberal problems of boundaries, liberties, and distributional justice, pluralist interests in multiplicity and diversity, deliberative democrats' interests in conditions of rational public judgment, utilitarians' concerns with efficient kinds and levels of organizations, realists' concerns with checking and balancing power, neo-Marxist interests in class structures, rational-choice interests in conditions of collective action, and postmodern interests in symbolism and spectacle. All these concerns are implicated in the multiplicity of associational attachments and the spaces they generate, and there are many potential books in each one. This book is, however, no more than a preface to any of these possibilities.

Although this is not a work of social science, I do have hopes it might aid in generating propositions that could bridge democratic theory and empirical research. It is possible to read this book as offering hypotheses as to how specific associational ecologies enhance or constrain democracy. If we can develop a good account of the associational ecology of the developed liberal democracies, we should be able to predict what kind of adjust-ments, inducements, laws, policies, movements, and other forces might, in aggregate, be good for democracy. This kind of project, however, goes far beyond the knowledge and resources I am able to marshal here.

My analysis is limited in another respect as well. Although I think my approach says something about all the developed liberal democracies, it is written from an American perspective. There are peculiar features of the American political system and social landscape that make the question of association more obvious, if not more important, than in other liberal democracies. Thus, in the colonization of America from the Mayflower Compact through the settlement of the frontiers, the associational form often preceded organized governement. American politics continues to be marked by this history. Americans have a propensity to create or join associations in response to perceived needs, threats, and conflicts—a pro-pensity often combined with a generalized suspicion of government. In part for the same reasons, "the state" in the United States is, in fact, a diverse patchwork of some eighty thousand or more units of government with their associated supports, clients, and cultures. Relative to most Eu-ropean states, the American state is decentralized and fragmented. Thus, especially at the local level and within functionally delineated policy areas (school boards, water conservation districts, transportation authorities, etc.), government often looks more like "association" than "state." Cer-tainly these qualities make the American state more open to the influence of associations—for better or worse, depending upon their purposes and powers.

Then again, there are also distinctive political functions for associations generated by American single-member-district electoral system when con-trasted to the proportional representation systems more common in Eu-rope. Because the single-member district denies representation to minori-ties, it produces, prior to elections, incentives for coalition-building under the umbrellas of the two major parties. In proportional representation systems, majority coalitions are formed after elections among smaller par-ties. In the American system, political associations have the infomal role in pre-election coalition building that is formalized in proportional repre-sentation systems. Thus, the American system is more likely to generate political associations than a proportional representation system.

At the same time, because the system of single-member districts tends to leave substantial minorities in different locales permanently without representation, it also generates incentives for these minorities to turn to associative venues not only for political voice, but also for redress of social needs that go unrepresented in political institutions. The "at-large" sys-tem of multimember districts in local government often has the same ef-fects. In addition, in contrast to parliamentary systems, the American system of checks and balances between the legislative, judicial, and executive branches means that any significant collective action requires overwhelming majorities, while powerful minorities can effectively block initiatives at multiple points within the system. The overall effect is a system that is less responsive to social needs and disadvantaged minorities than other institutional mechanisms would be likely to be. One celebrated effect is to reinforce the view among the less wealthy and educated that voting is not really very important. A less noticed effect is, again, to displace much collective action onto associations—either as means of influencing government through lobbying or public pressure or as means of addressing needs, threats, and conflicts when government does not respond.

These and other distinctive features of American politics suggest that associative means of collective action have been more prominent in the American case than in other developed liberal democracies. From the perspective of democracy this is not always a good thing, and I certainly do not mean to idealize the American example. As will become clear, a political system that diminishes the impact of the vote (in contrast to parliamentary systems) will tend to increase the power of those with the means to organize associations—usually those with money and education. Weak or unresponsive units of government, or those captured by associations, can fail to protect vulnerable members of society—as when they fail to enforce civil rights laws or worker safety regulations under pressure from conservative and business associations. Nonetheless, I think my analysis, with modifications, transcends the American case to encompass other developed liberal democracies.

My analysis speaks less well to countries where ethnic or religious communalism remains a dominant force—Afghanistan, Iran, some Balkan states, and many African states, for example. As will become clear in chapters 2 and 3, I am assuming an associational landscape that is pluralized in the two senses. First, the purposes of associations are segmented rather than encompassing, so that associations express discrete interests (or clusters of interests) or nonencompassing identities. When associational attachments become encompassing, no democratic process can mediate conflicts. Under these circumstances, every conflict or threat cues an entire universe of meaningful social attachments, which will tend to provoke (rigidly principled) war rather than deliberation, negotiation, and bargaining. Although the most prominent examples are abroad, the United States is not exempt from this pattern of attachment. The Christian Right comes very close to exemplifying such encompassing attachment, but is held in check by the fact that it exists within a pluralized society, meaning that its members will often have interests in and allegiances to jobs, public schools, regions, hobbies, and the like that are not encompassed. Fortunately, most associations in the United States are relatively discrete in the interests and identities they embody and express. Added together, they produce a pluralism of interests and identities that, ideally, check and balance one another in ways that make democratic responses to politics more attractive even for those involved in encompassing associations.

Second, the pluralism of discrete associations in the United States and other developed countries tends to be matched by individuals with complex identities. Most individuals inhabit a variety of roles with corresponding identities: those of parent, son or daughter, church member, employee, union member, consumer, sports fan, man or woman, lifestyle aficionado, member of a neighborhood, city, and region, parent-teacher association member, gardener, protester, Democrat, and so on. People are more likely to have some basis for understanding and empathizing with others in socieities where they inhabit crosscutting and overlapping roles. At the very least, complex identities disincline people to fight with arms—few threats are encompassing enough to justify this form of struggle, as compared to deliberating, demonstrating, bargaining, exiting, and other strategies that are the lifeblood of democracy. In contrast, those violent struggles that have occurred periodically in the United States almost always involve cases in which associational attachments are not overlapping, but are marked by cleavage. Historically, for example, discrimination against African Americans has extended to political enfranchisement, housing and neighborhoods, social associations, employment, career mobility, union membership, schooling, and religious worship. We should not be surprised that such a history coincides with associational attachments that rarely bridge race and provide too few incentives for democratic responses to conflict. The American case provides exceptionally rich terrain for conceptualizing the democratic possibilities of association not because it is exemplary, but because it combines a rich tapestry of associative venues for collective action with more than enough cautionary tales to give pause to anyone inclined toward uncritical celebration.

Two

Approaches to Association

THERE is a growing literature on association, much of it concerned directly or indirectly with its relationship to democracy. At least three broad kinds of issues now divide the literature. The first concerns whether or not it is possible to generalize about associations at all, given the diversity of their kinds and purposes. I shall argue that it is possible to generalize, if we make the right distinctions. The second has to do with the kinds of normative purposes that are attributed to association. Here I consider three: communitarian, liberal, and democratic, distinguished by their dominant purposes: community, freedom, and political self-governance. My analysis follows those who have placed the democratic effects of association in the foreground—a topic to which I return in chapter 4. This choice, however, should not be understood as implying a normative commitment to democracy *rather* than to freedom or community. No general trade-offs exist at this level of abstraction; conflicts tend to be specific, and should be treated as such. So, initially, my choice should be understood as a hypothetical: *if* we want to know what associations do for democracy, *then* we should foreground the question of their democratic effects. We should then be able to see how enabling the democratic effects of associations might affect their contributions to community and freedom—although I do not address these issues systematically in this book. Finally, democratic approaches are distinguished by the social theories within which they are embedded. In particular, Alexis de Tocqueville's *Democracy in America* has been centrally important but sometimes overwhelming. For this reason, I shall comment upon the strengths and weaknesses of the Tocquevillian paradigm, and suggest how we might go beyond it.

For and against Theoretical Generalization

A remarkable feature of much of the recent literature is the very general nature of claims for the desirable effects of association. John Rawls, for example, conceives of associations as venues for a generalized "morality of association," which includes the virtues of "justice and fairness, fidelity and trust, integrity and impartiality," virtues that will tend to be enforced by associates through the mechanism of guilt.[1] In *Making Democracy Work*, Robert Putnam views associations in Tocquevillian terms, arguing that they "instill in their members habits of cooperation, solidarity, and public-spiritedness" by drawing individuals out of their natural forgetfulness of their dependence upon public goods and public life. In addition, associations provide the spaces, venues, and opportunities for social collaboration and collective action.[2] Michael Sandel understands associations as schools of civic virtue, and judges associations according to their contributions to civic education.[3] Iris Young hopes that associations, in contrast to interest groups, can provide the social fabric that supports a harmonious negotiation of differences among groups.[4] More expansive and diverse expectations can be found in Joshua Cohen and Joel Rogers's influential work, "Secondary Associations and Democratic Governance": associations can underwrite democracy by providing information, equalizing representation, educating citizens, and providing alternative forms of governance.[5] In addition to these expectations, Paul Hirst conceives associations as replacements for state institutions.[6]

There is nothing wrong with such expectations in themselves, and I shall draw on these and others in my own analysis. But owing to the level of generality at which they are cast, they cannot fail to disappoint. Certainly this is why some commentators are beginning to sound notes of caution.[7] Most careful in this regard is Nancy Rosenblum, who has gone so far as to suggest that it may not be possible to generalize about the virtues, functions, and effects of associations at all. "There is no systematic answer to whether we can depend on the associations of civil society to cultivate the moral dispositions liberal democracy requires, or whether to use public incentives and the force of law to create and enhance liberalizing, democratizing groups. Associational pluralism and the vicissitudes of personal experience militate against a coherent answer."[8] Even the more limited classical liberal expectations that associations check government and facilitate representation are overdrawn. "These considerations support a general thesis in favor of pluralism," Rosenblum writes. "But they are of little help in identifying the associations that at any moment are salient for political self-defense of participation. That is a contextual, contingent question, and specific perceptions of danger give specific groups first place."[9] Even if it were possible to encourage through law or incentives those groups that produce democratic effects, these strategies would endanger goods that are valuable in their own right, the identity and character-forming goods that are irreducibly a part of the freedom of association. The only democratic virtue about which it is possible to generalize, in Rosenblum's view, is that associations enable "the experience of pluralism" itself, which in turn contributes to a democratization of everyday life.

Rosenblum's approach is uniquely valuable in that she emphasizes processes of group formation by focusing on the experiential impact of making and breaking associative ties. The experience of diverse associative connections in itself, aside from any other virtues or vices of association, contributes to the "democracy of everyday life," the "easy spontaneity" and relative equality with which individuals meet and greet one another in a democratic society.[10] But Rosenblum also overdraws the case against generalization, primarily because the generalizations she rightly criticizes are overly general in most cases, and not the right kinds of generalization in others. Her argument does not add up to a case for a pluralism that cannot be fathomed in theoretical terms, but rather to a case for more careful kinds of generalization. Moreover, Rosenblum's case for indeterminacy is closely connected with a *generalized* judgment that some kinds of associational effects are more valuable than others, in particular, the personality-forming and containing effects of membership. In a review, Alan Wolfe rightly points out that "the pursuit of indeterminacy can itself become determinate. In response to the algorithmic tendencies in some versions of liberal theory, Rosenblum finds herself in the position of arguing over and over that membership is always preferable to alienation or isolation."[11] One result is that *this* good (which may or may not always be good!) trumps all other goods, and the analysis of these other goods is obscured by general claims for their indeterminate plurality and specificity. The argument I offer here suggests that the associational landscape is indeed complex and pluralistic, but it is not theoretically indeterminate. There are theoretical reasons for plurality, and each kind, good, and structural location of association can be analyzed on its own terms, and then be related to the multiple goods required by a democracy.

A somewhat different case against theoretical generalization is made by Yael Tamir, who emphasizes the indeterminate effects of association in a critique of what she refers to as the "instrumentalist-democratic approach" to association—a view she associates with Stephen Macedo,[12] Young, Cohen and Rogers, Rawls, and Putnam. In somewhat different ways, each focuses on the effects of associations on the development of the civic capacities that underwrite democracy. Tamir's critique is based primarily upon the diversity of associational effects. If, as in the case of Rawls and Putnam, the associative structure of civil society is left free of state intervention, there is no reason to expect that "associational life will foster tolerance, modesty, and reciprocity; strengthen liberal democratic beliefs and tendencies; restrain the rule of the majority; balance the activities of the state; give individuals a public voice, and stabilize democracy. A few associations may indeed fulfill all (or most) of these functions effectively, but many will fail to do so."[13] In fact, more and more "illiberal associations, religious and others, are emerging in liberal democratic societies. This proliferation of illiberal associations suggests that the harmonious picture drawn by Tocqueville and reiterated by so many other social thinkers is inaccurate. . . . When allowed to associate, individuals quite often opt for illiberal, authoritarian, nondemocratic options."[14]

Of course the mere *fact* of diversity does not in itself cut against what are essentially normative arguments. But these normative generalizations can justify programs of state intervention in ways that make associations into instruments of a democratic system. This is, in different ways, what Cohen and Rogers, Young, and Macedo suggest—programs that add up to what Tamir calls *the* democratic case for associations. The case is weak, she argues, not only because of the diversity of actually existing associations, but also because of the diversity of effects associations can have within a liberal democratic system, many of which would be crushed by even a gentle program of state intervention. Potentially endangered associations include those that enable individuals to gain influence in government, protect against a "tyranny of the majority," balance the powers of government, underwrite peaceful and legal modes of resistance, and provide the social fabric for the autonomous development of civil society as a political and ideological force.[15] One might add that because the point of many kinds of association is precisely their freedom and spontaneity, state intervention cannot help but damage their effects. So those who level expectations at associations need to be mindful of the diverse potentials of associational life.[16]

While these points are well taken, Tamir's argument does not, in the end, cut against the democratic case for associations for three reasons. First, she equates the democratic argument with an argument for constructing associations as venues for civic virtue. This is only one kind of democratic effect, as she herself suggests. In any case, at least three of Tamir's targets—Cohen and Rogers, Young, and Putnam—do not equate an argument for the democratic functions of associations only with their effects on individual character. The argument works only because Tamir attributes a democratic theory to her interlocutors that they do not hold, one that reduces democratic systems to the aggregate effects of individual character—an argument that is more characteristic of neoliberal civic republicans (that is, American neoconservatives). It is primarily against this misplaced expectation that the diversity of associational life seems like an argument against theorizing the democratic effects of association. Second, what Tamir in fact demonstrates is that associations serve multiple democratic functions—although her list is itself overly general and incomplete. Third, even if we are mindful of the dangers of state intervention, there are no neutral states. We have no dispensation from identifying and assessing the effects of differing political and legal procedures and of the countless policies that constitute and affect associational life in today's liberal democracies. Tamir herself recommends various welfare state programs aimed at underwriting a robust civil society—quite rightly, in my view. Income supports, for example, can *increase* the voluntary character of association by decreasing social dependencies and increasing options for exit.[17] On Tamir's account, however, this counts as a liberal good. But why, we might ask, should we want state activities that support the liberal purposes of association while denying those that have democratic purposes?

In short, the case has been made against broad generalizations about plural associational landscapes, as well as against monocausal views of what a democracy needs to work. But it has not been made against theorizing the democratic effects of association.

What Do We Want from Associational Life?

Not everyone who writes about associational life is interested in same kinds of goods. We find, roughly, three kinds of clusters: those who seek communitarian goods; those who seek liberal goods; those who seek democratic goods. My point in this book is not to argue for democratic goods against communitarian and liberal goods. But it is important that communitarian and liberal approaches not be confused with *democratic* theories of associational life—the goods of which sometimes complement and sometimes conflict with these other kinds of goods.

Communitarian Approaches

Communitarian approaches emphasize the socially integrative functions of association, so it is not surprising the concept of association is often assimilated to that of community—a point I shall take up in chapter 3. The communitarian approach is driven by the perception that modern liberal societies are increasingly anomic, and associations are valorized because they combat anomie, providing individuals with their identities, horizons, and moral orientations. As Charles Taylor has emphasized, anomic individuals lack strongly constituted senses of moral identity, and are thus morally unpredictable and even politically dangerous.[18] Francis Fukuyama stresses the social weakness of anomic individuals: when individuals are disconnected from the moral discipline of "ethical communities," they are unable to form bonds of trust, which in turn disconnects them from capacities for collective action. Anomic individuals stand alone, as it were, against powerful state forces, and cannot form the social units necessary for success in the market.[19] For all communitarians, anomie is the dark side of a liberal society that emphasizes rights-based individualism and freedom of choice. Indeed, even the term *association* may evoke liberal dangers if misunderstood, especially when combined with the notion that association is always "voluntary." As Michael Walzer points out, many of the forms of association most essential to the self are not "chosen" in any meaningful sense of the term: families, religious affiliations, cultures, and citizenship are for most matters of birth that together form a nonvoluntary associational background on the basis of which persons develop their capacities for choice.[20]

These are the matters on which communitarian agree. Indeed, as general claims, the points about the social contingency of individuation should be matters of common sense. The interesting differences have to do with how these points shade over into democratic theory, and in doing so occlude certain democratic goods and effects.

Some communitarians equate community with the territorial nation-state, so that the state is viewed, as it were, as a community of communities. In *Democracy and Its Discontents*, for example, Michael Sandel judges the contributions of associations according to their propensity to develop civic commitments to a national community. Sandel envisages, in effect, a hierarchy of attachments in which the civic commitments would draw the polity together into a differentiated but strongly integrated community.[21] Sandel does not argue explicitly that the state should be the principle agent of integration, but one could be forgiven for drawing this conclusion, since one-half of *Democracy and Its Discontents* is devoted to criticizing what he takes to be overly liberal Supreme Court decisions limiting state intervention on behalf of civic commitments. Michael Walzer, in contrast, points out that many groups, especially in pluralistic, heterogeneous societies like our own, have the effect of *loosening* the bonds of citizenship on behalf of other desirable goods.[22] Individuals are, in fact, "encumbered" by the attachments of communities, as Sandel desires, but in ways that properly limit the attachments of citizenship. While Sandel conceives of a good society as embracing plural modes of citizenship, he does not distinguish among the variety of goods that attachments and encumbrances might bring, nor among their latent political effects. He is not prepared to say that groups that provide nonpolitical goods are not good, but neither is he willing to grant that they may compete with the demands of citizenship. Sandel's model demands, by default, that associational attachments contribute to civic virtue, whereas Walzer's more pluralistic communitarianism seeks a "community of communities," in which the bonds of citizenship are loose, but precisely because they accommodate a variety of other desirable encumbrances and goods. Walzer's model is centered on civil society, and allows that whatever democratic effects flow from association life may be indirect.[23] Both approaches foreground the community-constituting effects of association, but Walzer distinguishes these from other kinds of democratic effects, including those aimed at limiting domination. Because Walzer is quite clear that individuals ought to constitute communities centered on distinctive goods and that they ought to be empowered to patrol the boundaries of these spheres, his communitarianism underwrites a pluralized, robustly democratic theory.[24] Sandel fails to make the necessary distinctions, and so leaves us with an approach to association that could underwrite what would amount to a neoconservatism of the left—at worst a Jacobean-style politics energized by a vision an integrated, state-centered community. In this construction, community and democracy will indeed trade off against one another.

We find a similar emphasis on political integration through community in other communitarian works. Daniel A. Bell, for example, asserts as self-evident that "increasing civic virtue will likely have socially desirable consequences in the contemporary American context." Bell's approach follows from the widely accepted Tocquevillian claim that "intermediary associations are essential 'springboards' for civic virtue." Bell interprets this claim, roughly, as the propensity for associations to induce members to put aside their narrow self-interests in favor of broader attachments to political community.[25] Interestingly, he notes that local associations are often less virtuous than larger-scale, state-centered, national associations. Thus, the U.S. National Park Service (NPS)—which might count as an association under some versions of the concept—cultivates more civic virtue, especially pride in national community, than do the now burgeoning, local, face-to-face Residential Community Associations (RCAs), which tend to reinforce narrowly parochial neighborhood self-interest. Bell is quite right to reject the assumption—often associated with conservative brands of civic republicanism—that local association always cultivates more civic virtue than do larger-scale associations. Nor can one be "against" the kind of national pride cultivated through the NPS.

The communitarian assumptions embedded in Bell's analysis do, however, undermine a democratic account of associations in two respects. First, Bell assumes that the altruism that drives pride in a collective achievement such as a national park system is better than the self-interest that drives RCAs. But such an assumption is at best apolitical and at worst naive. Democracy is a response to politics—circumstances in which there are disagreements, reinforced by power positions, in the face of necessities.[26] Politics, among other things, is about sorting out individualistic and common interests. If we knew one from the other beforehand, we would not need processes of political judgment, and we would not have to suffer the uncertainties of democracy. We cannot say, from the perspective of theory, that individualistic self-interests are a priori bad or good; rather, the question is whether they are ultimately defensible, given the range of goods that people need to thrive. Many "selfish" interests *are* defensible, but are not encompassed by communitarian altruism—the interests in the exclusive intimate attachments, for example, out of which families and friendships grow. It is important that a democratic approach to association not prejudge the political question of what varieties, mixes, and ranges of interests are ultimately justifiable.

Second, civic identification is good only if the civic community is good. While few would deny with the goodness of a system of national parks, the example does not generalize. What collective actions require in a democracy is not civic identification, but political justification fueled by other kinds of democratic virtues, including capacities to resist, argue, enter into conflict, and even make mischief in order to push injustices and hidden damages into the public view.[27] As in the case of Sandel, we find that the communitarian emphasis on civic virtue too easily shades over into an apolitical image of community, a vision within which democracy loses its political functions.

It is also possible to harness liberal accounts of associational rights to communitarian aspirations, an approach exemplified by Aviam Soifer's argument for an independent right of association in *Law and the Company We Keep*. Soifer's key concern is with constitutional recognition of the fact that communities constitute persons, a recognition that would go far beyond current doctrine, which recognizes the right to associate primarily as instrumental to political and religious expression.[28] The freedom of association ought to protect our abilities to construct "our ideas of communities," through which we define "where we belong and who we are, as well as who we are not."[29] Soifer's approach has the advantage of recognizing—in contrast to Sandel's, which is critical of "rights-based liberalism"—that rights are not only, or even primarily, legal devices to protect the separateness of individual against the pressures of community, but are constitutive of communities. Rights have multiple effects in constituting power relations, depending upon the kind of right and the environment within which it is operative. Many rights serve to keep certain kinds of powers—especially those of the state, but also sometimes of the market—from displacing relationships formed through the associative media of norms, cultural habits, and language, ethics, and other social means of relating.[30] This being said, Soifer values associations primarily as a medium of self-constitution, and would tie their legal protection to a communitarian conception of self-constitution. What is missing is an argument as to why *this* function of association, fundamental though it may be, should be the primary focus of law.

Liberal Approaches

Liberal approaches to association are distinguished by their emphasis on the freedom to associate, which is in turn justified by the liberal commitment to the moral dignity and priority of the individual. Not surprisingly, most liberal approaches focus on questions of law, since laws provide the boundaries between individuals' freedom to choose their associational attachments and those attachments (or detachments) compelled by state regulation or intervention. Nancy Rosenblum's is one of the most interesting of the liberal accounts: in her view, we ought to value associations precisely because of the indeterminacy of their effects in constituting the moral dimensions of individuality. There is no reason to think that every association should contribute in the same way, a view Rosenblum refers to as the "logic of congruence" that characterizes much of the discussion of associational life.[31] Nor does she think—in contrast to Rawls—that moral effects generated in one associational context necessarily generalize to other associational contexts, what she refers to as a misplaced "liberal expectancy" for the benefits of associational life.[32] Because of the difficulties of understanding all of the moral effects of associational life, we should be careful about recommending legal regulation of association. Rosenblum's liberalism thus mirrors and complements her emphasis on the pluralism of associational life. Pluralism ought to be protected precisely because its moral effects are subtle and varied; these are not the kinds of effects that states are likely to be very good at regulating or instilling. Rosenblum's expectations are modest, but she directs them at the toughest cases. Although militia groups, for example, may not appear to possess any liberal or democratic virtues, they may serve to channel and contain pathologies that would otherwise undermine liberal-democratic processes.[33] More generally, it is the "experience of pluralism" within diverse societies that ultimately underwrites liberal-democratic values. There is more moral benefit to be had here than could possibly be gained from interventions designed to produce civic or other moral effects. Beyond this, associations only fail in moral development if "they cannot create the conditions for effective rules and settled expectations."[34]

Rosenblum's cautious liberalism forms an interesting contrast to that of Rawls, who views associations as necessary to the moral development of individuals, but in the directly substantive sense that he expects them to develop the social-psychological precursors of justice.[35] What distinguishes Rosenblum is that, unlike Rawls, she does not have impossibly high expectations for moral effects. At best, she has limited hopes for the moral experience of reciprocity built into associational expectations that "members must do their share." Associations that cultivate reciprocity of this sort may contribute to liberal ideals of justice, but only in highly indirect ways.[36]

From a purely liberal perspective, of course, it is not necessary to think of association as instrumental to liberal political processes or to justice or to any other end that is extrinsic to individual freedom. George Kateb argues the liberal case that freedom of association ought to be valued simply because it is intrinsic to the meaning and social reality of freedom.[37] The freedom to choose the purposes of association as well as those with whom one wishes to associate is essential to the proper meaning and uses of freedom. A strong and robustly protected freedom of association follows from the liberal valuation of the worth of persons; the presumption should always be against state interference in or regulation of associational life. To be sure, even on the purely liberal construction, freedom to associate is limited by duties not to harm others through one's associations.[38] Depending on one's understanding of social power relations and the potential harms that flow, say, from associations that restrict access to economic resources, such a duty may justify strict limits on some kinds of association.

While my analysis of the democratic effects of association is by no means illiberal, it does not center on the freedom of association. Although a democratic theory of association will, naturally, have much to say about the nature and limits of state intervention, as well as about the constitutional law relating to association in the United States, my emphasis here is on the range and variability of democratic goods. Indeed, freedom of association is not unproblematic from a democratic perspective. As commentators often point out, freedom to associate also implies the freedom to exclude and discriminate, which can have antidemocratic effects if an association controls significant resources.[39] When purely liberal principles are applied without attention to social and economic power relations, for example, a group of businesses with monopoly control over some essential good—telephones, local housing, the local supply of jobs, health care, or whatever else people need—can claim the freedom to associate and transform this freedom into a local tyranny. Associations exist within fields of power relations, and absolute claims for freedom of association can produce a society within which there are very few freedoms. Even the U.S. Supreme Court—which has developed only the most limited account of associational goods—recognizes this fact by restricting its deference to freedom of association to matters of political expression and religious conscience, while often supporting laws forbidding discrimination and exclusion where an association controls resources people need to thrive.[40] But the Court has never generalized such distinctions. In any case it would hobble a democratic approach to associations to remain too closely tied to American constitutional law, or even to the more general question of how far the freedom of association ought to extend. My point is not, of course, to opt for democratic goods over liberal rights (of which the Court has been a fickle defender), but rather to avoid building a democratic theory of association out of the peculiarities of American constitutional law. I do, however, return in chapter 7 to the question of the extent to which freedom to association ought to be defended by law. More generally, any democratic theory of associations will judge that there are more and less desirable mixes of associations, and that sometimes state regulation, intervention, or incentives may be appropriate means for adjusting the mix.

Democratic Approaches

Much of the literature on association follows Tocqueville's lead in focusing on the democratic effects of associations. What is most striking about this literature is the range and variety of democratic effects attributed to associations. My approach is distinctive not in that it adds another kind of democratic expectation. Rather, I shall argue that a democracy needs them all, but it needs them in mixes that maximize the democratic consequences of associational ecologies. Since my take on the issues relies on surveying these effects—a task I take up in chapter 4—here I shall settle for some general remarks.

Any democratic system, but particularly one in which politics has migrated beyond state-centered venues, depends upon multiple effects of associations—representation, deliberation, a counterbalancing of powers, alternative forms of governance, the cultivation of political skills, and the formation of public opinion, just to name a few possibilities. Associations play key roles at numerous points in what are now complex and multifaceted political systems, but it is prima facie unlikely, given this complexity, that any single kind of association could contribute at every point in the system. Nor does it make sense to expect associations to display similar democratic capacities and virtues. Democracies require advocacy groups to represent people within state arenas. But advocacy groups are unlikely to be very good at providing alternative venues of governance. This is not what they aim to do, nor are they organized to do. Likewise, associations that remind us of our commonalties—civic booster associations, for example—may be unable to partake of the mischief often necessary to push hidden injuries into the public eye. And yet democracies need groups that emphasize differences and injuries in order to form and extend public agendas. There is, in other words, every reason to approach

the diversity of associational types with an eye to the diversity of democratic functions that any associational ecology will embody.

Viewed from such a perspective, sins of the literature more often than
not prove to be sins of omission and overgeneralization, which in turn lead
to selective accounts of democratic effects. The result of omission is to
reduce theoretically the domain and scope of potential democratic effects
and the associational venues to which they are related. The result of overgeneralization is to look for democratic effects where they are not likely
to be found, thus setting up democratic expectations for disappointment.

This being said, I do not aim to provide a comprehensive democratic
theory. This, more than anything else, distinguishes my endeavor here
from two recent works that view associations as the heart of a democratic
theory—Paul Hirst's *Associative Democracy* and Joshua Cohen and Joel
Rogers's "Secondary Associations and Democratic Governance." Although I find these works very attractive, arguing as they do for pluralized
and varied forms of democratic governance, both seek to provide more
or less comprehensive normative visions. As befits works of normative
vision, they tend to imagine exemplary forms of association. My aim is
different: I am interested in theorizing the associational terrain that such
associative theories of democracy must take into account if they are to
have an impact within the developed liberal democracies.

I do assume that whatever democratic effects associations have, they
have within the contours of liberal-democratic constitutional states and
within the context of an economy that, for better or worse, will remain
essentially market-driven and capitalist for the foreseeable future. A comprehensive democratic theory would view the terrain of associational life
as elements within a democratic system, and would thus include accounts
of the state and markets that I cannot provide within the short space of
a book. I do not assume that associations can replace states. In fact, a
robust associational life demands a strong state—a state that is strong
enough to develop and enforce a systems of fundamental rights, to protect
the zones of freedom within which associational life grows, to support
citizens with enough basic income and services to ensure that they do not
become dependent upon one or a few associations for their life necessities,
and to deepen the democratic forms of governance within the state, into
which associations insert themselves. But the question of how, exactly,
our laws, governmental institutions, and economic structures might be
designed to support, regulate, encourage, and adjust associations to provide the social fabric of a robust democracy is also beyond the scope of
this book—although I shall provide some general considerations in chapter 7. Even more difficult is the task of identifying political agents that
might adjust the mix of associations in democratic directions. We cannot
assume that the state is the primary agent of adjustment and regulation

of associational life. Rather, I can only imagine that a more democratic mix of associations would be a result of cultural changes, political pressures brought by New Social Movements, legal challenges, fiscal supports, citizens' initiatives, and organizational innovations within workplaces. This being said, I turn to a brief survey of democratic approaches to associational life.

The Influence of the Tocquevillian Paradigm

Alexis de Tocqueville's influence upon the way we think about democracy and association has been deep and profound. *Democracy in American* established the channels into which most of the literature has flowed.[41] Tocqueville's appeal stems from the fact that he was the first to show in detail how the liberal-democratic constitutional government depends upon social mores, political culture, and habits of collective action cultivated by horizontal relations of association. The institutional face of Tocqueville's approach is not in itself remarkable: it repeats the classically liberal "protective" account of democracy that was already a dominant strain in English and American political thought. On the protective model of democracy, the purpose of democratic institutions is to guard against the potentially tyrannical powers of the state.[42] Tocqueville argued, however, that liberal-democratic constitutional design is not enough: democratic government depends upon associations that mediate between individuals and the state.

For this reason, the associations of greatest interest to Tocqueville were *secondary* associations with a *voluntary* character. These are the associations that stand between the powers of the state and the close, primary associations of friends and family. Tocqueville's emphasis on voluntary secondary associations followed from his view that a democracy needs the functional equivalents of the European estates, which he saw as providing venues of collective action, representation, and, if necessary, resistance to the political center. If only the right ethical sensibilities could develop, he argued, voluntary association among equals could replace the vertical ascriptive association typical of much of the European continent. Thus, Tocqueville searched America for the social conditions and "habits of the heart" that could underwrite these political effects.

Long before the current wave of interest in civil society and its associational structure, the literature of American pluralism followed Tocqueville's problematic in two ways. The first is the important but obvious emphasis on group representation of social interests within state-centered venues. While political parties are crucial, so are the wide variety of interest groups and other kinds of associations that populate the American social landscape. We find this emphasis carried through in more contemporary work, most notably in the extensive study of participation by Verba, Schlozman, and Brady, *Voice and Equality: Civic Voluntarism in American Politics*, where this function is especially prominent. These representational effects of association figure into virtually every democratic consideration of association.

The second Tocquevillian influence was more original and productive. Tocqueville linked capacities for mediation and representation to civic habits developed within the associational fabric of civil society, which he in turn related to a strong meaning of democracy located in associational capacities for collective action. Reversing the Madisonian and Rousseauian suspicions that associations are the social basis of political factions and "conspiracies against the public interest," Tocqueville argued that secondary associations draw individuals out of their primary associations, educating them about their dependence upon others. In this way, associations provoke a civic consciousness and displace narrow self-interest with a "self-interest rightly understood." In addition, associations cultivate reciprocity and trust among individuals, enabling them to accomplish tasks together they could not manage alone. Thus, for Tocqueville, the qualities of representative democracy depend on the qualities of the society within which it is embedded, especially upon the cultivation of civic virtues via associational ties. Democracy is centered, as it were, in the self-rule manifested in associational life and in the civic culture resulting from associational experiences.

The message handed down from Tocqueville is that social integration through associations is necessary for democratic institutions to work. Again, we find this emphasis in the American pluralist literature, exemplified by Robert Dahl's argument for the independent influence of culture on democratic institutions in *A Preface to Democratic Theory*.[43] The Tocquevillian paradigm was fully embraced in Almond and Verba's *The Civic Culture*, which directly related levels of associational life to the more robust civic values of tolerance and support for democratic institutions in the United States as compared to those in a number of other countries.[44] The more recent literature on associations and democracy has revived this emphasis on cultural function of associational life. Measuring these effects and relating them to civic and political participation, for example, is a central purpose of Verba, Schlozman, and Brady's *Voice and Equality*.

Robert Putnam's *Making Democracy Work* adds a bit of rational choice theory to the Tocquevillian idea. Putnam's thesis is that when citizens have capacities for collective action, they can monitor, attend to, and pressure governments for performance—a thesis he exemplifies by contrasting the good governments in the autonomous regions of the north of Italy with the corrupt and ineffective governments of the south. What distinguishes north and south is the amount of "social capital"—a term Putnam borrows from James Coleman, who uses it to indicate situations in which individuals have found normative solutions to the free-rider problem that plagues many forms of collective action.[45] The solution involves a close relationship between experiences of horizontal association and the development of norms of reciprocity and trust. Where these exist, citizens can form associations in response to collective problems. When they form associations, they reinforce norms of reciprocity and trust, thus promoting a "virtuous cycle."

One of the more important features of Putnam's approach is that he is able to explain the importance of Tocqueville's emphasis on social and economic equality by pointing to their effects in limiting hierarchical dependencies. While independence may threaten anomie, it also means that associational bonds are formed under conditions of relative equality. They are therefore more likely to be horizontal and voluntary in nature, and thus capable of generating an ethical character that cannot occur within vertical relationships of dependence. Under conditions of dependence, norms of reciprocity and trust are either superfluous or naive. "A vertical network," writes Putnam,

> no matter how dense and no matter how important its participants, cannot sustain social trust and cooperation. Vertical flows of information are often less reliable than horizontal flows, in part because the subordinate husbands information as a hedge against exploitation. More important, sanctions that support norms of reciprocity against the threat of opportunism are less likely to be acceded to, if imposed. Only a bold or foolhardy subordinate, lacking ties of solidarity with peers, would seek to punish a superior. . . . Patron-client relations, for example, involve interpersonal exchange and reciprocal obligations, but the exchange is vertical and the obligations asymmetric.[46]

This is why, for pluralists influenced by Tocqueville, the internal structure of an association is key to its civic effects.[47]

Beyond Tocqueville

The Tocquevillian paradigm has been powerfully suggestive, owing to its emphasis on the complementarity of civil society and political institutions—an emphasis that highlights the democratic effects of association in underwriting representation, pressure, subsidiarity (devolving collective actions to their appropriate levels of organization), and the cultivation of organizational skills and civic virtues.[48] Yet omission and overgeneralization are also built into the paradigm in the following respects, each of which I elaborate in subsequent chapters.

The Bipolar Model of Civil Society

Tocqueville worked with a relatively simple bipolar model of state-civil society relations, and conceived of associational effects within this model. The model assumes two basic social media of social organization: (1) the coercive, legal, and administrative powers of the state and (2) the social media of norms, cultural habits, discussion, and agreement that character-ize nonstate relations. The model thus differentiates society into two spheres: one characterized by power, the other by social and economic interactions with the voluntary forms of association they imply. The prob-lem with such a model is that it assimilates market interactions and struc-tures to a civil society characterized by social integration. But, of course, markets organize social relations and make "decisions" through price mechanisms, which may depend on social media for their existence (as they do on the state for a stable money supply, contract law, and so on), but work in fundamentally different ways.[49] In a phrase, Tocqueville did not understand the structural qualities of markets.

The costs of the bipolar model are numerous. First, the model detracts from the ways in which nonstate arenas are characterized by power rela-tions, albeit power relations that are different from the kinds of powers associated with the state's monopoly over the means of violence. Because of this omission, the Tocquevillian model leans toward characterizing all nonstate forms of association as "voluntary," when, in fact, associations always work within fields of power relations, given by their different kinds and levels of control over the resources that people need to thrive— not only economic resources, but also the resources of organization, social networks, and even identity. This is a defect carried over into American pluralism, manifest in its (theoretical) indifference to nongovernmental forms of power.[50] Moreover, the Tocquevillian model makes it difficult to conceive the (real) possibility that associational life might replicate, reinforce, and even enhance power relations among groups, even if they develop and reinforce egalitarian norms within associations.[51] Many of the antidemocratic effects of associational life, as I shall argue in chapters 5, 6, and 7, follow from circumstances in which associations can use their social and economic powers to produce relations of dependence.

Second, because the bipolar state–civil society model fails to conceive economic and social power effects, it produces a limited conception of what counts as "political."[52] Thus, the democratic effects of associational life are conceived as those orientated toward state or government venues. This is so even if, as in the case of Putnam, nonpolitical associations like "choirs and soccer clubs" are understood to contribute to the forms of trust and cooperation needed for effective political action. On Putnam's account, "making democracy work" really means "making government efficient and responsive," surely an overly restrictive account of democracy.

Third, associations are now thoroughly entangled with states and markets, so much so that the imagery of distinctive domains of state versus associational organizational types can be misleading. To be sure, the Tocquevillian image of associations as inhabiting the sphere of civil society, and even comprising modes of collective action that replace state action, still describes a wide variety of associational types. What it misses, however, are the modes of association that have developed with and within interventionist welfare states. As states have become more interventionist, they have endowed associations with statelike regulatory functions, as with bar associations' regulation of lawyers. Massive numbers of associations, especially in health and welfare, provide social services by government contract. In addition, associations are increasingly involved in affecting the ways markets organize collective actions, as when consumer groups work directly with companies to ensure safe or high-quality products. Numerous public-private partnerships such as Community Development Corporations (CDCs) bring together market forces, government regulators, and community groups. In the United States associations have increasingly become a factor in the administration of government policy, partly in response to an ideological drive in favor of privatization of services and partly as a means to increase flexibility and experimentation in social policy. In the United States, the number of tax-exempt (and hence presumably nonadvocacy) organizations, excluding religious organizations, increased from 389,415 in 1987 to 576,133 in 1995, an increase of 48 percent. Government grants to these organizations amounted to about $23 billion in 1987 and rose to about $36 billion in 1992 (an increase of 57 percent), with human services the biggest spending category.[53] A recent study of several U.S. metropolitan areas by Julian Wolpert has shown that far from government activity crowding out associational activity as one might predict from a neoconservative interpretation of Tocqueville's model, precisely the reverse occurs. Government attention to particular policy areas produces a "crowd in" effect, increasing the numbers of associations and their activities.[54] As these and many other kinds of examples suggest, we shall have to look closely at how distinct kinds of associations are entangled with various media of decision making if we wish to gauge their democratic effects—a topic I address in chapter 5. Because the Tocquevillian model is, as it were, pre–welfare state, it obscures the ways in which so much associational life today is intertwined with the powers and resources of governments.

Fourth, and closely related, the bipolar model obscures the senses in which associations can, and often do, serve as alternative modes of governance (as opposed to policy administration), a function that figures heavily into the "associative democracy" approaches of Hirst and Cohen and Rogers. The Tocquevillian model does, of course, conceive of voluntary collective action as an alternative to state-organized collective action, but fails to capture other possibilities. Thus, there are associational models of collective action that are state-enabled but not directed (as in the case of labor unions). Even more interesting are the ways in which governments seek to deflect political problems and issues onto corporatist or quasi-corporatist structures (that is, representative relations organized on the basis of sector or interest rather than territory), many of which have associational qualities. Often, government officials will seek "voluntary" self-regulation of an industry (such as the media) through industry associations in response to political problems rather than seek a direct resolution of the issues. In this way, problems of governance are deflected onto associations, which in turn operate under the implied threat of direct intervention. Examples such as these represent a devolution of politics, but through venues that would not develop "voluntarily" without the attention of government.

The Associational Fabric of the Public Sphere

One class of democratic effects hardly appears in the Tocquevillian paradigm at all: the ways in which associational life forms the social infrastructure of public spheres. *Public spheres* are spaces within which public opinion and public judgments are formed through argument, as distinct from the spaces of political judgment that are designed into liberal-democratic constitutional states by providing for legislative debate. Public spheres generate the "force" of persuasion, as distinct from the forces of coercion and money. Although the conception of a public sphere can be found as early as Kant, only recently has it been combined with democratic theory, most notably in the work of Jürgen Habermas. No doubt the reasons for the oversight have to do with several factors. (1) The genesis of much democratic theory from the protective model of early liberalism has led to a focus on the strategic and power functions of democratic institutions more than on their ability to form and guide political judgments. (2) In an era of less interventionist states there was much less for publics to be concerned with, and so they were, on average, less politicized. (3) An overly volunteerist conception of associations can, in effect, replace a conception of political judgment with a marketlike conception of judgment. Within civil society, political judgments can be viewed as an aggregate effect of membership and exit. In a situation of "perfect liberty" (to borrow loosely from Adam Smith), political judgments are nothing other than the equilibrium result of associational voices and their political representatives.[55] Habermas has focused attention on the role of associations in political judgment, however, by conceiving them as the social infrastructure that supports public spheres of opinion formation.[56] Indeed, this democratic effect of associational life has become, in some philosophical circles, so dominant that it threatens to crowd out the more "classical" democratic functions of associations. Will Kymlicka, for example, asserts that the two key questions about ethnic associations from the perspective of liberal-democratic citizenship is whether they develop "the ability to question authority" and "the willingness to engage in public discourse."[57]

Resistance and Counter-Hegemony

Because the Tocquevillian paradigm focuses heavily on the kind of social integration that enables cooperation, it can deflect attention from hidden injuries and injustices, as well as from the functions associations may have in bringing these into the public view. Put differently, without a convergence of interests, trust and reciprocity are foolhardy—a point Putnam makes that really deserves to be generalized beyond the issue of the internal structure of association. One of the defining features of politics is that interests diverge, or at least are perceived to diverge, and so must be worked out. So trust and reciprocity—good for generating some kinds of democratic effects—should not be generalized to encompass all democratic effects.[58] Mischief on behalf of hidden injuries, Andrew Szasz puts it, is an effect that democracy could do without only in a just society with convergent interests.[59]

The Social Psychology of Developmental Effects

For those working within the Tocquevillian paradigm there is a tendency to generalize a single set of social-psychological effects of associational experience, namely, those that integrate potentially anomic individuals by increasing their sense of reciprocity and trust of others. Indeed, this is a sin of overgeneralization that Tocquevillian pluralists often share with participatory democrats, who often hold the view that more participation makes citizens more virtuous.[60] But the social psychology of an association is likely to vary in its purposes and structural location. Identity-based groups may increase in-group solidarity, but do so by demonizing outgroups—a technique displayed by the fundamentalist Religious Right, as well as groups consolidated by conspiracy theories.[61] Purely social associations may not be able to withstand much internal dissent, while associa-

tions devoted to some external purpose—CDCs fostering urban development, say—will have a less delicate social-psychological balance. In these
latter kinds of associations, people are kept at the table by interests they
bring with them, and they need not be motivated to remain associated
through friendship or other social attachments.

Fortunately, democracy requires a variety of social-psychological effects—not just trust and reciprocity, but also, in different contexts, capacities for dissent, argument, and resistance. It may even be the case, as Rosenblum argues, that apparently antidemocratic effects such as in-group
solidarity may contain pathologies that would otherwise be unleashed in
more destructive ways. The problem, then will be to recognize the variety
of social-psychological effects of association, and then to assess their impact on the several dimensions of democracy within a society's associational ecology.

The Democratic Effects of Undemocratic Practices

Putnam's emphasis on the effects of horizontal relations among individuals within associations in cultivating the ethic of reciprocity is a staple in
the literature on the democratic effects of association. The reasoning is
straightforward and important: if democratic character can be molded by
experiences of reciprocity, trust, and mutual respect, then associations
with horizontal, relatively egalitarian structures will do more to generate
a democratic culture. This point is undeniable. Nonetheless, it can often
lead to the overgeneralization that democratic systems work because of
the effects of association on political culture. But this is just one of many
democratic kinds of things associations can do, some of which may militate against internal reciprocity. For example, advocacy groups are often
embedded within strategic relationships in ways that produce incentives
for associations to represent their members with a clear public voice. But
this incentive can also induce associations to encourage the exit of dissenters rather than to suffer the weakening of their public voice that internal
dissent might cause. This is hardly a democratic way of responding to
dissent. And yet it is not at all obvious that democratic systems would be
better off if advocacy groups were more inclusive and internally democratic: public spheres need clear voices to establish and alter the parameters of public agendas. Should the Sierra Club or Greenpeace be compelled
to admit representatives of the mining industry as members and provide
them with a public platform? Clearly, the public voices of these associations would be muddied and they would cease to be effective participants
in the public sphere. What democrats should be more concerned about,
rather, is that each individual experience a mix of associational attach-

ments; some of these should be robustly democratic. Those that are less democratic should, in compensation, have higher possibilities for exit and fewer opportunities to monopolize the livelihoods of members—points I discuss in chapters 5 and 7.

A Note on Functionalist Language

Throughout this book, I refer to the "democratic effects" of associational life rather than, say, to the "democratic purposes" of association. This is, of course, functionalist language of a sort, indicating that the democratic functions of associations may differ from the motives and purposes of members. Or—to use the terms of now classical sociology—the manifest functions of an association do not exhaust, and may sometimes contradict, its latent functions.[62] I have three reasons for using this distinction.

First, any purpose can be judged from the perspective of the agent, or from the perspective of the consequences of pursuing it in a multifaceted environment. Ideally, individuals become attuned to these consequences, and are able to engage both perspectives—itself a civic achievement—as when someone says: "I disagree with what you say, but I defend your right to say it." Even then, an individual's recognition of the opinions of another may be nothing more than a gesture of recognition, but, in aggregate, such recognition functions to enable discursive approaches to political conflicts. Similarly, a church may exist for the sake of a biblical mission, and its members will understand its manifest purposes in this way. Nonetheless, it may serve the latent democratic functions of teaching organizational and verbal skills. It may serve as a means of representation of moral issues to a broader public, thus enlivening democratic discourse. Its members may find that for broader effect they must convert biblical language into secular terms, thus building bridges to other perspectives. The church may serve to devolve certain desirable social tasks, such as providing welfare to those who fall through the "official" safety net, and so on. The family, to take an example of primary association, tends toward insularity, and individuals do not enter into these intimate relations for any remotely democratic purpose. As Hannah Arendt noted, a family is even "antipolitical" in the sense that its constitutive good, intimacy, cannot become a common good by its very nature.[63] But the family can and (we hope) often does serve to develop the most basic structures of reciprocity and empathy. Such ethical dispositions can underwrite generalized forms of empathy with and attentiveness to the needs and perspectives of others.[64] The general point is that societies and political systems are not just the aggregates of the dispositions of their members, but something more—and this is what functionalist language indicates.

Second, distinguishing the purposes and goals of associations from their functions guards against the reductionist view that associations are good *only* if they have democratic goods and goals. The term *democratic effect* points toward the good of a democratic society and politics, but does not imply that people undertake (or should undertake) their associational attachments for democratic purposes or, indeed, for any broader social purpose whatsoever. Nor does it imply that the democratic functions of associations exhaust the goods of association, which are many and varied. After all, democracy may be good, but it is not exhaustive of all goods. What the terms "function" and "effect" do imply, however, is that associations may be judged from a democratic perspective, assuming that what this means is spelled out.

Third, ethical potentials with democratic implications exist, often counterfactually, in the structures of interaction necessary for association. In this sense, individuals may unintentionally pursue, say, a democratic ethos of reciprocity as consequence of intentionally pursuing other goals.[65] Habermas shows convincingly, for example, that bargaining and negotiation depend upon a prior consensus about the rules of bargaining, the appropriateness of the matter at hand for a bargained resolution.[66] In many cases, these (latent) criteria may themselves become topics for discussion or matters of political conflict. Importantly, the distinction between the latent and manifest functions of a social action or relationship helps to reveal possibilities for immanent criticism of beliefs and practices.

Three

The Concept of Association

LACK of consensus about the concept of democracy for the most part reflects distinctive visions and theories that are well understood. Although the concept of association is likewise contested, the conceptual terrain has not been worked enough for us to know exactly what is at stake—this, despite the fact that the modern pedigree of the concept goes back at least as far as Locke.

As a matter of description, of course, we know what we mean by "associations." We ordinarily mean those kinds of attachments we choose for specific purposes—to further a cause, form a family, play a sport, work through a problem of identity or meaning, get ahead in a career, or resolve a neighborhood problem. Our most common theoretical take on associations relies on a distinction between the thickness or thinness of associative relations.[1] Thus, families and friendships constitute a web of *primary associations*, while less immediate but nonetheless close social attachments count as *secondary* (or *intermediate*) associations—civic groups, sports clubs, religious associations, and the like. In *tertiary* associations— the membership-based interest groups and professional organizations that populate Washington, D.C., for example—members are relatively anonymous to one another and have little in common beyond the specific purpose they are pursuing.

The (Tocquevillian) assumption embedded in this kind of distinction is that the democratic virtues of association follow from their mediating ("intermediate") role between state and society. As I suggested in chapter 2, the Tocquevillian state-society dualism limits our understanding of the democratic effects of association. But it nonetheless reveals a core idea: shared purposes achieved by voluntary attachments are, under another description, the intrinsically democratic way to relate normative purposes and collective action. In contrast to markets and bureaucracies, association is the form of social organization that thrives on talk, normative agreement, cultural similarity, and shared ambitions—that is, forms of communication that are rooted in speech, gesture, self-presentation, and related forms of social interaction.

At the same time, such classifications often involve an assumption that these social means of organization are best effected through thick association based on face-to-face relations—reflecting the localism embedded in

Tocqueville's rendition of America. This assumption is most certainly wrong: it injects an unnecessary parochialism into the concept, while over-looking the democratic benefits of socially "thin" associations.[2] Tertiary associations, for example, may be better at underwriting public dialogue than secondary associations can precisely because they do not bear the burden of face-to-face social integration, a point I discuss in chapter 5.

Nonetheless, classifications based on the thickness of associative attach-ments provide still another important clue to the nature of modern associ-ation. Modern associations are selective in their purposes. Unlike strong communities or inclusive corporate bodies, modern associative attach-ments are rarely all-encompassing of individuals, but are taken up by them in different ways, for different purposes, at different times in their lives. That is, associations are *modern* (post–seventeenth century) and *pluralistic* forms of social organization.

Hobbes and Locke: The Modern Concept of Association

The notion of a distinctively modern associational form is not new. We find the idea of a discrete associative purpose as early as Hobbes, who gave it a rough start in *Leviathan* by conceiving the state on the principle of association rather than as a corporate, organic body. Owing to their natural weakness and fear, individuals associate for purposes of mutual security. Hobbes's approach implied, of course, that political association is closely related to individuals' capacities to decide, and that association is discrete rather than all-encompassing. Individuals choose association as a purposively rational means for pursuing the specific good of security. Hobbes did not, however, understand social resources as distinctive means of association: indeed, promises made for the sake of collective security are effective only if enforced by the sword. Hobbes in this way identified emerging individualism with anomie (to use Durkheim's term anachronistically), so that while association is a distinctively modern form of attachment, it also lacks any motivational force except as an in-strument of individual purposes. There is no indication in Hobbes that association can produce its own kind of social order when differentiated from the coercive order imposed by the state.

This Hobbesian form of liberalism—the notion that society becomes an anomic aggregation of egoistic self-seekers when detached from corpo-ratist communities—provided fodder for the shallow view of modern as-sociation found in Ferdinand Tönnies's well-known distinction between Gemeinschaft (community) and Gesellschaft (association-based civil soci-ety).[3] By linking associational relations with anomie, Tönnies suggested that fluid, association-based social organizations lack the capacities for social integration necessary for individuals and societies to reproduce themselves.

If we look to Locke, however, the modern concept of association emerges more vigorously, now incorporating the view that different kinds of social order are appropriate to different kinds of purposes. In *An Essay Concerning Toleration*, Locke distinguishes between social order imposed by force and that emerging from conviction, opinion, and conscience.[4] Force, the key resource of the "magistrate," is appropriate for securing external regulation of behavior, but can have no impact on convictions and opinions. Indeed, Locke suggests that when magistrates seek to extend their powers beyond the goal of maintaining civil order, they will tend to disrupt social order rather than secure it. The suppression of religious expression in particular causes men to hold their convictions more strongly, forcing them away from peace and toward war.[5] But if the magistrate allows men to follow their convictions in matters of conscience, it follows that most religious associations will likewise limit themselves to matters of conscience. Locke's ungenerous view that toleration ought not to extend to "papists" reinforces this point: followers of the pope fail to distinguish religious and political order, and are thus unable to extend toleration to others.[6]

Locke generalized this distinction in *Two Treatises of Government* by conceiving society as a contract among equals.[7] In contrast to the contract of Hobbes's *Leviathan*, Locke's does not include a state but only agreement among equals. The primary legitimacy of social organization flows from autonomous and uncoerced consent, and voluntary association moves to the heart of social order. A second contract establishes the state as a trustee of society, necessary to achieve those things that cannot be achieved by individuals through voluntary association alone. To be sure, with Locke the religious dimension remains essential to voluntary association: the ethical force of Protestant commitments provides a background of assurances that promises are, as it were, enough to ensure social order.[8] Nonetheless, association now takes on its own ethical meaning as a social space within which things can be done through agreements among equals. Although Locke was no democrat, the strong connection between self-governance, association, and democracy can already be found in his work.

The notion that associations express a distinctively moral ordering of social relations was developed and reinforced by Adam Ferguson, in *An Essay on the History of Civil Society*.[9] In Ferguson's account of civil society, Locke's Protestant precepts drop out and are replaced by an emphasis on the social and benevolent nature of humans. Left to follow these inner-worldly resources, humans will by nature organize virtuous spheres of social interaction.

Tocqueville: The Associational Democracy of Everyday Life

It was Tocqueville, however, who filled out the modern concept of association by providing it with a sociology. In particular, secondary associations can integrate and socialize, producing attachments that might replace hierarchical corporatist organization with horizontal attachments. Anomic individualism will occur if the corporatist hierarchies that defined feudal social orders are replaced *only* with *primary* associations of friends and families. *Secondary* associations, in contrast, draw individuals out of their primary attachments, enabling beneficial collective actions as well as cultivating the ethical sensibility of "self-interest rightly understood," which would direct individuals to appreciate their extended interdependencies. Associational attachments of this sort enable new, "democratic" forms of social integration.

Two features of association are especially prominent in Tocqueville's analysis. First, there exists a relative social equality of individuals given by the fact that inequalities are sphere specific and do not map onto generalized ascriptive status. Tocqueville is quite taken with the fact that in America, unlike in France, a worker and his boss can mingle socially after work. Second, attachments are much more likely to be chosen by individuals, a fact in part explained by the availability of land, increasing as it did the opportunities of exit from relations of dependency—at least for white males. The fact of choice, combined with a relative equality of members, however, makes the ethical dimension of association more robust. Although Tocqueville does not provide an analysis, the availability of exit means that those forms of association that do exist must be based on "voluntary" resources—that is, the consent of those within the association. Consent provides a form of social organization that alters, develops, and democratizes the ethical sensibilities of individuals, at least in contrast to European ascriptive hierarchies. "When the chroniclers of the Middle Ages, who were all by birth or assimilation aristocrats, relate the tragic end of a noble, there is no end to their grief; but they mention all in a breath and without wincing massacres and tortures of the common people." In democratic ages, "men rarely sacrifice themselves for another, but they show a general compassion for all the human race. One never sees them inflict pointless suffering, and they are glad to relieve the sorrows of others when they can do so without much trouble to themselves."[10] Ethical sensibilities in America—especially empathy with others—tend to move across classes and strata, although not, as yet, across racial lines.[11]

For Tocqueville, then, associations stem the dangers of anomic individualism by drawing individuals out of their primary associations, providing alternatives to ascriptive forms of social organization, and by inducing ethically transformative experiences—a point that later figures prominently in Durkheim's *Professional Ethics and Civic Morals*.[12] These are the Tocquevillian insights into the nature of association I wish to build upon here.

Nonetheless, a purely Tocquevillian conception of association is not entirely adequate for two reasons. First, although Tocqueville noticed the distinctiveness of associational organization of society when compared to state-imposed organization, he did not generalize the idea that there exist distinctive media of social organization. As I suggested in chapter 2, this left him with a bipolar, state-society model, which—at the level of theory—generalizes by default the idea that the state is the sole agent of power within a society of otherwise voluntary relations. Thus, he modeled economic relations on the concept of voluntary association, without grasping how markets might structure social organization or affect the distribution of economic power in society. Similarly, although Tocqueville often comments on the ways in which bias is mobilized within local associations against outsiders, free blacks, and others, he does not develop a general account of how social media can produce hegemonic influence. As a result, Tocqueville overgeneralized the democratic effects of associational life. Second, in part because Tocqueville did not develop a general account of the social media of association, his conception of association is instead tied to a spatial conception of social connection—consistent with the ways that associations were rooted in the face-to-face relations of small-town life in early-nineteenth-century life in America, but less useful in today's societies.

G. D. H. Cole: Association versus Community

Tocqueville's notion that democracy and association are closely related was revived by G. D. H. Cole, the English guild socialist. His aims were democratic and pluralist: collective actions ought to be organized around specific purposes, and organizations should be pluralized in accordance with the wide variety of purposes that people pursue. For Cole the democratic significance of associations resides in their segmented and differentiated purposes, in contrast to the encompassing purposes of communities. This is a key point: in contrast to the encompassing relations of communities, modern associations can become means of pluralizing power and devolving politics, decision making, and governance. Limited in their purposes and added together, they constitute a decentered political fabric of crosscutting and overlapping organizations.

Cole defines an association as "any group of persons pursuing a common purpose or aggregation of purposes by a course of cooperative action extending beyond a single act, and, for this purpose, agreeing together upon certain methods and procedures and laying down, in however rudimentary a form, rules for common action. At least two things are fundamentally necessary to any association: a common purpose and, to a certain extent, rules of common action."[13] Cole's definition is broad: associations describe any group of people that combines a purpose with organization. Thus, associations range from families, with their informal and traditional means of organization, to schools, unions, and firms.

Cole's definition may be broad, but it is distinctively modern in drawing attention to the segmented character of association. Associations organize society differently than do communities, which Cole conceives as encompassing (and thus nonpluralistic) means of organization. "In order to be a community," writes Cole,

> a group must exist for the good life and not merely for the furtherance of some specific and partial purpose. Thus, a cricket club, or a trade union, or a political party is not a community, because is it not a self-contained group of complete human beings, but an association formed for the furtherance of a particular interest common to a number of persons who have interests outside of it. A community is thus essentially a social unity or group to which human beings belong, as distinguished from an association with which they are only connected.[14]

To be sure, the concept of community is notoriously slippery, and there would be little gain in taking Cole's distinction too literally. In ordinary usage, the notion of community at best indicates common feelings of attachment and identity, and in this sense is not in opposition to association, which can evoke similar common feelings.[15] Often the concept of community is used as a pointed rhetorical device to evoke dimensions of commonality—the "community of Spanish speakers" or "communities of faith"—that by virtue of their "community" status imply that ethical or affective attachments are the primary adhesive of association. Used in this sense, a community is actually something less than an association; its basis consists only in evocative ideas and images, and seems not to depend on actual contacts among people or on any organizational structure. This conception of community is so devoid of content that there is little point in using it at all.

If, however, we revert to the stronger definition of community used by Cole—communities as ethically integrated, "self-contained" groups of people—then we can learn something more about association. To a far greater extent than communities, modern associations are contrived and justified for the purposes they serve. Associations are, to use Paul Hirst's terms, "communities of choice" rather than "communities of fate."[16] This is what makes associations rather than communities (of fate) the primary means of social organization in modern pluralistic societies. As Nancy Rosenblum rightly observes, the experiences of joining and quitting, multiple memberships, and the restriction of some kinds of memberships to distinctive stages in individuals' life-cycles suggest a society of highly social (that is, not anomic) people who are nonetheless not ordered according to an overriding community or way of life. This is the modern pattern of social integration not grasped by Tönnies, nor, for that matter, by many contemporary communitarians. Associations are not as malleable as suggested by Cohen and Rogers's characterization of them as "artifactual."[17] Nonetheless, when compared to communities, they are intrinsically more fluid in the sense that they can be brought into existence in response to a problem or opportunity without requiring social and psychological integration with every other social attachment. As Cohen and Rogers's term suggests, associations can be "built," whereas communities cannot. Associations can also evolve in new directions as their purposes, missions, and aspirations shift. Or they can be dissolved when they either decisively achieve or fail to achieve their purposes.

There are, of course, many forms of association that seek to emulate self-contained communities. Such associations are, to borrow Rosenblum's characterization, "greedy" of their members' time, commitment, identity, and even property—as are cults, militias, and fundamentalist religious sects. But these forms of association are limiting cases, and difficult to maintain in isolation from other attachments members inevitably have or from needs that are life-cycle specific. Plural encumbrances can be controlled by greedy associations only by encompassing design—having members renounce past beliefs, give away their property, disconnect from family and friends, and live communally in isolated areas.

There is a sense too in which associations provide better soil for democratic collective action than do communities. Because communities are less fluid and more encompassing than associations, they are inherently more conservative. In contrast, owing to the fluidity of associational attachments, individuals are less likely to view their associations as invested with encompassing and authoritative pasts, which in turn makes it more likely that associations can orient toward novel problems and new futures. Moreover, all other things being equal, the relatively discrete nature of associational purposes makes it easier to bracket other purposes and arrive at consensus about a single purpose. As the American pluralists pointed out, if I can agree with a number of others that we should stop a freeway or a toxic dump or reduce global warming, we can associate for these purposes, even if we are of differing religions, nations, occupations, ethnicities, and so on. In contrast, in any complex and pluralistic society, the (encompassing) communitarian impulse to connect every issue and identity tends to stop collective action in its tracks.

Outside of questions of desirability, in complex and pluralistic societies associations in fact tend to erode communities as venues for collective action and decision. The vast majority of individuals are connected to one another in multiple, crosscutting ways, so that there are now fewer opportunities for the tyrannies as well as the comforts of community. Not only are individuals freer in their social attachments, but even in associations in which individuals are less free (as in families and unions), they are more likely to demand justifications in terms of purposes. In this sense too, associations are more likely than communities to entail democratic possibilities, since the burdens of choice and of self-crafting through associations are now left to individuals whose futures are no longer ascribed by thick communal location. Associations are, in this sense, intrinsically connected to the strongest meanings of self-governance, a point long appreciated, if not always defended, in First Amendment constitutional law.[18]

A closely related point is that because associations can be distinguished by discrete purposes, they can be judged in terms of their ideals and effects. This is a key moral and discursive resource for democracy. Although the fluidity of associations may tend to externalize dissent through exit, in principle associations are better able to respond to dissent through deliberation. Because associations are not encompassing, members can bring perspectives from the outside. And when associations are voluntary, repression of dissent induces exit—a dynamic that can produce incentives for associations to use persuasion rather than force. Although even strong communities inevitably have their share of dissent, they are usually ill equipped to respond in democratic ways. A strong community is constituted in such a way that its practices and traditions are securely interconnected with its social functions, which are in turn closely integrated with its members' identities. When expressed, dissent too easily evokes threat, which in turn provokes repression. S. N. Eisenstadt and L. Roniger, for example, argue that the relative lack of freedom to criticize in Muslim societies stems in part from the fact that they are strongly integrated as communities, meaning that criticism of cultural or religious tenets also threatens economic and political integration.[19] The functional costs of cultural disorder are high enough that communal traditions are strongly and often violently defended against "moral corruption."

In contrast, associations provide modes of interconnection within societies that differentiate cultural from economic and political reproduction. A key effect of differentiation is that different spheres of activities and different institutions can be measured in terms of their intrinsic criteria (art for art's sake, production for needs, marriage for the sake of intimacy, raison d'état, and so on), which can in turn be compared and contrasted to other criteria. These comparative vantage points afford individuals the opportunity for critical perspectives and choices that are not possible in undifferentiated, encompassing communities. It is not accidental, for example, that when liberal contract theorists beginning with Hobbes conceived the state as an association devoted to specific purposes (rather than as an encompassing community), they could also put the questions of the legitimacy of the state and obligations to the state, as well as conceive of strict limits to the justifiable domain of state violence. Nor is it accidental that the notion of tolerance dates from this era in which the relationship between association and differentiation was first discovered.

What we can gain from Cole's approach to associations, then, is an appreciation for their modern character, in contrast with the attachments of (premodern) community. Cole does not, however, provide a conception of association that is sufficient for the purposes of democratic theory. One defect is that Cole overgeneralizes association as a means of social integration and reproduction in modern societies. He views the state, for example, as simply one more form of association. Cole misses the fact that the state—even the most democratic state—also uses nonassociational means of getting things done, namely (following Weber), coercion based in a monopoly over violence within a given territory. If the state has an associational dimension, it resides in the fact that it draws on associational relations (deliberative decision making within legislatures, for example) to codify, legalize, and legitimate the violence it monopolizes. But this does not make the state an association, and we shall need to maintain the distinction among associational ways of integrating society and those based on coercion embedded in law, as well as those that work through markets. Only then will we be able to conceptualize how, exactly, associations can support democratic effects both outside and within these other modes of integration—a topic I address below and then again in chapter 5.

A second difficulty with Cole's approach is that he embeds his concept of association within a teleological functionalism, in terms of which associational purposes carry out their roles in reproducing society. In Cole's view, the "purpose or group of purposes is the basis of the *function* of the association which has been called into being for its fulfillment."[20] Added together, the functions served by associations ought to constitute a "coherent" society, which in turn allows associations to be judged more or less essential. Cole grants that the functions are themselves socially constructed and contestable according to different conceptions of value.[21] But even then his functionalism attributes an overriding desirability to a "coherence" that should not be theoretically prejudged. Moreover, there is no need to equate associational purposes with their contributions to a "coherent" society at all. The contributions associations make to the overall functioning of society (or democracy for that matter) neither exhaust the purposes of associations nor are they even necessarily important to associational purposes. We may, for some purposes, wish to judge the effects of associational activities in terms of criteria grouped around a single idea—as I do here with democracy. But it is an entirely different matter to judge associational purposes in terms of their contributions to a global vision, or even to assume that the purposes of an association exhaust their effects. As I suggested in chapter 2, it is important to distinguish the manifest and latent functions of a social form. What members of an association intend, the purposes they pursue, and the justifications they proffer may have little if anything to do with the democratic functions their association serves.

Parsons: Three "Types of Operative Organization"

Although Cole is sensitive to the distinctively modern qualities of association, we shall need to turn to Talcott Parsons for a generalized conception of association that will allow us to identify democratic effects within differentiated societies. For my purposes, what is most important about Parsons's approach is that he distinguishes "associational structure" or "associational relations" as one of three central "types of operative organization" in modern societies, along with markets and bureaucracies.[22] Modern societies are distinguished by the extent to which these three means of organization form distinct axes of differentiation, each with distinctive modes of operation, organization, and normative criteria. Parsons's approach is important for at least three reasons.

First, because no organization is purely associational, the distinction avoids the confusion of actual associations with particular kinds and means of social organization. Although *associational means* of organization are dominant within *associations* (families, churches, sports clubs, political interest groups, New Social Movements, etc.), "the associational principle" (in Parsons's terms) may be found in organizations within which other types of media (markets and bureaucracies) are at work as well—within firms, labor unions, legislatures, and even government bureaucracies. Thus, for example, Parsons can speak of associative structures becoming more common within government, bureaucracy, and even market-oriented firms. To the extent that associative structures have democratic effects, we may find a sociological basis for identifying these effects not just within society, but in states and markets as well.

Second, associations exist not only within environments populated only by other associations, but also by markets and states. These other means of organization constrain associative relations in diverse ways, which in turn influences their democratic effects. We should not expect, for example, that an association entangled with the state—a professional society with state-sanctioned powers to license its members for practice, for example—to have the same kinds of democratic effects as, say, a New Social Movement that organizes its members through the social media of norms and identity formation. We need the conceptual tools to identify the different kinds of entanglements with distinctive "types of operative organization" (to use Parsons's terms) if we are to know what kinds of democratic effects to expect of different kinds of association.

Third, if we can distinguish these distinctive entanglements, we shall also be able to decipher the confusions that surround the notion that the important associations for democracy are "voluntary." Each operative type of organization has its distinctive mode of forcefulness, combined with environments that make exit more or less difficult. These in turn combine to affect ways in which associations deal with conflict, which in turn makes a difference in their democratic effects—a topic I discuss in chapter 5.

On Parsons's view, modern associational relations develop as societies evolve from the "more primordial bases of religion, ethnicity, and territoriality" as ways of organizing "social solidarity."[23] With their move away from these premodern bases, modern societies organize some spheres in ways that do not depend directly upon cultural forms of integration, nor upon territorially based force. Perhaps most fundamental is the emergence of market structures, where the operative organization is through price structures—a "delinguistified" mode of communication (to borrow Habermas's accurate if inelegant term) among individuals and organizations separated in time and space. Agents communicate impersonally through the signals given by prices, resulting in market structures that coordinate extensive and vastly complex divisions of labor and modes of cooperation.

Markets are, of course, enabled by the political development of rights, especially rights over unconstrained and "free" use of property, including property in one's own body, skills, and mind. Markets also require an environment of predictable laws and rules. These political and governmental developments involve a second kind of differentiation or operative organization, the bureaucratic administration of law within constitutional orders. In the Weberian terms Parsons uses, the bureaucratic type of organization is based on the development of (enforced) rules—rules that provide regular and knowable environments for actors in markets and civil society. Bureaucracies do this in part by cutting ties of patronage, ethnicity, religion, and other personal relationships, by developing "offices" filled under merit-based procedures, and by holding officers to their job descriptions. Accountability of officials is enforced by hierarchy. The combination of written code and control over organizational capacities produces a distinctive type of operational organization that depends neither on the direct, particular face-to-face coordination of social relations nor on responsiveness to price mechanisms. Bureaucratic organization dramatically increases the capacities of institutions (not only state institutions but also firms, labor unions, political parties, and many other large-scale associations) to extract, control, and organize resources of collective action. When combined with the coercive powers of the state, bureaucratic organization produces a binding system of administrative procedure and law. When combined with control over means of production, bureaucratic organization produces the modern form of the firm.

Associations constitute the third type of operative organization in modern societies. They retain the more primordial social and cultural bases of organization, but shift these onto distinctively modern ground—what Habermas refers to as the "rationalization of the life-world."[24] The prototype of associational structure, Parsons writes, is perhaps "the societal collectivity itself, considered as a corporate body of citizens holding primarily consensual relations to its normative order and to the authority of its leadership."[25] If we focus on the point that association involves *consensual* relations to a *normative* order, we can see that it is essential to association that cultural resources are purified of their coercive and economic elements. Only then can associations develop according to the logic of their normative potentials. Modern associations rely on attachments that are held and justified in terms of the intrinsic criteria of the norms—and herein lies their distinctive means of influence, their ethical vitality, as well as their dynamism. When marriage, for example, is freed of its economic functions it can develop and express its intrinsic potentials for love, intimacy, and friendship. In modern societies, associative relations are constrained less from within through the melding of social functions and more from without by the systems from which they are differentiated.[26]

The democratic functions of associations I discuss in chapter 4 depend upon this prior differentiation of means of social organization.[27] Without this differentiation, there is no *distinctive* contribution of associational relations, whether this amounts to providing normative leverage over or within states and markets, underwriting normative discourses within public spheres, developing civic and political capacities, or providing alternative forms of governance.

Parsons identifies three trends in modern association relations that help to develop these characteristics. The first is an increasingly inclusive citizenship of a sort that displaces ascriptive association. "Citizenship can be dissociated from ethnic membership, with its strong tendency toward nationalism and even 'racism,' which provides a sharp ascriptive criterion of belonging. The alternative has been to define belonging in universalistic terms, which inevitably must include reference to voluntary 'allegiance,' although probably no societal community can be a purely voluntary association."[28] This trend involves increasing equalities that define the terms of citizenship, especially expanded rights against the state and rights to participate in public affairs, both of which tend to increase attention to the welfare of individuals.[29] These trends have been complemented by the development of universal education, which likewise challenges parochial bases of membership, loosens ascriptive ties, and provides more alternatives for individuals.[30] In the United States, Parsons argues, these dimensions of inclusive citizenship have been enhanced by two cultural factors: the universalism of ascetic Protestantism and the drive to mastery of various social environments.

As a general diagnosis, Parsons's account is problematic. Protestant universalism has two faces: one inclusive of those who bend to its variety of university, the other exclusive of those who do not fit. Mastery likewise has two faces: extending value systems and social structures functions to control through inclusion, while it also justifies violence against those who cannot be so disciplined. In addition, there are other forces, such as the development of markets beyond any Protestant origins, that loosen ascriptive forms of membership.

Nonetheless, if we make allowances for Parsons's optimistic and somewhat one-sided assessment of the United States, his general point is worth noting. The trend toward equality in associational relations indicates a trend toward modes of social organization that are less greedy of identity, and thus produce modern forms of "community"—if that is what they are—that include crosscutting and plural forms of attachment. This is why as the "societal community" extends it also loosens communal allegiances, which in turn encourages the development of procedures of negotiation among and between differences. Such developments enhance the democratic qualities of political culture—the key Parsonian insight incorporated into the sociological strains of American pluralist theory. The point remains valuable today, but only if we do not mistake (as American pluralists often did) these tendencies for realities. On average, increasingly inclusive equalities tend to pluralize relations of dependence, which in turn mitigates their impact on individuals. While such developments do not produce social or political equality in themselves (which requires affirmative action of one sort or another), they do provide many more chances for individuals to escape relations of dependence. They pluralize dependencies, as it were, which increases the number of bonds that can be re-formed on more consensual grounds.[31]

The second trend Parsons identities—toward increasing voluntariness in associational structure—depends on this structural background of equality. Although "an element of bindingness is essential to all collectivities," Parsons notes, "voluntariness" describes the decision "to accept and retain membership, an alternative to compliance always being resignation."[32] Although Parsons merely hints at the relationship, differentiation pluralizes the resources of power so that possibilities for exit increase. In a purely associational tie, association is voluntary, meaning not that there is a lack of commitment (as communitarians often mistakenly argue),[33] but rather that the means through which the association is bound together into a collectivity consist in the social resources of consensus, shared goals, and norms.

The voluntary or consensual nature of associational relations is essential to defining their distinctive quality as a means of social organization. They affect organization through *influence* rather than through money or power. Influence, in Parsons's usage, is "a generalized symbolic medium of interchange, in the same general class as money and power. It consists in capacity to bring about desired decisions on the part of other social units without directly offering them a valued quid pro quo as an inducement or threatening them with deleterious consequences. Influence must operate through persuasion, however, in that its object must be convinced that to decide as the influencer suggests is to act in the interest of a collective system with which both are solidary."[34] That is, influence is exercised by building normative consensus.

In this sense, increasing voluntariness also increases the domains of society that can be regulated by ethical attachments—not generally, but within those domains in which associational relations are dominant. As Kant and many others in the liberal tradition have emphasized, norms enforced by external means lack intrinsically motivating force, and thus lack moral value. Because associational relations tend toward voluntariness, they must also rely to a greater extent upon the force of norms. As I shall suggest in the next section, however, *associational relations* that have an intrinsically consensual basis should not be confused (as they often are) with the idea that *associations* are for this reason voluntary in other respects, a quality that depends upon their structural entanglements, which may bring other kinds of force to bear. This distinction becomes important, as we shall see, in determining how differently situated associations handle conflict, and hence serve as "schools of democracy" (chapters 4 and 5).

The third trend Parsons identifies—toward increasing proceduralism within associational relations—is especially interesting because of its simultaneously progressive and problematic aspects. In spite of the fact that they have their origins in legal systems, "procedural institutions" are central to the functioning of associational relations. Parsons conceives procedures as consisting in two levels, one involving discussion, the other decision making. "Discussion within association is a primary sphere of the operation of influence as a medium for facilitating social process. From the viewpoint of an interested party, discussion serves to improve the chances of having his view prevail; from the viewpoint of the collectivity it facilitates an approach to consensus."[35] The second level is the process of deciding itself, which often means that there are formal rules for voting to which members have previously committed themselves.

As an account of democratic process, of course, this is standard stuff. The points become interesting, however, when viewed in the context of associative relations as a means of operative organization. Differentiation, insofar as it pluralizes dependency, *in itself* pushes toward procedure. And procedure, far from being "neutral" (as communitarian critics often suggest) displaces money and power in favor of influence as a means of social organization. There exists a close relationship between pluralizing dependencies and movements toward modes of decision making based on influence—if not directly through normative agreement, at least secondarily through prior commitment to the outcomes of decision-rules such as voting.[36] This point gets at the question as to why democratic procedure alone makes effective the normative question What shall we do?—a point rightly emphasized by Benjamin Barber when he characterizes democracy as the *most political* of political theories.[37]

Parsons is especially taken with the extent to which associations mimic these processes of constitutional government. From a theoretical perspective, we can account for this by noting that because associations rely primarily on influence as a medium of social interchange, they must find means of continually renewing a normative consensus. Where members can exit in response to conflict, associations that seek to retain members find they must devise ways of repairing the tears in the normative fabric. This often means that associations must develop procedures that provide the chance for members to discuss differences and to renew the normative consensus. All other things being equal, pluralized dependency leans toward conflict resolution through democratic procedures. At the same time, as I will argue in chapter 5, the same mechanisms can depoliticize a *purely* voluntary association, because exit can serve as a means of gaining consensus that avoids discursive resolutions in favor of a marketplace in associational attachments.

Associations versus Associational Relations

Following Parsons, we can sketch another piece of the theoretical picture by distinguishing associations from associational relations. *Associations* are organizations whose force is derived primarily from associational relations—that is, relations based on normative influence. *Associational relations* refers to one of the three general means of organizing societies. It follows that the distinction between state, economy, and civil society is one of institutional domain, while the distinctions between bureaucracy, market, and associational relations refer to types of operative organization. The sets of distinctions are related in that each kind of institutional domain is centered, as it were, on a type of operative organization, of which no institution is a pure exemplar. No institution can work purely through market transactions, nor through hierarchical command. Likewise, few associations, owing to their entanglements with power and money, exhibit the purely voluntary and consensual qualities of associational relations.

The distinction between association and associational relation is important because (1) it will allow us to show how associational relations can inhabit institutions that are not themselves associations; (2) it will allow us to show how state/government bodies or firms can be structured to be susceptible to or to include associational relations and thus to develop their democratic potentials; (3) it will allow us to show how associations (as organizations) are structured by their relations to power and money (the other two types of operative organization) in ways that influence their democratic effects; and (4) last but not least, the distinction will allow us to define the relationship between the topic of association and that of civil society.

With regard to the first point, Hobbes notwithstanding, states are not associations; neither are firms or other kinds of market-oriented economic organizations. Such institutions are primarily structured by the media of (legal and administrative) power and money. Associations, in contrast, are constituted primarily by shared purposes or interests, and the dominant means of organization is influence. Nonetheless, associational relations can be found to greater or lesser degrees in all organizations. Thus, while maintaining the distinctions between the institutions of state, market, and civil society, Parsons can also speak of an increase in associational relations within the state. In particular, procedural institutions tend to mitigate the organizing effects of power and place a premium on influence. Thus, although states are primarily organized by legal-administrative power, legislative bodies are structured (by constitutional law) to be arenas of associative relations in which influence is (or ought to be) paramount. Legislative decisions must be taken on associational grounds through procedures that enable bargaining or consensus among equals. Ideally, the powers of members of a legislature are equalized by the institution itself, so that associational relations become the residual means of organization, despite conflict and despite the fact that decisions are ultimately empowered by state coercion. In this way, we can see that the state is not an "association," but also that in democratic states associational relations do their work within the coercive shell of law, in this way generating legitimacy for state coercion. Likewise, as Parsons notes, bureaucratic means of organization are receding in many kinds of bureaucracies, being replaced with associational relations. The notion of having "colleagues" in the workplace with whom one cooperates can take up residence within the shell of bureaucratic command and control, especially in sectors where there are higher degrees of education and professionalism.[38] Moreover, even firms and other market-oriented organizations can have significant associative qualities. This is so when firms function less as command hierarchies and more as cooperatives or partnerships in order to enhance internal solidarity and communication or as a result of members' identification with the intrinsic worth of the firm's products or services. For some purposes it may make sense to view such firms as associations operating within the economic constraints of markets. Of course, even firms such as these remain subject to the tensions and crisis possibilities inherent in the fact that they serve the imperatives of a system of economic reproduction that is not sensitive to the normative integrity of associative relations.[39]

With regard to the second point, the fact that associational relations can take up residence, as it were, within institutions that are not themselves associations provides linkages between the spheres of civil society, state, and economy. As both Parsons and Habermas emphasize, a society with differentiated media must, somehow, coordinate their effects. A *democratic* approach to coordination will lean toward associational relations as means of coordination—again, because this is the only type of operative organization that can relate the political question "What should we do?" to collective decision and action. On the assumption that democracy involves more than mere preference aggregation, the democratic project depends upon identifying ways in which systems organized by power and money might be guided by associative relations. Cohen and Arato, for example, speak of state and economic institutions that incorporate "sensors" or "receptors" that are sensitive to the normative discourses of civil society.[40] What this means, theoretically, is that associational relations have a presence within these institutions in ways that can contain and guide their effects while enabling some normative leverage of civil society associations over the "steering" effects of legal-administrative systems (the state) and markets. The oldest model of such a sensor is, of course, the legislative body, which is (ideally) sheltered from the powers of the state by the separation of legislative and executive powers—although often inadequately sheltered from the force of money. Unions provide another example. Because unions are legally empowered to leverage control over labor against owners of means of production, owners must default to negotiation and develop associative relations with labor in order to organize production. The effect is to insert into market-oriented bureaucratic firms associative sensors that empower goods that have no means of being registered in markets. Corporatist arrangements in Sweden and Austria have similar effects, since various labor and community interests have some direct input into corporate management.

With regard to the third point, associations (as organizations) are variously and ambiguously embedded within the three generalized media of social interchange: power, money, and influence. Different kinds of embedding produce different structural constraints on associations and associational relations, which in turn influence democratic effects. Thus, some kinds of associations rely purely on the influence of norms for their cohesion: churches and recreational soccer clubs, for example. Other kinds of associations—advocacy groups, for example—are oriented toward influencing the state. When advocacy groups gain in influence, they are sometimes cut into power arrangements, as when professional associations gain the power to regulate their members' professional activities. Or they gain representatives within government through elected representation, appointments, or corporatist means of influence. Working on the "inside" may make groups more prone to insider bargaining and less likely to seek influence through public discourse. Or associations may be empowered to enforce government policies, as they were by the Clean Water Act of 1970, which enabled civil suits to be brought against polluters. Still other kinds of associations are implicated within market structures. Business associations find that their internal associative relations are highly constrained by the interests imposed by the market positions of their member firms. Such associations will prefer, all other things being equal, not to go public with their interests. Taken together, these different entanglements lead to a highly complex and pluralistic web of democratic possibilities.

The Concept of Civil Society

With regard to the fourth point, I have so far made only passing reference to the concept of civil society. I have avoided the term because it is primarily a *sectoral* concept, whereas I have sought the more precise conceptualization that follows from looking at kinds of social *relations*. There are,

TABLE 3.1
Locating civil society

Closeness of Social Relations	*Means of Social Coordination*			
	Legal coercion		*Social (norms & communication)*	*Money*
Distant	States	Mediating associations: "political society"	Mediating spaces: Publics	Mediating associations: "economic society" Markets
Intermediate			Civil society Pure associative relations	
Intimate			Families, friendships	

of course, important dialogical advantages to connecting the topic of association to that of civil society, given its rich and evocative history. I am less sure there are theoretical advantages. Without careful usage, the concept of civil society obscures more than it clarifies, and in any case whatever conceptual work it does follows from its associational core.

Still, beginning with the concept of association, it is possible to develop a relatively precise conception of civil society: Civil society is the domain of social organization within which voluntary associative relations are dominant. This definition identifies civil society by combining the distinctions between Parsons's "types of operative organization" or "media of social coordination" with those of the closeness or distance of social relations, as represented in table 3.1.

Several features of this definition deserve comment. First, this definition follows common usage by excluding intimate relations among friends and family. The reason for excluding these conceptions from civil society is that there is nothing "civil" about such attachments—they are "private," and operate below the threshold of common collective action. In addition, as Hannah Arendt often emphasized, these private relations are "antipolitical" in that intimacy is corrupted when it becomes, as it were, common property or is put to common purposes. If we grant these points, it becomes clear why the concept of civil society is inadequate to understanding the associative terrain of democracy. It is within intimate relations that we hope to find the ethical dispositions of reciprocity, empathy, and care developed that, injected into political domains, can underwrite de-

mocracy. Spatial/sectoral conceptions obscure what the relational conception of association makes obvious.

Second, this definition identifies what is normatively compelling about
the concept of civil society—namely, that it indicates a domain in which
the voluntary social qualities of associative attachments are dominant, as
compared to the legally compelled attachments of the state or money-
based attachments to the market. This being said, the domains of civil
society and association are not coextensive. One advantage of conceiving
of civil society as the domain in which associative relations are dominant
is that we can then see that these relations are *also* present within nonassociative organizations—within and between firms, in legislative bodies,
and so on. Thus, we need to think of civil society as the domain of associations that is *centered* on associative *relations*, and that shades into associative domains which interact with states, markets, and intimate relations.

Third, although we should conceive civil society as consisting in associations that are centered on associative relations, *for problems of democracy* the associational kinds that mediate between "pure" association,
states, and markets are often the most interesting. Mediating forms of
association—political parties, unions, and consumer cooperatives, for example—connect civil society proper to the market and state sectors
through the associative sensors that exist within market and state organizations.[41] Translated into sectoral language, these domains of association—sometimes termed *political society* and *economic society*—are "of"
civil society but not "in" civil society.[42] These mediating domains serve as
the conduits through which associative relations can potentially affect
markets and states, and are thus key to a number of democratic potentials.

Finally, it is worth noting that public spheres have uniquely spatial locations. Publics are often distant from pure associative relations, which are
constituted as they are by forms of communication that span vast reaches
of time and space. Flows of communication within and among associations and other organizations produce public spaces that are irreducible
to the associative relations upon which they depend. Publics are, as it
were, spheres enabled by the associative structures of civil society, but exist
in ways that keep them from being the exclusive preserve or property of
any associational form. These spaces become detached from their agents,
and come to exist as public conversations not subject to the spatial, structural, and social limits on the associational form, but rather to the logics
of argument, rhetoric, and symbolism. In a somewhat different way, then,
we should also conceive of publics as "of" civil society but not "in" civil
society.

In sum, conceptualizing the democratic effects of associational life depends a good deal on what kind of thing association is. Perhaps most
importantly, despite Tönnies, association is not a kind of anomie.

Rather—as Tocqueville appreciated—association represents a new, distinctively modern form of social attachment. Modern associational attachments have ethical possibilities that do not exist in premodern forms because they exemplify chosen attachments rather than ascriptive integration into society. Willing attachment, however, presupposes the possibility of exit; hence the pattern of pluralized dependencies—what Tocqueville loosely called "equality"—that typified the life of white males in the frontier atmosphere of early-nineteenth-century America. But we can see that this close connection between voluntary attachment and normative influence that is essential to the associative relationship is not limited to this stratum nor to this time and place. Association and equality are interrelated more generally, a point G. D. H. Cole understood when he based a democratic theory on association. He also understood that association does not produce strong community, but rather plural and overlapping attachments, enabling the close relationship between social attachment and self-rule that robust forms of democracy demand. It is Talcott Parsons, however, who provides the theoretical tools for unraveling the possibilities of association in contemporary societies. Parsons understands association as a distinctive means of social organization within differentiated societies. Differentiation frees associations from the economic and political functions they have in premodern societies, which in turn leaves normative attachments as a residual means of social organization. Differentiation thus enables the moral potentials of associational life. At the same time, differentiation produces constraint: associations must contend with legal-administrative and economic constraints from without, producing the paradoxical patterns of normative potential and structural constraint that typify modern societies. Associations are strategically located within this tension, which in turn enables the multitude of potentially democratic effects to which we now turn.

Four

The Democratic Effects of Association

MORE DEMOCRACY is a good thing, and the right mix of associational attachments can help to provide more democracy—or so I have been suggesting. But I have said little about what democracy is, why more of it should be a good thing, or what kinds of democratic effects might be enhanced by associational life. At the highest level of abstraction, of course, democracy is straightforward: it means (and is usually taken to mean) collective self-rule under conditions that provide relatively equal chances for citizens to influence collective judgments and decisions. Embedded in the notion of democratic self-rule are two complementary ideals, one involving equal distribution of the *power to make collective decisions* and the other equal participation in *collective judgment*.[1]

One of the two ideals, equal participation in *collective judgment*, itself has two distinct but complementary meanings. First, democracy implies processes of communication through which individuals come to know *as individuals* what they want or think is right. Individuals should be the owners of their beliefs and preferences, meaning that beliefs and preferences should not be the result of manipulation or received opinion but rather the result of considered adherence. Second, democracy implies processes of communication through which a collectivity comes to know what it wants or thinks is right *as a collectivity. Collective* judgment indicates that individuals have given due consideration to what each wants *as a member of the collectivity*, enabling the collective to formulate a will or "public opinion." Democracy thus involves institutionalized procedures and protections that enable the expression, demonstration, argumentation, and justification through which individuals decide what they want or think is right both as individuals and as members of collectivities.

Both dimensions of judgment depend upon institutions that distribute power democratically, in ways that equalize individuals' chances to influence collective decision making. Voice depends upon the potential veto powers of participants. The most basic power mechanism is, of course, the vote, which amounts to the distribution of the power of decision to each individual in the collectivity. Democracies that include basic rights also distribute an indirect veto power by virtue of the fact that rights tend to constitute sites and capacities for collective action in ways that cause collective decisions to depend upon the cooperation, acquiescence, or indifference of many different actors. In one form or another, broadly distributed powers complement citizens' capacities to partake of collective judgments and decisions.

The normative perspective I adopt here is relatively simple and follows from these dimensions of democracy.

- Democracy is good because it enhances individual and collective self-rule.

- A political system is more democratic the more equally its institutions enhance individual self-rule and the more equally it underwrites individual chances to influence collective judgments and decisions.

Although rather generic, these two ideals (democratic judgment, differentiated into its individual and collective aspects, and democratic distributions of power) do what we need them to do: identify the three general ways in which associations might produce effects that are potentially "democratic."

- Associations may contribute to forming, enhancing, and supporting the capacities of democratic citizens. I shall refer to these as the *developmental effects* associations have on individuals. Ideally, associations would underwrite the capacities of individuals to participate in collective judgment and decision making and to develop *autonomous* judgments that reflect their considered wants and beliefs.

- Associations may contribute to the formation of public opinion and public judgment, especially by providing the social infrastructure of public spheres that develop agendas, test ideas, embody deliberations, and provide voice. I shall refer to these as *public sphere* effects. Ideally, public spheres provide *political autonomy*, that is, the public reasoning through which collective judgments are justified.

- Associations may contribute to *institutional* conditions and venues that support, express, and actualize individual and political autonomy as well as transform autonomous judgments into collective decisions. They can do so by providing political representation, enabling pressure and resistance, organizing political processes, facilitating cooperation, and serving as alternative venues for governance. These effects work through the empowerments associations can provide, and which can directly influence the extent to which the institutions of voting and representation work in democratic ways. But there are also indirect institutional effects: when the institutions of state and market are limited by rights and procedures, associations can enable individuals to affect them in democratic ways through resistance or simply through exit to alternative venues of collective action.

Democratic Self-Rule as Autonomy

Before elaborating these democratic potentials of association, however, I
should like to provide an account of the norm of "democratic self-rule,"
which I associated above with the term *autonomy*. Autonomy means that
individuals—both individually and collectively—hold their interests with
due consideration, and are able to provide reasons for holding them. The
choice of autonomy as the fundamental democratic ideal may seem unusual.[2] More commonly, democracy is viewed as a direct expression of
egalitarian ideals—whether ideals of equal dignity in the deontological
rights-based traditions that stem from Kant or the natural rights traditions; the egalitarian ideals implied in the utilitarian view that individuals
have equal claims to happiness; or the views that derive from the Aristote-
lian and civic republican notion that democratic self-rule is essential to
developing one's humanity, to which each is equally entitled. My presumption that autonomy describes the essential meaning of democratic
self-rule by no means excludes a concern with equality. Indeed, autonomy
is descriptive of *democratic* self-rule only when individuals are conceived
to have equal (moral) claims to autonomy. Other senses of equality, however, are instrumental to individual and political autonomy, including
equal protections, equal personal rights, equal political rights, as well as
resource distributions that are not so unequal that they undermine the
development of autonomy.

Autonomy is a fundamental good, however, only in a limited sense: it
is a fundamental *political* good. It does not encompass all goods, but is
good in relation to demands of *political* relationships—and these are
often quite different from the demands of social relationships more generally. Most social relationships are routinely nonconflictual. When conflicts do arise, they are often resolved by simple clarifications of intent or
by bargaining or even by exit. Social relationships are politicized, however, when individuals *must* decide and act in the face of conflict—even
if the "decision" is a subconscious acceptance of subordination, as in
relationships of domination.[3]

These are the circumstances that place a premium on clarifying interests
and seeking influence through argument, thus making the concept of autonomy essential to that of political self-rule. It would be a mistake to
generalize autonomy as a fundamental good beyond the domain of political relationships. There are many kinds of social relationships where autonomy is inappropriate. Friendship, for example, requires a trust that
questioning and clarifications of motives might very well corrode. The
cathartic effects of a movie or a play essential to its aesthetic appeal might
very well not survive the conscious self-examination inherent in auton-

omy. The virtues of autonomy, in other words, are most evident under circumstances of conflict that call for consciously critical responses.

If we recognize that autonomy is *not* a general account of the good life—that its virtues are closely related to the demands of politics—we can also avoid a normatively reductionist account of associations. That is, if we are explicit about the democratic good of autonomy, we can also avoid overgeneralizing to other domains, which embody other virtues, such as those of love, friendship, loyalty, or beauty. Again, associations may be valuable for their democratic effects, but they need not be judged solely in these terms.

Individual Autonomy

Autonomy in its individual dimension has nothing to do with separateness, anomie, individualism, or even self-sufficiency. Rather, it has to do with individuals' capacities to take part in critical examination of self and others, to participate in reasoning processes, and to arrive at judgments they can defend in public argument—capacities that are, in the end, delicate and valuable social and political achievements.[4] An autonomous self is self-identical, not in the trivial sense of being a distinct physical object, but in the reflexive sense that one can identify oneself as an individual who maintains a biographical continuity in time and who is distinguished by a unique life-history.[5] One maintains identity in this sense by projecting goals into the future and organizing one's present in terms of these goals. Autonomy is experienced as self-location in terms of biographical projections and retrospections, so that the continuous core of the self resides in the reflexive traces of relations with the world that have been desired, projected, maintained, or broken.[6] These reflexive characteristics of autonomy in turn imply capacities of agency, the ability to initiate projects, to bring new ideas, things, and relations into being—capacities for "natality" (to borrow from Hannah Arendt) we usually consider to be uniquely human.[7] Capacities for origination in turn imply capacities to distance self-identity from circumstances. Autonomy in this sense describes the kind of freedom that follows from abilities to adopt a reflexive attitude toward one's own internal impulses—interpreting, transforming, censoring, and providing names for needs, impulses, and desires, as well as expressing them to others as interests and commitments.

With regard to the social world, autonomy implies that one can distance oneself from traditions, prevailing opinions, and pressures to conform by subjecting elements of one's social context to criticism. Autonomy describes the capacities for the critical distance that enable social assessment. Such capacities develop in part through the imagination—the ability to think of alternatives—and in part through the expression of these alternatives to others through reason-giving. In this sense, autonomy depends on public representations of imagined futures. These complementary dimensions produce psychological reinforcements of autonomy: public expression works more forcefully for those able to develop consistency between their thoughts, words, and deeds. Consistency in self-presentation underwrites trustworthiness, responsibility, and promise-keeping, which in turn produce social fabrics of attributions—"reputations." These attributions can reinforce autonomy by placing a social premium on an individual's capacities to relate intentions, speech, and actions.

In these ways, the autonomy of the self depends upon and requires participation in intersubjective processes of reason-giving and response. Autonomy, in other words, implies communicative competencies that cannot exist as individual properties, but only as a part of a shared fabric of communicative understandings and interactions.[8] Even the linguistic subject "I" must be recognized by others as a condition of self-identification.[9] Because autonomy requires participation in linguistic interaction, it also implies reciprocal recognitions of the identities of speakers, if only as a condition of language that depends on the intelligibility of linguistic subjects such as "I" and "you." Without some degree of reciprocity individuals would lose one of the pivotal resources of their autonomy. Autonomy thus implies and requires equality in the sense of a reciprocal recognition of speaking subjects—the "democracy of everyday life," as it were, commonly expressed in conceptions of civic virtue.[10] In this way, moral equality is intrinsic to autonomy.

Clearly, autonomy in all of these senses is presupposed by democracy *if* there is a strong and meaningful sense to the notion that democracy involves self-rule. This is certainly the sense behind the common claim that democracy involves *authenticity* in judgment—indicating that in a democracy, individuals' political judgments should really be their own. Unless the interests and commitments individuals express are their own, unless they can justify the positions they take with reasons and do so in situations free of coercion or economic dependency, unless they have access to adequate information, it is just as possible that their opinions are the result of unreflective beliefs, propaganda or other unreflective modes of influence, coercion, or forced collusive interest.[11] Individual autonomy, in other words, names the kind of authenticity democracy requires for the notion of self-rule to have meaning.

There are a number of associational effects that count as contributions to democracy because they contribute directly to individual autonomy or to its conditions. These include developing individuals' sense of efficacy or political agency, developing their organizational and political skills, developing their cognitive and deliberative skills, and developing their civic virtues—by which I mean the capacities for reciprocity and recognition of others that underwrite and condition the relationships that contribute to autonomy. I examine these effects separately below.

Political Autonomy

With the development of deliberative theories of democracy, it has become more common to refer to *political autonomy* as the democratic ideal that complements individual autonomy.[12] The root idea is very much the same as that of individual autonomy: judgments are autonomous when they are held with due consideration and can be justified by the giving of reasons to others. The notion of *political* autonomy suggests that *collective* judgments ought to have these attributes as well: they should be the result of a process of public reasoning and justification. Political autonomy is not, however, reducible to the sum of individual judgments, no matter how autonomous. It is a distinct ideal because it involves modes of validity (and hence influence) that are not, shall we say, "epistemological": the influence of political judgments does not derive from the relationship between mind and object (whether fact or norm), but rather from interactions among individuals who recognize the validity of a claim and thus its authority.[13]

Hannah Arendt develops a similar point (with her characteristically idiosyncratic use of words) by contrasting the validity of "truth" with that of political judgment.[14] "Since philosophical truth concerns man in his singularity," she writes, "it is unpolitical by nature. If the philosopher nevertheless wishes his truth to prevail over the opinions of the multitude, he will suffer defeat, and he is likely to conclude from this defeat that truth is impotent—a truism that is just as meaningful as if the mathematician, unable to square the circle, should deplore the fact that a circle is not a square."[15] By "philosophical truth," of course, Arendt means those claims that seek epistemological modes of validity, and for that reason short-circuit the opinions that constitute public judgments. It is crucial for the autonomous characteristics of political judgment that Arendt does *not* mean that there are no *cognitive* criteria of validity within public opinion itself. So, on the one hand, she argues that "all truths—not only the various kinds of rational truth but also factual truth—are opposed to opinion in their *mode of asserting validity*."[16] On the other hand, she claims that "the very quality of an opinion, as of a judgment, depends upon its degree of impartiality."[17] Opinions can be better or worse, but they cannot be judged to be so by "modes of validity" associated with "rational truth."

What kind of criterion is impartiality if it does not refer to "truths"? Arendt's answer is that impartiality arises out of inclusiveness, itself a feature of democracy. "Political thought is representative. I form an opinion by considering a given issue from different viewpoints, by making present to my mind the standpoints of those who are absent; that is, I represent them. . . . The more people's standpoints I have present in my mind while I am pondering a given issue, and the better I can imagine how I would feel and think if I were in their place, the stronger will be my capacity for representative thinking and the more valid my final conclusions, my opinion"[18] Taking her lead from Kant's *Critique of Judgment*, Arendt notes that impartiality is gained by traversing opinions, not by measuring them against external criteria, which would miss the kind of "objectivity" possible in political judgment.

Arendt's account of political autonomy is not complete. In particular, she never fully develops her insight into the fact that political judgment relies on distinctive modes of validity, which leaves her notion of impartiality without a referent. Does impartiality require only a survey of viewpoints? Or is it that by means of inclusively inserting viewpoints into public dialogue, the interests, needs, and beliefs of participants not only come to light, but also become subject to public justification? The concept of political autonomy implies the latter, which in turn requires an account of political validity.

Habermas, who agrees with Arendt's insights into the irreducible qualities of communicative validity, does provide an account of political validity. The elements of Habermas's approach that are important here focus on the nature of the authority of political judgments, that is, their influence on participants or their *forcefulness*. The forcefulness of collective judgments can ultimately be traced to the pragmatic effects of communication in enabling individuals to reproduce themselves.[19] Referents invoked by participants—whether facts, norms, or inner experiences—come to have political influence only mediated by argument and persuasion. Influence is not given independently of common judgment by appeal to facts, norms, or inner states, but rather by agreement about the validity of statements that make reference to the truth of facts, the rightness of norms, or the sincerity of expressions. In short, the political influence of truth, rightness, and sincerity depends upon opinion. Judgments are disciplined primarily by the pragmatic consequences of accepting statements as valid, rather than by an objectivity that can in any case be influential only through agreement.

As Arendt also understood, the importance of this point to collective self-rule—the fundamental core of democracy—cannot be overstated. Facts, norms, or inner experiences may be held as true or right or authentic by individuals. But if they are then empowered by coercion or money rather than argued in public, they lose their qualities of truth, rightfulness, or authencity. This point renders oxymoronic the notion of the philosopher-king and all related models of political guardianship on behalf of truths: truths imposed by sovereigns lose their qualities of truth and reduce to imposition.[20] They reduce to failed rationalizations of power: subjects are not motivated by the compelling qualities of the truth, but by the coercion that evokes acquiescence. It is only when truths (factual, normative, or expressive) are converted, as it were, into the force of public opinion that they exert their influence *as* truths. As Habermas puts it, "The political influence that actors gain through public communication must *ultimately* rest on the resonance and indeed the approval of a lay public whose composition is egalitarian. The public of citizens must be *convinced* by comprehensible and broadly interesting contributions to issues it finds relevant. The public audience possesses final authority, because it is *constitutive* for the internal structure and reproduction of the public sphere."[21]

This point gets at the essence of democratic governance: it is only when power arrangements enable and protect processes of argument and persuasion, and do so inclusively, that politics can be guided by the force of talk rather than by other kinds of force. It is only *this* mode of forcefulness that individuals will not experience as external to self-rule, but rather (as Rousseau was the first to grasp) as extensions of self-rule into the collectivity. This is why the ideal of political autonomy taps the strongest normative meanings of democracy.

In democracy, political and individual autonomy are co-determining. This co-determination is already embedded in the concepts: democracy means deciding together. Individual judgments have no force *as* individual judgments; they must be transformed into public reasoning, and gain their influence in this way no matter how well considered from an individual perspective. At the same time, individual autonomy is protected and enhanced by political autonomy: public reasoning processes remain *reasoning* processes only if they are built on the protection of individual autonomy, both in the negative sense that every exclusion of voice damages political autonomy by limiting its reach, and in the positive sense that political autonomy *is* autonomous only insofar as it builds on recognitions of individuals as speakers.[22] From this perspective, democracy involves shifting the means through which collective decisions are taken away from money and coercive power and toward communicative power or influence. This is "democratic" in that what constitutes communicative power is agreement, which intrinsically relates self-rule to inclusion and its egalitarian conditions. Every exclusion shifts power back toward money and coercion.

Individual and political autonomy thus depend on political institutions that simultaneously protect and constitute them. What Habermas and others[23] refer to as a "system of fundamental rights" secures their co-dependency or co-originality. The pivotal nature of this relationship has been missed by most liberal defenders of rights: they have tended to see individual autonomy as fundamental and political autonomy as derivative. That is, individuals can exercise political judgment only if their rights to private autonomy are guaranteed prior to political interaction. Rights, on this view, should not depend on political processes, for they would in this way be dependent on the will of a sovereign, even if this sovereign is the people. On the liberal view, individuals possess (or should possess) rights *pre-politically*, prior to their entrance into democratic politics. Individual autonomy rights are logically and morally beyond the reach of politics, and thus constitute the limits of democracy.

The liberal formulation, however, detaches rights from their conditions of realization—some of which include the reproduction of their social conditions within associational life. We do better to recognize that individual and political autonomy are symbiotic, and that rights provide one set of points around which the symbiosis pivots.[24] Individual autonomy requires political autonomy, but likewise, political autonomy depends absolutely upon the protection of individuals as private persons, thus enabling the independence necessary for individuals to enter as equals into processes of public judgment.[25] *Logically*, a right is a claim against others for some performance or forbearance. Without acceptance by the Other, the right cannot exist. *Sociologically*, rights are claims for recognition, and come into being when claims are recognized by others. And so it should not be surprising that politically and historically the existence and enforceability of rights depends and has depended upon their recognition by others. Without public recognition of private rights, they have little or no impact or existence. As Habermas puts it,

> At a conceptual level, rights do not immediately refer to atomistic and estranged individuals who are possessively set against one another. On the contrary, as elements of the legal order they presuppose collaboration among subjects who recognize one another, in their reciprocally related rights and duties, as free and equal citizens. The mutual recognition is constitutive for a legal order from which actionable rights are derived. . . . In one way or another, the intersubjective meaning of legally defined liberties is overlooked, and with it the relation between private and civic autonomy in which both moments receive their full due.[26]

Associations are not politically self-sufficient, depending as they do upon an elaborated system of rights. At the same time, because they provide the social infrastructure of communicative influence, associations also provide the social media that join individual and political autonomy. In doing so, they can contribute to the social and ethical substance of the rights that constitute the spaces within which they thrive.

From a democratic perspective, the most important political autonomy effects of associations stem from the many ways they enable the public spheres from within which persuasion, argument, and other forms of communicative power are generated. More specifically, associations can constitute public agendas by communicating information and developing issues, enter into public deliberations, represent marginal and excluded voices, and often remind us of our commonalities. All of these count as distinctive contributions to political autonomy, and I shall examine each as a possible *public sphere effect* below.

Institutional Empowerments

The focus of much democratic theory is institutional: voting, representation, distribution of powers among branches of government, proper venues of governance, and the like. I have shifted the emphasis to the normative criteria of individual and political autonomy in order to suggest that what ought to count as a "democratic" institution should be determined by its contributions to these ideals, either directly or as a condition. Likewise, we can judge the effects of associations to be "democratic" by the ways and extent to which they contribute to the institutional conditions of individual and political autonomy. Thus, the third general class of democracy effects of association involves institutional empowerments.

Since these democratic effects are familiar, I shall simply list some possibilities, reserving elaboration for later. Thus, associations may serve to actualize voice in representative institutions. Enabling individuals to be heard within the state by combining their voices is perhaps the most familiar of democratic effects. In addition, associations empower citizens by enabling the collective actions necessary to resist, cause mischief, organize votes, initiate lawsuits, withdraw support or resources, and engage in other tactics that increase the force of the message within strategic contexts of power. When voices are heard and the channels of communication are effective, associations become a key to the democratic legitimacy of institutions. And when self-rule might be better achieved in nonstate venues, associations may provide the means for devolving collective decisions and actions or for coordinating among people in different sectors, regions, or issue areas. Each of these effects is potentially "democratic" because each potentially enhances individual and political autonomy—the normative meanings of democratic self-rule. As with the other two classes of democratic effects, I discuss each distinct possibility below.

I turn now to a closer look at these potentially democratic effects of association. Again, the point is that if we want to know what associations might contribute to democracy, we should know exactly what to look for. Remarkably, there is no literature on association that details the multitude of potential democratic effects. Nonetheless, there does exist a range of expectations that, when summed together, will fill out the picture we shall need to proceed.

Developmental Effects on Individuals

Tocqueville was the first to consider the possibility that modern associations might cultivate individual autonomy. His aim in *Democracy in America* was to locate the functional equivalents of aristocracy within democracy—not so much with respect to leadership, but rather to the confidence, capacities, and skills that nobles bring to collective action. The democratic equivalent of aristocratic bodies, Tocqueville argued, is association. "In democratic countries knowledge of how to combine is the mother of all other forms of knowledge; on its progress depends that of all the others."[27] Associational experiences might provide the habits of collective action that can keep equality from aligning with atomistic individualism, which—Tocqueville believed—had caused the budding democracy in France to take a despotic turn under Napoleon Bonaparte. "If men are to remain civilized or to become civilized," he wrote, "the art of association must develop and improve among them at the same speed as equality of conditions spreads."[28] Associations are the "schools of democracy" that provide not only the confidence and knowledge to undertake collective actions that was, perhaps, typical of the obsolete aristocratic stratum in France, but also the ethos that replaces noblesse oblige, turning individuals away from their natural self-possession and toward their obligations to others. The opportunity to act together, in Tocqueville's view, is the experience that turns individuals toward "the public welfare" and convinces them that "they constantly stand in need of one another in order to provide for it."[29] "Understanding its own interests, the people would appreciate that in order to enjoy the benefits of society one must shoulder its obligations. Free associations of the citizens could then take the place of the individual authority of the nobles, and the state would be protected both from tyranny and from license."[30]

While Tocqueville's expectations are by no means unfounded, they are so general that they could not possibly be met. But they might be met sometimes, in some ways, by some kinds of associations if only we could refine our expectations—and not level all of them at every kind of association. I suggest we do so by distinguishing the following dimensions of individual autonomy, any one of which might be enhanced by association: a sense of efficacy or political agency, information, political skills, capacities for deliberative judgment, and civic virtues.

Efficacy

Perhaps least problematic is the effect that contemporary behavioralists refer to as the psychological disposition of "efficacy."[31] Efficacy is the feeling that one *could* have on impact on collective actions if one so chose to do so. It is the self-confidence necessary to action, and the habit of doing something about problems when they arise. In Tocqueville's terms, efficacy is the confidence possessed by the nobleman, which might be replicated by associational experiences. "Efficacy" does not, of course, refer to objective outcomes, but rather to the reflexive effects of experiences, sedimented in individuals' biographies over a lifetime and expressed as a psychological disposition. In part, feelings of efficacy (or inefficacy) can be accurate readings of one's chances of making a difference, which will depend upon resources, institutional venues, and opportunities. One can be trained, as it were, for confidence, assertiveness, and agency, primarily through experiences in which one does have some impact. In developing efficacy, nothing succeeds like success. But success is not always necessary: some kinds of associations, primarily New Social Movements, may even specialize in developing feelings of efficacy as a part of more general strategies of consciousness raising. But one can also be trained otherwise: a history of discouragement and failure produces passive and fatalistic individuals; they come to lack the psychological resources to act even when circumstances permit.

Information

Associations often serve as collectors, organizers, and conduits of information that educate individuals about matters relevant to them. Information empowers citizens to demand transparency and public accountability of government institutions, as well as of other powers such as corporations. Especially when they are involved in advocacy, associations provide key informational resources, concentrating on issues related to their purposes or sometimes on monitoring governments and other powers for compliance with agreements, laws, and treaties. The membership-based advocacy and public interest associations—the National Organization for Women (NOW), the United States Public Interest Research Group (USPIRG), the Institute for Global Communications (IGC), and

Common Cause, for example—provide focused information to their members, in contrast to mass media organizations that often tend to disperse attention. In addition, larger and more highly organized associations often have their own experts and professionals who can assimilate and convey information in ways that would be far too costly in time, expertise, and attention for individuals to accomplish on their own. In short, associations can provide what might be called an epistemic division of labor, without which individuals would be more overwhelmed by the amount and complexity of information than they already are.[32] Associations whose primary reason for existence is to effect change—that is, public interest advocacy groups or New Social Movement groups as opposed to soccer clubs, for example—will be especially effective in this respect. Likewise, associations with federated structures linking local, state, and national organizations, such as the National Audubon Society, will have the infrastructure and resources for collecting, focusing, and disseminating information.

Political Skills

Closely related are the political skills individuals may acquire in associations, including speaking and self-presentation, negotiation and bargaining, developing coalitions and creating new solutions to problems, learning when and how to compromise, as well as recognizing when one is being manipulated, pressured, or threatened. Such skills are likely to be cultivated by any association that deals with problems of collective action—not just by associations directly involved with political causes.[33] In fact, it may be that dealing with workplace problems, organizing parent-teacher association activities, or participating in neighborhood watches provide more opportunities for developing political skills than do political associations, which are typically organized on larger scales, focused on distant seats of government, and less internally democratic and more professionalized owing to the strategic environments within which they operate. Other factors will constrain these effects as well: associations organized around charismatic leaders who seek followers rather than partners—some kinds of religious movements, for example—may do little to enhance political skills.

Civic Virtues

The Tocquevillian expectation that associations will cultivate civic virtues is widespread and can be found in the writings of all democratic theorists who emphasize the developmental impact of democracy on individuals, including associative democrats,[34] participatory democrats,[35] deliberative democrats,[36] and civic republicans.[37] The list of potential civic virtues is a long one: attentiveness to the common good and concerns for justice; tolerance of the views of others; trustworthiness; willingness to participate, deliberate, and listen; respect for the rule of law; and respect for the rights of others.[38] The received list of civic virtues is far too long to allow any general conclusions about the effects of association. In any case, were we to expect these effects of associations, we would be disappointed. It is quite clear, for example, that most associations make few contributions to liberal concerns for justice, and many "cut against strong claims of justice."[39] Moreover, it has long been evident that associational membership increases with socioeconomic status, so that in aggregate, associations mirror existing injustices and may even multiply them.[40] To take another example, while there is a correlation between higher rates of membership in associations and tolerance, Verba, Schlozman, and Brady suggest higher rates of education cause both.[41] Amy Gutmann does well to note that not "every association can reasonably be expected to cultivate even the most basic civic virtues."[42]

We will do better to narrow the list of civic virtues to those *moral* effects of association that contribute to *democratic processes*—a somewhat different matter than seeking to generalize about the impact of associational experiences on specific virtues or ethical goods. Thus, although still overly general, Cohen and Rogers identify a more discrete and relevant cluster of civic virtues when they suggest that "associations help foster the 'civic consciousness' upon which any egalitarian order and its deliberative politics depend. That is, they promote a recognition of the norms of democratic process and equity and a willingness to uphold them and to accept them as fixing the basic framework of political argument and social cooperation, at least on the condition that others do so as well."[43]

This remains a tall order, and I expect that if these expectations were applied rigorously, we would find only modest effects from some kinds of associational experiences. Nonetheless, there may be some generic effects that are, as it were, precursors of these democratic virtues. Nancy Rosenblum's analysis of the "morality of association" is suggestive in this respect: "The chief and constant contribution of associations to moral development is cultivating the disposition to cooperate. On my view, that is what we can reasonably expect as a regular matter. . . . Voluntary associations fail, then, only if they cannot engage members in cooperation."[44] There is, on Rosenblum's account, no *necessary* relationship between cooperation and *civic* virtue. "Cooperation enables the worst as well as the best social actions—'force and fraud are most efficiently pursued by teams.' "[45] But there are indirect supports for some civic virtues embedded within these moral effects. The disposition to cooperate is part of almost any associational relation, assuming it is voluntary, owing to the ways in which individuals ascribe responsibilities to one another. Such ascriptions motivate individuals to "live up to the ideal of their station as a result of ties of friendly feeling and trust."[46]

These effects bear closer scrutiny. In Rosenblum's terms, the primary moral effect of association is the experience of reciprocity built on mutual expectations of performance. Insofar as association has a voluntary dimension, reciprocity is the basic sociological building block of cooperation. That is, there is a generic "democracy of everyday life" built into association, albeit in segmented and pluralized ways. There is no necessity, of course, that such relationships will generalize, but they may provide developmental experiences upon which civic virtues might be built. One is trust, at least when combined with its reciprocal virtue, trustworthiness. Robert Putnam's account of the democratic effects of association is built almost entirely on this virtue. Trust enables individuals to overcome problems of collective action, which in turn enables them to organize politically, pressure governments, and get the things done that "make democracies work."[47]

To be sure, there are forms of trust that undermine democracy. But these forms are built not out of reciprocity but rather out of group identity or ascription. One trusts (or distrusts) others not because of their demonstrated trustworthiness (or untrustworthiness), but rather because of their race, ethnicity, family, religion, and so on. Such forms of trust are rarely virtuous since they are not built on any morally praiseworthy performance by individuals. These forms are rarely good for democracy because they must be complemented by an ascriptive distrust of outgroups, which is likewise unaffected by their performance.[48] Trust built on reciprocity, however, can develop into robust cooperative relationships. Associations focused on common tasks (as opposed to ascriptive identities) can provide for these possibilities, as well as build upon them.

Rosenblum emphasizes somewhat different effects of cooperation built on reciprocity: its contributions to self-respect within the context of pluralism. Individuals have a great variety of abilities and capacities; these abilities and capacities are also unequal. In liberal democracies, the great variety of associations provides a great variety of arenas within which most any ability can be appreciated and recognized by others. The insults and psychic injuries sustained within the workplace, for example, do not need to encompass one's entire sense of self-worth if one is also a breeder of Siamese cats and recognized by other cat breeders, or if one belongs to a church that reminds each of his or her intrinsic worth, or if one is a good soccer player. Each venue keeps the virtue of reciprocity alive by linking it to self-respect through cooperative investments. As long as the respect one gains is the result of reciprocities and the "personal contributions" these imply (and not, Rosenblum says, the result of vicarious identification with a group),[49] then the resulting self-respect is valuable for its own sake. Importantly for democratic pluralism, self-respect also enables recognition of others. The "experience of pluralism," as Rosenblum puts it, also means experiencing places for oneself; the self-respect that follows enables a liberality that can extend to recognizing the distinct accomplishments of others. But the experience of pluralism is also valuable as a condition of individual autonomy: recognition for one's particular abilities makes individuals more secure in their identity, which in turn makes it easier to investigate one's own preferences and beliefs without threat of destabilizing the core of one's personality.

Reciprocity, trust, and recognition, then, are the virtues we should look for in association. They are "precivic" or simply "civil" virtues in the sense that they are not immediately (or merely) civic, but should nonetheless support (in Cohen and Rogers's terms) "norms of democratic process and equity" while motivating individuals to "uphold them and to accept them as fixing the basic framework of political argument and social cooperation."[50] Not every kind of association will contribute to these generic effects: some will undermine them, while others will go beyond.

Critical Skills

While efficacy, information, political skills, and civic virtues may be necessary to individual autonomy, it is a different question as to whether associational attachments cultivate individuals' cognitive capacities for autonomous judgments. One can feel effective, have information, possess political skills, relate to others with reciprocity and trust, and *still* fail to reflect on one's own interests and commitments and their relationship to those of others.[51] The opportunities to develop critical and cognitive skills are key to the possibility that participants in political processes will change their preferences in ways that are truer to their needs (that is, more individually autonomous) and are more likely to contribute to stable consensus, bargains, or coalitions because they know what they want. This possibility, however, is likely to occur only under rather specific conditions: what is needed is some degree of conflict under conditions that enable conflict to be resolved by deliberative means.[52] As I shall argue in chapter 5, when there is conflict, the temptations to leave an association will often overcome the difficulties of staying, engaging in battle, defending one's positions, and listening to the arguments of others. These activities are especially difficult when they chafe against the normative purposes of association and fray the friendliness and good feeling that provide the social fabric of many associations.

The democratic effect of critical skill development is often mentioned in the literature, although not always with an appreciation of its exceptional qualities. Parsons is among the least cautious, as he sees this effect as among the most prominent of the modern effects of association. Modern associations tend to institute procedures that structure discussion as "a primary sphere of the operation of influence as a medium for facilitating social process."[53] Joshua Cohen is somewhat more cautious, although optimistic that associative structures might serve as "schools of deliberative democracy" outside of the formal political process. He focuses especially on associations that deal with "functional" issues, primarily workplace and neighborhood issues, because associations structured so as to bring diversely situated individuals together are more likely to use deliberative approaches to problem solving.[54] Likewise, Amy Gutmann suggests that other things being equal, "the more economically, ethnically, and religiously heterogeneous the membership of an association is, the greater its capacity to cultivate the kind of public discourse and deliberation that is conducive to democratic citizenship."[55] Ironically, it may be that associations best suited to cultivating civic virtues because of their reliance on normative resources—civic organizations devoted to worthy causes, for example—may, for this very reason, find it difficult to resolve internal conflict through deliberation. Unless there is a deep reservoir of loyalty, members disenchanted with an association's purposes, tactics, leadership, or activities will drift away rather than bear the social costs of conflict. I shall return to this issue in chapter 5, but it is clear that these developmental effects are more likely to be found in associations that have incentives to resolve internal conflicts through discourse owing to structural location (egalitarian workplaces and CDCs), ethos (a Quaker congregation), or purpose (associations specifically devoted to coordination and conflict resolution).

If associations cultivate individual autonomy—a democratic self—it is because they provide a variety of developmental experiences relating to a number of dimensions of autonomy. A democratic individual feels effective, is informed about the issues, possesses the ability to organize with others for a collective action, can trust others if they are trustworthy, recognizes and respects others even if they differ on issues, and responds to conflict with reasons and reasoning. Distinguishing these dimensions of individual autonomy makes the important point that no associational venue can, or should be expected to, contribute to all of these developmental effects. We shall want to know is what associational kinds are likely to contribute to which effects. What democrats should hope is that individ-

closely related. Information needs to be related to problems and issues, selected for relevance, connected to matters of public concern, and solidified into public agendas. In Habermas's terms, the "associational network of civil society" generates public spheres that serve as sounding boards

> for problems that must be processed by the political system because they cannot be solved elsewhere. To this extent, the public sphere is a warning system with sensors that, though unspecialized, are sensitive throughout society. From the perspective of democratic theory, the public sphere must, in addition, amplify the pressures of problems, that is, not only detect and identify problems but also convincingly and *influentially* thematize them, furnish them with possible solutions, and dramatize them in such a way that they are taken up and dealt with by parliamentary complexes. The capacity of the public sphere to solve problems *on its own* is limited. But this capacity must be utilized to oversee the further treatment of problems that takes place inside the political system.[63]

Although public spheres can be sensitive to problems generated within individuals' life-worlds, they are not specialized for reproduction of the life-world (in contrast to religion, education, and the family) or for dealing rigorously with validity claims. "Rather, the public sphere distinguishes itself through a *communication structure* that is related to a third feature of communicative action: it refers neither to the *functions* nor to the *contents* of everyday communication but the *social space* generated in communicative action." Thus, the "public sphere can best be described as a network for communicating information and points of view (that is, opinions expressing affirmative or negative attitudes); the streams of communication are, in the process, filtered and synthesized in such a way that they coalesce into bundles of topically specified *public* opinions."[64]

In the parlance of cognitive psychology, associations constitute public spheres when they *frame* issues by making public assertions or taking public positions—that is, when they attempt to constitute the terms by means of which an issue is understood. As participants in public dialogues, for example, businesses with international markets will seek "free" trade, casting their opponents as against freedom. Unions and businesses threatened by cheap foreign goods will speak of "fair" trade, casting their opponents as against fairness. Likewise, anti-abortion groups prefer the term "pro-life," while groups seeking to keep abortion legal employ the term "pro-choice." That such rhetorical strategies select and frame information is entirely appropriate: in seeking to change minds and solidify support, they signal matters of normative significance, and in this way provoke deliberative justification of normative positions. One consequence can be that the meanings of normative ideals such as *freedom, fairness, life,* and *choice* are better understood by more people, and more people are able to relate these normative ideals to specific policies. In these ways, associations constitute public spheres and make contributions to political autonomy.

If associations are conduits and constituents of the public voices of individuals, they also reproduce the norms of public influence themselves. By seeking influence through public arguments and representations, individuals reproduce the norm that collective decisions ought to be made on the basis of communicative power, in contrast to the powers of money or coercion.[65] Of course there is no need for associations to *intend* to constitute public spheres and the norms that sustain then—although there are some who cast their missions in precisely this way, such as the Kettering Foundation, which seeks to induce public dialogue by organizing forums on current issues, and Common Cause, which seeks to stem the electoral influence of money in favor of public justifications of policies. Most, however, will simply wish to make their views known and seek communicative power through public presentation of their cause. In any case, it is not even necessary for associations to have public influence as their primary purpose for them to produce public-sphere effects. Nancy Rosenblum, criticizing the view that associations merely aggregate the voices of their members, notes that often "association precedes voice": public voice can develop as a consequence of association—a point well illustrated by the history of Black churches in America, which evolved from religious organizations into public voices, as well as by feminist consciousness-raising groups.[66] As I shall suggest in chapter 5, there is no necessary positive relationship between an association's internal propensity toward deliberation and their contributions to public dialogue. In fact, there may be an inverse relationship: the public voice of an association may be weakened just to the extent that open dialogue occurs within an association, which often nuances or confuses the message in ways that reduce its impact within a broader public. In contrast, associations with a high capacity for public voice may, for the same reason, have difficulty resolving internal conflict through deliberation, which may be viewed by members as a challenge to the association's core identity and mission. In short, the associations that can best cultivate individual autonomy may be quite different from those that underwrite political autonomy.

Representations of Difference

Associations may have symbolic functions in the public sphere that do not contribute directly to deliberation, but serve to alter the parameters of the public conversation. Importantly, when associations "go public," they can leverage their influence in ways that can compensate for lack of other kinds of power. Silence serves the wealthy and powerful well, and public argument is one of the few resources through which poorer and weaker members of society can exert influence. Historically, association "has been the resource of groups without the votes; before they achieved suffrage, women successfully fought for legislative protection for children and other social policies through their associations. It is the critical resource for those who lack influence based on economic resources, cultural hegemony, prestige, and so on."[67] "Voluntary associations are indispensable for nudging issues into public consciousness or offering reasons that supplement, reinforce, or oppose the terms dominant in public discussion."[68] This is why a group will often consider it a considerable achievement merely to have placed an issue before the public eye; the influence of the wealthy and powerful is compromised to the extent that their positions, possessions, and actions are subject to public tests of legitimacy.

To set a public agenda in a way that an issue becomes a topic of deliberation is even a more difficult feat still. *Deliberation* requires reciprocal recognition of individuals as *speakers*, meaning that individuals respond to the arguments, information, representations, and demonstrations of others *as issues*—that is, as matters that deserve response in their own terms. Deliberation depends on achieving an important kind of equality, equality as a partner in a dialogue. This is a significant but difficult and sometimes fragile achievement. Deliberation cannot be a starting point for a democratic theory that, no matter how deliberative in orientation, must attend to the political achievements necessary to transform an issue into a topic of deliberation. It is always to the disadvantage of those who benefit from the status quo to recognize a discursive challenge, since responding to an argument already legitimizes it *as* an argument, thus bringing benefits and privileges into question. So it is important to identify as distinct contributions those activities of associations that change the parameters of the public debate. Associations that lack recognition typically cannot change debate through dialogue, but must do so by means of other kinds of symbolic resources—demonstrations, protests, civil disobedience, theater, literature, and the like. These groups might be called, following Nancy Fraser's Gramscian term, *subaltern publics*—publics that specialize, as it were, in counterhegemony.[69] This democratic effect is even more important when public spheres are under the influence of money (via the commercial mass media) and power (through state-sponsored deliberations), both of which will tend to seek and represent a mainstream consensus—a consensus that will, for that very reason, often exclude the weakest and most poorly organized members of society.

Representations of Commonality

Finally, it is worth emphasizing that representations of commonality are distinctive contributions to political autonomy. They are, as it were, symbolic preconditions of public spheres. Many associations specialize in symbolic commonality, emphasizing inclusive membership in the polity and, often, our common humanity and shared human risks. In distinctive ways, civic booster clubs, associations constituted to celebrate national holidays or centennials, associations that focus on nonstigmatized diseases (leukemia rather than AIDS) that link people through their shared biological risks, and associations that focus on child poverty (everyone was once a child, and most have a reflexive empathy with the vulnerabilities of childhood) all emphasize commonality. Many international nongovernmental organizations (NGOs) such as the World Health Organization (WHO), CARE, Oxfam, and Amnesty International portray people as members of a world community, often by evoking empathy with others on the basis of shared experiences—of childhood, family, insecurity, health, and death. To be sure, symbolic commonality can be relatively empty of content or cynically emphasized for reasons of economic gain (as in the civic boosterism of the many chambers of commerce). Or, worse, it may be deployed to define a "we"—the respectable mainstream— against marginal others. Whatever the intentions, however, such associations inject into the public realm a common claim to membership, and thus an entitlement of voice with respect to matters of common concern. As the history of universal ideologies from Christianity to liberalism has shown, it is very difficult to justify exclusive privileges and communities in universal terms. So although it is unlikely that associations that use oppositional strategies—ACT UP (the AIDS Coalition to Unleash Power), for example—will also be effective at emphasizing commonalities, they can nonetheless leverage commonalities against a mainstream by pointing up hypocrisies and sometimes attempting to shame.[70]

Institutional Effects

Far more familiar within democratic theory are the effects of association on the institutions of democratic governance. By *institutional effects* I mean the effects associations have on the institutions through which collective decisions are made and collective actions organized. In contrast, the developmental effects I have identified have to do with associations' contributions to individuals' democratic capacities and dispositions. Public sphere effects have to do with developing public opinion and forming collective judgments. Here, the question has to do with the institutions of governance that translate the capacities of individuals and judgments of publics into collective decisions and actions. What, in other words, might associations contribute to the democratic functioning of institutions such as legislatures, administrative units, federal structures, partnerships, and other rule-based means of decision making and organization?

The most familiar of these effects are at the core of American pluralist theory, which views associations as a primary means through which interests are represented to the state and states are pressured to respond.[71] More recently, associations have been called upon as well to provide alternative modes of governance on the assumption that associations can often undertake collective actions with greater flexibility and creativity than the state. As governance becomes more complex, associations may have a greater role to play in developing, administering, and coordinating public-sanctioned policies. In addition, associations may help to legitimate the state, in part through contributing to public justifications, but also by devolving the locus of action, and thus the locus of expectation.

Representation

Representation is one of the two classically recognized democratic effects of association, figuring into Madison's view in *The Federalist* that the primary functions of groups are to connect individuals to government and to resist when its powers threaten to become tyrannical. Representational effects are central to the American pluralist understanding of the political functions of association, although the pluralists expanded the notion by emphasizing its communicative dimension. On the pluralist model, associational representation complements voting with information, since votes are at best crude instruments of direction. Associations speak on behalf of their member-voters, communicating the meanings of votes to representatives. When associations can combine votes with messages, they can even hold representatives accountable for specific policies—as, for example, in the areas of Medicare funding, Social Security, gun control, and abortion. In addition, associations can and often do serve to overcome the territorial bases of representation—which is, after all, only one, increasingly narrow basis of interest representation. For better or for worse, the American Association of Retired Persons tells its members in Virginia that they have more interests common with retirees in Florida than they do with shipbuilders in Norfolk or parents with school-age children in Arlington. The National Organization for Women and the American Federation of Labor and Congress of Industrial Organizations (AFL-CIO) unite people on the basis of their interests as women and as workers.

Primarily because of associational organization, territorial representation takes into account a broader range of interests and aggregates them at higher levels than it would were people connected only on the bases of residence.[72]

Associations also have the potential to *equalize* representation in systems like our own that are under the sway of money. The most important resource for associations is the time and commitment of its members, and these resources are more widely distributed than money. Importantly, time and commitment can be pooled, but cannot be accumulated like money.[73] This means that, in principle, associations can help to level the playing field, organizing pressure and votes in ways that can compete with money.[74] In the United States, however, this democratic effect has, with some important exceptions, mostly remained unrealized, as inequalities of membership tend to mirror other inequalities. Indeed, as Theda Skocpol argues, it is likely associations now multiply the influence of those who already have resources.[75] Those who have education, money, and skills are also able to more effectively associate, which in turn increases their abilities to accumulate other resources. "Social capital"—the networks of trust and reciprocity that facilitate collective action—seems to be as maldistributed as other resources.[76] Whether or not social capital is becoming more or less equally distributed in the United States, however, remains unclear.[77]

Whatever powers associations have to represent their members depends in part on their capacities to communicate the interests, norms, and identities of members to public officials. One condition of representative communication is that there exist organized communication between members and those who claim to speak for them. As Max Weber emphasized in developing the concept of a "party"—that is, a collective political agent—class situation or other sociological commonalities are not sufficient for political unity and action.[78] There must be connections among people focused upon particular issues, problems, or grievances, and they must be made effective through an organizational structure. Nancy Rosenblum makes much the same point in criticizing associations that claim to represent individuals based on ethnicity or identity: "Shared experiences may be a starting point for representation, but it is not politically directive. In the absence of goals generated and communicated through associations, shared experience is likely to be politically incoherent or vacuous. *Associations* serve representative purposes, not cultures or communities."[79] They do so when they establish representative structures within the association, so that the goals, purposes, and norms of members are represented by those who speak on their behalf. While (representative) democracy within an association is not always necessary to other democratic effects, it is decisive in the representation of members.

Resistance

Within contexts of power, communication becomes representation only when combined with inducements. Associations can provide inducements through their capacities for resistance. This is why, of course, one of the first goals of any would-be totalitarian or authoritarian state is to remove rights of association—forbidding meetings in public places, smashing the offices of political and cultural groups, arresting activists, closing newspapers and radio and television stations, closing universities that house student groups, outlawing unions, and so on. As Hannah Arendt argued so cogently, authoritarianism can thrive where individuals are isolated and atomized, each left to face the power of the state on his or her own. Totalitarianism goes one step further, seeking to reintegrate individuals into state-sponsored associations. Tocqueville already anticipated these developments, fearing that the American case might go the way of France, where an atomized society nourished Napoleon Bonaparte's authoritarianism. Absent association, individuals would withdraw into themselves, becoming "unaware of the fate of the rest." Into the vacuum of association would step the state,

> an immense, protective power which is alone responsible for securing their enjoyment and watching over their fate. That power is absolute, thoughtful of detail, orderly, provident, and gentle. It would resemble parental authority if, father like, it tried to prepare its charges for a man's life, but on the contrary, it only tries to keep them in perpetual childhood. It likes to see the citizens enjoy themselves, provided that they think of nothing but enjoyment. . . . Why should it not entirely relieve them from the trouble of thinking and all the cares of living?[80]

Because associations provide people with the capacity to organize collective actions, they also provide the capacity to resist what they do not like—sometimes politely, through the vote or through gathering and disseminating information, sometimes less so, through demonstrations, strikes, civil disobedience or through setting up competing ways of providing services that threaten to draw public money into their wake, as in private school alternatives to public schools. Most state policies require the willing cooperation and skills of most people, most of the time. This is why the capacity to resist can also produce state responsiveness, increase the transparency of state and corporate activities and process, and sometimes even produce organized dialogue. None of these institutional effects is likely when people are passive recipients of administered policies. The capacity to resist provides incentive for representatives to represent and for state officials to respond, and to be more transparent in the ways they respond.

From a democratic perspective, capacities for resistance are very often but not always a good thing: powerful organizations such as corporations can use their control over social resources—often amassed with the help of willing workers, sympathetic communities, and reliance on public resources and infrastructure—to bypass democratic representation and impose their will by threatening exit. On the other hand, appropriately protected by laws, other kinds of resources can be leveraged against powerful social actors—resources such as labor (via unions), information, democratic control over public infrastructures (via local and state government), and coordination among local governments to increase the costs to those who threaten capital flight. Clearly, from a democratic perspective, the capacities of associations for resistance can work for better or worse, depending upon the kind of association and the resources it controls. Because associations have capacities and control resources, in aggregete they constitute an intricate system of power that is more or less democratic depending upon how power is dispersed and who has it.

Subsidiarity

It was with bemused admiration that Tocqueville observed that Americans, faced with problems of drunkenness, formed temperance societies to educate and reform by example and peer pressure.

> The first time that I heard in America that one hundred thousand men had publicly promised never to drink alcoholic liquor, I thought it more of a joke than a serious matter and for the moment I did not see why these very abstemious citizens could not content themselves with drinking water by their own firesides.
>
> In the end I came to understand that these hundred thousand Americans, frightened by the progress of drunkenness around them, wanted to support sobriety by their patronage. . . . One may fancy that if they had lived in France each of these hundred thousand would have made individual representations to the government asking it to supervise all the public houses though out the realm.[81]

Tocqueville's contrast between association as the site of collective action and individual representations to a state understood as the sole agent of collective action is telling in two respects. First, associations provide nongovernmental ways of organizing collective actions. The American example, Tocqueville speculates, suggests that "instead of entrusting all the administrative powers taken away from corporations and from the nobility to the government alone, some of them could be handed over to secondary bodies composed of private citizens. In that way the freedom of individuals would be safer without their equality being less."[82] Second, sometimes collective actions are more appropriately and effectively pursued by associational means. Tocqueville's example of collective testimony against public drunkenness is especially to the point because it involves a public problem with individual vice. Associations can make good use of normative influence. But when the state undertakes a task, Tocqueville notes in another context, it is often difficult to tell the difference "between its advice and its commands"—displacing of course, whatever normative influence the advice might have.

Tocqueville's comments point toward a principle sometimes referred to as *subsidiarity*—a term borrowed from Catholic political thought and meaning that problems ought to be addressed at the lowest appropriate level of organization. The notion of subsidiarity is different from the federalist idea that the best government is small and close to the people. Unlike the federalist idea, subsidiarity suggests that units of collective action should be matched to the scale and nature of the problem. It makes no sense, for example, for a national state to directly administer local schools; but it might make sense for a national state to redistribute funds to local schools that lack a tax base or to set minimal standards for performance. Smaller, in this case, is not better but simply ineffective. The idea of subsidiarity applied to association takes this notion one step further, focusing on subsidiarity with respect to associational function rather than (as in federalist thought) applying the notion only to territorial units of government. As G. D. H. Cole appreciated, most associations are not territorial at all, but rather based on profession, common problems, shared identities, or other commonalities not based on residence. The functions of government can be, and sometimes are, devolved to functionally-organized associations: charities that provide welfare but depend in part on government grants, professional associations that set standards for licensing, and so on. There is, of course, ample precedent in the United States. The number of associations devoted to specific social functions has grown dramatically with government spending, in large part because much of this spending is channeled through nonprofit entities. This is especially true in the area of medical care (almost one-half of all nonprofit expenditures is devoted to medical care and related services), but also in various arenas of social service.[83] Nancy Rosenblum gets the picture exactly right in noting that it is incorrect to refer to the myriad of "semipublic/semiprivate organizations—churches and neighborhood groups, ethnic associations and civic charities, commercial and for-profit organizations" as engaging in "self-help" or "volunteerism":

Since the 1960s, almost all of the groups delivering social services, from Catholic Charities to the Boys Clubs, have been publicly subsidized, often on the order of 70 percent or more of their funding. Goals are set or endorsed by public policy, and the rationale for delivery by a profusion of associations has a good deal to do with moral and political education as well as efficiency. . . . The "welfare state" is a misnomer, not only because it falls short of securing welfare, but also because it is not coextensive with the state.[84]

The idea that associations can and often do serve as the social infrastructure of subsidiarity is central to the emerging school of "associative democrats" as well as others who have come to view associations as a means of restoring the radical meaning of self-governance.[85] Associations can provide alternative structures of governance, which can in turn provide more opportunities for participation and greater responsiveness. The possibilities are attractive because of apparent limits to state-centered administration which, by its very nature, tends to be inflexible (owing to accountability through universal rules) and sometimes arbitrary (as when universal rules produce different results under different circumstances). Because of their distance from social actors, states often have to resort to complex systems of inducements and monitoring to achieve results. In contrast, associations can draw upon social resources such as the trust and goodwill of members in ways that can stand in for regulations and monitoring.[86]

But while there are enormous democratic potentials in subsidiarity-based strategies, there are also clear dangers. Devolving responsibilities also empowers associations—and this may not be a good thing when associational ties are linked to inequalities in control over economic resources, knowledge, professional skills, and the like.[87] Issues concerning the distribution of power, equality of voice, and the protection of individual autonomy via rights remain here just as in the more formal venues of representative democracy. Indeed, devolution on behalf of "democracy"—conflating it with the "closeness" of government—is the preferred tactic of those who wish to escape public accountability. They often do so by actively seeking a mismatch between the problem and the scale at which it is addressed—itself a violation of subsidiarity. Because many problems—those of environmental destruction, labor markets, and the like—require large-scale collective action, devolving conflict in these issue areas can amount to disempowering the political units with the scale and capacity to address the issues. Local political units are more susceptible to the blackmail effects of local economic powers, the parochialism of local cultures, attachment to livelihoods that involve unsustainable environmental destruction, and sometimes local violence. Historically in the United States, much of the support for federalism and local control has come from those who are interested in disempowering collective actions, from slaveholders to industrial polluters. In short, the democratic possibilities of subsidiarity are enormously promising, especially in large-scale, complex societies. But precisely because powers are involved, it is an effect that bears close scrutiny for its consistency with democratic principles.

Coordination and Cooperation

Likewise, we shall wish to look closely at the effects of devolving *politics* (as opposed to specified functions or contracted services) into associational venues. It is often assumed that associations can do better at resolving conflict than can formal political institutions. In part because of the scale and complexity of many problems today, and in part because of the pluralism of forces and interests that bear on most problems, collective decisions and actions require negotiated coordination among a multitude of groups, each with different resources and often with different interests, identities, and values. Owing to these characteristics, many areas of policy have become difficult to manage and administer on the bureaucratic model favored by the state, while market solutions cannot respond to political (as opposed to monetary) demands.[88] Public education, welfare, management of public resources, environmental issues, occupational health and safety, public health, urban planning and development, research and development, and agricultural policy are just a few of the policy arenas that have these characteristics. Many of these areas of policy have become so politicized that policy can be made only piecemeal, in response to particular forces and without any locus of political responsibility.[89]

The problem is inscribed into the structure of late-modern societies. As Günther Teubner puts it, "Centralized social integration is effectively ruled out today and cannot be achieved by legal, economic, moral, or scientific mechanisms. A decentralized mode of integration is inevitable because to maximize the rationality of one subsystem is to create insoluble problems in other functional systems."[90] By default, much of the work of coordination and cooperation has shifted to associational venues. Networks of associations, as Habermas notes, "have arisen among public agencies and private organizations, business associations, labor unions, interest groups, and so on" that now "fulfill certain coordination functions in more or less opaque social sectors."[91]

Associations have potential capacities for coordination and cooperation that governments and markets do not. Cohen and Rogers trace these capacities to two factors. First, the very existence of associational connections "reduces the transaction costs of securing agreement among potentially competing interests. The background of established forms of communication and collaboration they provide enable parties to settle more rapidly and reliably on jointly beneficial actions. Second, groups help establish the trust that facilitates cooperation. They effectively provide assurances to members that their own willingness to cooperate will not be exploited by others."[92]

Cohen and Rogers conceive of these effects as policy making "in the shadow of the law," a notion that points to the strategies that states can use to structure and monitor associational venues of policy making. This line of thinking has been developed by Teubner under the concept of "reflexive law"—that is, laws that structure political processes at subgovernmental levels without imposing goals or preferred outcomes. Instead of directly insisting on and enforcing particular goals to be achieved in a regulated area, "reflexive law tries to establish norms of procedure, organization, membership, and competence that can alter decision-making, change the weights of different parties and members, and make overall processes of decision sensitive to side effects and externalities. Common to all these devices is the desire to achieve new effects through an alteration of procedures, that is, through procedural rather than formal or substantive law."[93] Or, as Habermas puts it, "With this type of regulation, the legislator no longer directly seeks to achieve concrete goals. Rather, the procedural norms are supposed to regulate processes of will formation and enable the participants to settle their affairs themselves."[94]

While my aim here is not to deal directly with the "secondary rules" that can make associations into *democratic* agents of cooperation and coordination, I am interested in the increasing functional pressures for associations to serve these roles, as well as in their differing capacities to do so. Clearly, there exist models of political devolution that are highly questionable from a democratic perspective. The American two-party system, for example, encourages conflicts to be brokered and resolved into two competing agendas prior to their entrance into formal institutional representation. In this way, much political conflict is pushed to subnational levels, where it is worked through within party caucuses, state and local governments, and other venues. Historically, the fact that these venues often reflect the inequalities of local contexts has meant that political conflict is often suppressed and displaced rather than devolved, so that devolutions of politics damages democracy. On the other hand, government policies can be devised with the goal of democratizing procedures to deal with conflicts that had been suppressed. As of 1997, for example, the state of Oregon has mandated that employers establish Workplace Safety Committees consisting of equal numbers of employee and employer representatives. The committees are charged with developing and enforcing safety plans that accord with OSHA (Occupational Safety and

Health Administration) regulations. By mandating committee composition and goals without dictating the specific means by which the goals are to be achieved, the state clearly hopes to structure associative resolutions to worker safety issues. In this case, "democracy" means empowering workers to deal with conflicts while providing negative incentives for businesses to do so as well. The result should be flexible, appropriate, and efficient approaches to workplace safety and monitoring that could not be achieved through direct state regulation. Clearly, as these two examples suggest, the extent to which the capacities of associations for coordination and cooperation are *democratic* depends upon contexts of vulnerability—contexts that can be altered by careful institutional design.

Democratic Legitimation

Last but not least, associations may have the potential to underwrite the legitimacy of the state, directly as well as indirectly. I argued in chapter 1 that state capacities are increasingly limited by a number of forces that are likely to remain with us. This point, however, does not imply that strong states are unnecessary for increasing democracy. Even a democracy that is no longer exclusively centered in and within state institutions needs a strong state, but one that focuses less on global collective actions and more on the conditions of democracy, including enforcing systems of rights, engaging in economic redistributions, and equalizing the power positions of social actors.

As I suggested in chapter 2, however, these conditions of democracy cannot be conceived as *pre*conditions, since to do so would beg the question of the political agency that would put such conditions into place and act upon them. So a state that establishes these conditions must continually draw its capacities to do so from democratic legitimacy. Ideally, democratic legitimacy would flow directly from public spheres: institutions are (democratically) legitimate if the policies they enact enjoy the support of public opinion. If public discourse results in political judgments that are then mirrored by political institutions and policies, they are, by definition, democratically legitimate. So clearly, one way associations can contribute to democratic legitimacy is by generating communicative power within public spheres (a possibility I discussed in connection with public sphere effects), which in turn provide *substantive* democratic legitimacy to policies.

But this mode of legitimacy is only one possibility. We need to ask whether associations might make contributions to legitimacy short of considered agreement with the outcomes. Why do those who lose not only acquiesce, but often consider the outcome legitimate? The standard (and still good) answer is that they consider the processes legitimate, even if they do not like the outcome, and are therefore likely to see the outcome as legitimate. When political processes are legitimate, they stabilize political conflict in ways that keep democratic processes open and fluid without producing uncertainties so severe that they would undermine the system as a whole. So a second possibility is that democratic legitimacy is enhanced if associations enable citizens to have equal chances to influence outcomes, even if they do not get their way. The opportunity to seek influence, even if it fails or is only partially effective, can nonetheless provide legitimacy for both processes and outcomes.[95] In their large study of participation, Verba, Schlozman, and Brady present the interesting finding that those who participate in politics through associations judge their actions to be effective.[96] In contrast, giving money is not experienced as effective, and most individuals vote not because they think it will make a difference, but out of civic obligation. Associations seem to be uniquely important in tying participation to the experience of efficacy, which in turn should lead individuals to be more supportive of political processes and their outcomes. Associations may in this way underwrite the *process* legitimacy of political institutions.

Third, as suggested in the discussion of subsidiarity above, associations may *devolve* the locus of decisions, and thus the locus of normative justification, in this way lowering the threshold of legitimation. This potential function is especially interesting because it speaks to the confluence of two contradictory developments. On the one hand, the rise of the welfare state has been accompanied by increasing demands on the state, which have translated into higher thresholds for legitimacy. On the other hand, as Max Weber already observed, these same societies have become increasingly differentiated in ways that cause distinctive normative discourses to inhabit different spheres.[97] Günther Teubner is surely correct when he writes that in "light of functional differentiation, one can neither hope for universal legitimation structures, for a generally applicable morality of discourse, or for a common procedure of reflexion. The legal prerequisites for reflexion processes in, say, the economy or in politics differ greatly from what will be required by the educational system."[98] Insofar as associations can provide venues through which conflicts may be resolved according to criteria appropriate to different spheres, they may lower the expectations people direct toward the state, and thus reduce the pressures of legitimation.[99] Clearly, associations that have capacities for subsidiarity, coordination, and cooperation will be most likely to produce this effect.

These, then, are the key kinds of democratic effects associations may have—"democratic" because they contribute to individual autonomy, to political autonomy, and to their institutional conditions. A democratic system requires all these effects, but associations are never so constituted and situated that any one kind could provide them all. Instead, we shall want to look for mixes of associational types that, in aggregate, enable democracy. We cannot do so, however, without an account of the features of associational types that make a difference for their potential roles in a democratic associational ecology.

Five

The Associational Terrain: Distinctions That Make a Difference

DEMOCRATIC THEORISTS have attributed a large number of democratic effects to associations. Most of these attributions are warranted, but only under limited conditions and with due consideration for the mix of effects democracy now requires. In the last chapter I sought to make two related points. First, the associational terrain of the advanced liberal democracies is highly pluralized. Democracies today depend upon a multitude of distinct and often apparently contradictory effects of associational attachments. If we expect associational life to contribute to democracy, we shall need to understand what potential effects might exist and how they function. Second, I suggested that the effects of associational life can be judged "democratic" insofar as they contribute to any of several dimensions of individual and political autonomy, or to their institutional conditions.

In this chapter and the next, I address the question that naturally follows: What kinds of associations are likely to provide which kinds of democratic effects? In this chapter I explore the terrain within which associational attachments form, the results of which will enable an analysis of associational types in chapter 5. Here, I begin with the assumption that potential democratic effects are just that: *effects* of other factors. I conceive of these factors in three dimensions:

- the degree to which an association is voluntary or nonvoluntary;
- the kind of medium—social attachments, money, or power—within which an association is embedded or toward which it is oriented; and
- the goods or purposes of the association.

In the overly mechanical language of social science, I am experimenting with the possibility that the democratic effects can be treated as dependent variables, while these three classes of factors serve as independent variables. If we can characterize associational types in each of these three dimensions, we will also have some theoretical basis for expecting specific kinds of democratic effects, as well as for identifying specific kinds of dangers to democracy. Not surprisingly, it will turn out that this formulation is indeed too crude—democratic effects are themselves causal insofar as they generate support for the very features of association important for democracy.

My focus here is theoretical: I am interested in those factors about which it is possible to generalize. There are factors that will have an independent impact but which are more difficult to treat with any generality. One of these is *organization*. A voluntary association, for example, might choose a democratic structure in order to cultivate the loyalty of its members or simply in order to divide labor and spread responsibilities. Or, it might not: if an association's purpose is clear, then loyalty can be guaranteed by ensuring that those who disagree are also encouraged to leave. In many cases, organization seems to be an independent choice, affected by the strategies and ethos of an association's leaders and activists. But it is difficult to generalize about these choices, and analysis is best left to case studies.

But sometimes organization is dependent on structural factors about which it is possible to generalize. The hierarchical structure of the National Resources Defense Council contrasts with the more democratic, federated structure of the Sierra Club. But this may have as much to do with the fact that the primary mission of the NRDC is advocacy and litigation. Although the Sierra Club has similar political goals, it combines these with social activities based in local chapters. This particular combination of purposes encourages a more democratic organizational structure. That is, organization may often reflect the variables of purpose and strategic location.

Leadership is another key factor about which it is difficult to generalize. Good leaders can make all the difference in terms of developing loyalty to an association, refining an association's purpose and normative center, focusing and efficiently using resources, motivating others, and making difficult strategic choices. On the other hand, leadership qualities are highly variable. In seeking more federal money for AIDS research, should ACT UP have taken the highly confrontational approach to AIDS researchers that they did? One could argue that in doing so they misunderstood what AIDS research is like, undermining their credibility as partners in the endeavor and diminishing their influence. But this was a leadership choice that could have been otherwise, and is best approached through a case study.

The factors I treat here are "determining" only in the sense that they identify specific challenges and constraints to which the members, activists, leaders, and employees of associations can react with more or less wisdom and finesse. Associations can rise to these challenges by choosing good leaders and appropriate organizational structures—or not. But even if we exclude the factors that do not readily admit of generalization, we can still generalize about a large number of potentially significant factors that, when combined in chapter 6, should give a baseline set of ideal types that we can then assess with an eye to their potential democratic effects.

Voluntary versus Nonvoluntary Association

Those who see associations as having an important role in democracy almost always focus on *voluntary* associations. The reason for doing so seems so clear that this characterization rarely has been challenged.[1] Associations, on the common liberal view, are the means through which people freely pursue their goals within pluralistic societies. One reason for the (classically) liberal caution in assigning social functions to the state is precisely it is a *compulsory* association.[2] Thus even those state actions that are beyond reproach from the perspective of democratic process but fall short of universal consensus threaten the freedoms of at least some individuals. Associations, because they are voluntary, do not have this ambiguous relationship to freedom. They thus are held to be the ultimate social expression of freedom, a view that easily slides over into the Tocquevillian view that voluntary association is also the ultimate expression of democracy.

This almost universal view, however, overlooks a key structural factor that influences a number of democratic effects: There is a close relationship between the ease with which members can exit, and the pressures within associations for voice. Ease of exit is determined by the extent to which the association is nonvoluntary (or, if one prefers, where the costs of exit are high), which is in turn determined by the extent to which an association controls the resources individuals need for security, livelihood, or identity. As Albert O. Hirschman argues in his now classic *Exit, Voice, and Loyalty*, the greater the chances for exit from an association, the lesser the chances that voice will have an impact within the association. The more nonvoluntary the association, the more important democracy becomes—which is why democracy is very important with respect to the state.

Exit, on the other hand, makes democracy within association less important, because unhappy members can always go elsewhere. As the saying goes, people vote with their feet. And as Hirschman emphasizes, a system based on exit is a marketlike way of making decisions, where pressure is exerted on associations by members moving out of the associations that displease them and into those they prefer. So voluntary associations will, all other things being equal, tend to displace internal politics onto marketlike mechanisms. Considered from the perspective of democracy within an association, exit is a *silent* way of making collective decisions within associations—beyond the message sent by the act of exit itself. When exit is easy, voluntary associations will lack the incentives to ensure its members, voice over time. All other things being equal, the alignment between an association and its members will be an artifact of members joining and quitting. Nonvoluntary elements, on the other hand, can induce associations to cultivate their members' voices, which can encourage important kinds of democratic effects, such as the development of deliberative and political skills.

To be sure, there are two very important mitigating dynamics, the first of which is central to Hirschman's analysis. It is possible for voluntary associations to combat exit by cultivating loyalty. And it is possible to cultivate loyalty through the device of internal democracy. If an association consciously cultivates an ethic of deliberation and encourages members to speak up, register opinions, and bring conflicts to the fore, then democracy can be used as a device to match the goals of the association to those of its members. Yet in an environment that offers alternative associations the temptations for members to exit will be high, given the costs and uncertainties of internal political processes. More likely, even in the most democratic associations, loyalty depends on a high degree of self-selection among the members.

The second mitigating dynamic is important for understanding trade-offs between democratic effects. When members "vote with their feet" rather than speaking up within an association, the effect is—as Hirschman argues—silence within the association. But the aggregate effect for the public sphere dimensions of democracy may be quite the opposite of silence. Associations that purify their goals through self-selection and exit may have capacities to represent their members more loudly in public, so that the politics displaced by exit may reappear in broader public forums. Because voluntary associations can externalize conflict, those with political purposes may be better able to speak with one voice in public spheres, and may be able to claim more legitimately to represent their members' beliefs and preferences.

The Meaning of "Voluntary" Association

What counts as "voluntary" and "nonvoluntary" association? Discussions are sketchy, not surprisingly given the almost universal assumption that voluntary association is the kind best for democracy. We will find little help in the standard (liberal) division of nonvoluntary and voluntary association into state and civil society/economy: the division is misleading because it construes civil society and economy as spheres of unrestricted freedom of association. What is at issue here is not simply state compulsion, but rather a whole range of factors that limit individuals' abilities to exit their associational ties.[3]

Nor is the voluntary/nonvoluntary distinction captured simply by contrasting the normative qualities of social attachments to those attachments affected by economic and political systems. Following Parsons, I argued in chapter 3 that volunteerism is essential to the very concept of the associational relationship. What *voluntary* means in this context is that the associational bond is held together by *chosen* normative allegiance rather than by other kinds of force. But not just any kind of normative influence is sufficient to this meaning of *voluntary*. Voluntary associative relations are modern in the sense that they do not reflect ascribed roles within fixed social orders, but rather choices within contexts that offer alternatives. *Voluntary association* implies normative allegiance within the context of a normative pluralism dissociated from nonnormative enforcement of ascriptive roles. In contrast, although the Catholic Church of the late Middle Ages was centered on the normative goals of Christianity, it made liberal use of its vast political, military, and economic powers, as well as quasi-judicial punishments that included torture and execution.

I also distinguished between *associational relations* and *associations*, the former an ideal type of "operative organization" and the latter referring to organizations within which associational relations are dominant, but which are embedded within social structures that often exert other, nonnormative kinds of force. What distinguishes "pure" voluntary associations is their almost exclusive reliance on associative relations; but in fact most associative relations are embedded within other kinds of forces such as those of biology, economics, legal compulsion, or—in the case of criminal organizations such as the Mafia—the threat of bodily harm. Each of these forces increases the costs of exit to individuals. So, in actual associations, purely associative relations combine with compulsions, fatalities, and inertias to produce a range of nonvoluntary effects following from exit costs.

I contrast *voluntary* with the term *nonvoluntary* rather than *involuntary* because it captures a broader range of the constraints that induce exit costs, which in turn affect individuals' motives to remain within or exit an association. The term *involuntary* suggests that individuals would choose to exit an association if they could do so—and so indicates compulsion against their will. The term *nonvoluntary* can include compulsion, but extends to circumstances that simply happen to impose exit costs. Owing to biological fate, for example, we do not choose our most important primary associations—relations with parents and siblings—and they can be exited only at high cost. The biological aspects of race and sex are fated, introducing nonvoluntary elements into associations based on these traits. On average, workplaces have nonvoluntary elements for workers, given the difficulties and dislocations of changing jobs for most. Workers are not legally bound—that is, *compelled*—to remain with their job, and so the workplace is not an involuntary association (as would be for indentured servants and slaves). But neither is exit without cost, especially if other jobs are not readily available in the same location. If other jobs are not readily available, a worker in a firm with a flat hierarchy may be more inclined to speak up in the face of conflict; a worker in a firm with an authoritarian structure is more likely to remain silent and suppress the injuries of conflict.

The point is that we should not abstract associational effects from the fields of forces, fatalities, compulsions, and sunk costs within which they come to be. Many of these forces enable power relations to be replicated within associations, depending upon the control an association has over means of physical force, economic livelihood, or—in some cases—social resources of identity. Similarly, the degree of nonvoluntariness can be represented by the costs to individuals of exiting the association. These costs may involve, for example, security (exiting the state), livelihood (exiting a workplace), identity (exiting a church or social movement where there are no alternatives, given an individual's psychological makeup), or care and shelter (exiting a family). The reason that the state is a nonvoluntary association is that exit is difficult and risky, which is evidence not only of the state's power, but also—where states are legitimate—of the key goods it provides: collective security and hedges against life-risks. The degree to which a workplace is nonvoluntary depends upon the supply and demand for an individual's skills, combined with the many costs to the worker of breaking social ties with her coworkers, and perhaps uprooting herself and her dependents from a place of residence. On the smallest scale, families are nonvoluntary for children, who are usually linked to them by biological fate and socialization, a link that translates into control over livelihood, security, and identity. The Catholic Church is nonvoluntary for those whose identity is molded through church membership in such a way that there are no perceived alternatives. Churches that are less successful in maintaining a monopoly over the interpretative resources of religious identity—most Protestant sects, for example—are more appropriately characterized as voluntary associations. Public schools are nonvoluntary for the children of parents who lack the resources for private schools, and this compulsion intrudes on the nature and structure of the more voluntary associations that attach to schools, such as PTAs.

The extent to which an association is voluntary does not always depend on the existence of alternative associations. What counts are the costs of exit *to the individual*. The nonvoluntary effects of association depend as much or more on the individual's investment in the associative tie as they do on whether or not there are alternatives. One may be in a position to choose from an number of workplaces; but having chosen one, one organizes residence, career skills, schooling for children, and many other things around this choice, reducing the ease of exit. One may be in a position to choose from a number of potential mates, but having chosen one, one becomes invested in the relationship, not only emotionally, but through shared children and property.

Michael Walzer is one of the few to have considered nonvoluntary aspects of association, although he does not define the issues as I do here.[4] Walzer notes four ways in which association can be constrained. First, we are born into associative relations, especially those of family and religion from which, later in life, we may choose to dissociate, but often at high cost. Second, voluntary association is limited by available cultural forms, such as the prevailing form of marriage, or even the standard forms in which associations' by-laws are written. "There is . . . a radical givenness to our associational life. We meet for a purpose, discover a common interest, agree more or less on a line of argument, and form an organization. Ours is very much like all the other organizations, *and that's how we know what we are doing. . . .* We arouse conventional expectations, and these are our passport to civil society."[5] We are, in other words, both aided by cultural inheritances that provide common associational templates and expectations, but also limited by their very conventionality. The third form of nonvoluntary association is political: we are compelled to associate in political units given by the state or, sometimes, to belong to a union in a workplace with a closed shop. These forms of compulsory association provide, Walzer notes, modes of security that make other forms of association possible. Finally, association is constrained by moral obligation. Because people often try to do the right thing—they follow their "inner voice"—they may find that they feel morally obligated to retain an associational connection, so much so that their obligations constrain their freedom to exit.

Although these four kinds of constraint do indeed limit the voluntary qualities of association, Walzer tends to trivialize the notion of "voluntary" by conceiving it as the equivalent of being unconnected, indeed to the point of pathology if not logical impossibility. On the conception of "voluntary" I use here (and which I think more closely reflects the normative insights of common usage) some of these constraints increase volunteerism, others decrease it. Thus Walzer's fourth kind of constraint, moral obligation, is (under the more Parsonian conception I have in mind) of the essence of associative volunteerism insofar as it signals the essentially normative quality of associative relations. The second kind of constraint, that of available cultural forms, far from producing nonvoluntary association, provides the associative skills necessary for voluntary association. Available cultural forms constrain in much the same way as language: their constraints empower by providing the means through which individuals can become influential in social contexts. What *does* makes a difference are the kinds of cultural forms and their availability: modern forms encourage self-reflective choice more than do premodern forms, and modern contexts are populated by a pluralism of alternatives. But, as Walzer knows, to be "free" of cultural forms *as such* is as meaningless as to be "free" of language: these are freedoms indistinguishable from utter helplessness.

The constraints represented by membership in political units, on the other hand, *do* count as constraints in the sense I mean here—more specifically, they are forms of compulsion based on the state's monopoly over resources of security and other aspects of livelihood. Finally, associations representing biological fate also count, since we do not choose our biological heritage and the close attachments that follow in their wake. These cannot be altered, although parenting can be transferred, often at high cost, to unrelated adults. These attachments are different yet from those of religious identity into which most are also born. We may inherit religious identities involuntarily, but they can be (and very often are) altered as children mature into adults and interrogate their faith. Religious identity can migrate, as it were, from a fate given by circumstances of birth into a voluntary attachment, chosen or reaffirmed later in life in the face of alternatives—a ritual played out by born-again Christians. It is in this sense that most kinds of religious institutions in religiously plural societies count as voluntary associations.

To be sure, there is a tricky issue here. *Some* kinds of identity-based attachments do have compulsory qualities of the sort that induce individuals to remain within associations, even in the face of conflicts. The Catholic Church, for example, exercises an identity-based power in the relevant sense. The church seeks to maintain control over the beliefs, lifestyles, and even some of the economic resources of Catholics, and does so in part through repeated threats of dire consequences in an afterlife believers perceive to be real. When combined with the lack of passable alternatives, the Catholic Church produces something like an identity-based monopoly over those raised in the faith. No doubt this has something to do with fractious nature of Catholic politics, especially within the United States, where Catholics are likely to experience the conflicts between the church hierarchy and the more egalitarian norms in other walks of life. Ironically, it is precisely such internalized conflicts that can cultivate individual autonomy—as evidenced by the willingness of many parishioners to challenge church authority without leaving the faith.

If Walzer's conception of nonvoluntary association is too broad, Nancy Rosenblum's is too narrow, resting primarily on a distinction between voluntary and *compelled* association, that is, circumstances in which states regulate associative life in ways that determine membership. To be sure, there is an important point to the way Rosenblum draws the distinction. Thus, in the case of freedom of religious association, she notes that "government nonintervention rests on the assumption that membership in a religious association is voluntary and based on faith. . . . Volunteerism and religious faith together are the key."[6] In this context, the term *voluntary*, Rosenblum rightly notes, does not imply an ontological doctrine, or nor does it necessarily mean that members of a religious association experience their faith as a "choice." What it does imply is that the influence wielded by the association is precisely that of faith and other social obligations, and not power over livelihood or security. Consistent with Parsons, *voluntary* implies, simply, that the key mode of attachment is normative and not coercive.

But Rosenblum does not, I think, consistently apply this point, especially in her discussions of the well-known U.S. Supreme Court case *Roberts v. Jaycees*,[7] in which the Court compelled the Junior Chamber of Commerce (the "Jaycees") to admit women. Rosenblum disagrees with Justice Brennan's majority opinion, which focused on the ways in which the stigma of second-class citizenship followed from nonadmission of women. "If associations cannot limit eligibility and control admission, their particular projects and expressive aspects will be inhibited, diluted, or subverted."[8] This would be exactly right *if* the Jaycees were primarily a normatively bonded association, and their primary purposes were expressive of moral aims. And, indeed, the Court's majority opinion, in focusing on *stigma*, allowed the regulation of what are in essence moral purposes. But if the Jaycees use the normative resources of association primarily to further *economic* ends—which they do—then the nature of the association is quite different. It was Justice Sandra Day O'Connor's concurring opinion that got the issue right: O'Connor emphasized the fact that the Jaycees provide avenues to local economic power. The Jaycees are not a church or merely a social club, but an association that wields economic influence—indeed, close to a monopoly influence over business opportunities in some places in the United States.[9] To exclude women is to alter their economic prospects, and this calls for regulation in a way that a social club does not—with whatever injuries to the identities of the excluded it may entail. The point is that although Rosenblum is quite right to conceive of voluntary relations in terms of the normative medium of associational life, she overdraws the extent to which they are embodied in associations. This is perhaps because her framework focuses primarily on state compulsion, often diminishing or excluding the impact of other sources of involuntarism, especially economic power.[10]

Rosenblum also overextends the notion of compulsion. The state may compel an association to admit a certain class of members as it compelled the Jaycees to admit women. But as long as exit options remain, the compulsion exercised against the association does not translate into compulsion against members. No male member of the Jaycees is *compelled* (in Rosenblum's legal construction of the term) to associate with women, since membership in the Jaycees remains voluntary.

Rosenblum does, however, make vital points about two other sources of nonvoluntary association. The first concerns the constraints of residence in the cases of Residential Community Associations (RCAs), an increasingly ubiquitous feature of American housing arrangements. Upon buying a house, one finds oneself formally associated with neighbors in matters having to do with the use and upkeep of common property, exterior colors of houses, landscaping, regulation of pets, snow removal, and a host of other neighborhood issues. Even if one initially chooses a place of residence *because* it is regulated by an RCA, once the investment in housing is made, exit is constrained. Thus, past material investment, as with other kinds of investment, serves to reduce the voluntary qualities of some kinds of association.

Rosenblum also makes the subtle but important point that ascriptive identities can produce nonvoluntary effects in an otherwise voluntary environment. Borrowing Anthony Appiah's distinction between ethnic and racial identity, Rosenblum notes that for those Americans who are not African American, ethnicity is an "option"—one can choose to emphasize elements of ancestry selectively, in order to associate with elements of that culture that are often placed along side a myriad of other identities—religious, professional, gender based, and so on.[11] For the African American, however, race is an ascriptive identity that he or she automatically has, the significance of which is already decided by the history of slavery, Reconstruction, segregation, civil rights movements, and economic stratification. The identity is, as it were, imposed from without on the basis of biological fate. Prior to desegregation, of course, associations such as black churches, schools, and universities were "Black" by virtue of state-enforced segregation. Beyond this history, however, common experiences and expectations imposed from without become, by default, a nonvoluntary basis for association. So there is an important sense in which some kinds of identity groups, most importantly those subjected to ascriptive roles based on race, are nonvoluntary.

Voluntary Association and Conflict

Each of these nonvoluntary qualities affects the ways in which an association is likely to handle internal conflict. When conflicts develop within associations, individuals have the choice of (1) speaking up, (2) maintaining the association at the cost of suppressing the conflict, or (3) leaving the association. The choice, clearly, will be influenced by the ease of exit combined with the costs of voice. Voice, writes Hirschman,

> can be viewed as residual—whoever does not exit is a candidate for voice and voice depends, like exit, on the quality of elasticity of demand. But the direction of the relationship [can be] turned around: with a given potential for articulation, the actual level of voice feeds on *in*elastic demand, or the lack of opportunity for exit. In this view, the role of voice would increase as the opportunities for exit decline, up to the point where, with exit wholly unavailable, voice must carry the entire burden of alerting management to its failings.[12]

What is most striking about *voluntary* associations is that they are subject to dynamics of self-selection that will tend to favor relatively homogeneous memberships, at least with respect to the purposes of the association. For the same reason, conflicts over purposes, or the strategies relevant to purposes, may be the exception rather than the rule. Dissenters may find themselves subject to the consensus of the majority combined with pressure either to be silent or to leave. The bias against voice may even be multiplied in associations that maintain close social ties or ties of an encompassing identity. Civic groups, religious groups, and even New Social Movements can often view those who speak up as *introducing* a conflict and thus threatening the solidarity, mission, or purpose of the group.[13] To be sure, within voluntary associations it can often happen that loyalty enables some degree of conflict. A church member of incontestable devotion may thereby earn the right, as it were, to argue tactics without having his devotion questioned. But conflict would, in such cases, be limited to ways, means, and strategies, as when religious fundamentalists disagree about how they ought be associated with other fundamentalists within the Christian Coalition—a religious advocacy coalition—for purposes of magnifying their political impact.

In addition, as Hirschman notes, voice within associations suffers from the uncertainties of success inherent in its future orientation.[14] While "exit requires nothing but a clear-cut either-or decision, voice is essentially an *art* constantly evolving in new directions. This situation makes for an important bias in favor of exit when both options are present: customer-members will ordinarily base their decision on *past* experience with the cost and effectiveness of voice, even though the possible *discovery* of lower cost and greater effectiveness is of the very essence of voice. The presence of the exit alternative can therefore tend to *atrophy the development of the art of voice.*"[15] Since the "decision to exit will often be taken *in light of the prospects for the effective use of voice,*"[16] exit will often be the preferred option for dissenters unless voluntary associations actively seek to reduce the burdens of voice. Over time, whatever little heterogeneity remains after members self-select is further reduced by the structural bias against voice and in favor of exit whenever there are issues to be resolved, *even* when exit is not favored by leaders as a way of avoiding criticism. For these and other reasons, in voluntary associations the costs of voice may seem unduly high to members when compared to those of exit.

Perhaps perversely, the pressures for voice within associations will tend to be less where there is a diversity of associations, since the availability of alternatives makes exit less costly for members while at the same time offering greater chances that individuals can find comfortably homogenerous attachments. Hirschman suggests that loyalty to associations may, in fact, keep exit from being as attractive an option when associations face internal conflicts, and this is certainly a mitigating factor. Yet where associations are truly voluntary, the dynamic of self-selection and homogeneity is there from the start, in part because loyalty to the purposes of an association is itself a factor in self-selection—indeed, the *major* factor for voluntary associations since they are formed for specific purposes and held together by normative forces. The result may be that within voluntary associations individuals' voices are prescripted for harmony; those who sing out of key may be encouraged to mouth the words or to drop out. But easy exit is not necessarily good for voluntary associations. In Hirschman's terms, those who exit are often the most "quality sensitive," so exit can drain an association of its most active and vocal members.

The matter is quite different when associations involve some nonvoluntary qualities. In these cases, Hirschman suggests, the structural pressures will tend to favor voice, if only because the voice option is "the only way in which dissatisfied customers or members can react whenever the exit option is unavailable."[17] There is, of course, nothing necessary about voice when associational relations are circumscribed by nonvoluntary factors. At the limits of compulsion, association as a means of social organization disappears altogether, since associative relations build on normative resources that are crowded out by compulsion. Authoritarian states work at this limit when they use their powers to deny voice as well as exit. The same kind of situation can exist within firms in capitalist markets, where economic power over employees can have the effect of suppressing voice altogether. Firms often have a close to monopoly control over their employee's livelihoods at any point in time—not just because jobs may be scarce, but because a worker taking a new job will often face uprooting from a locale, breaking ties with friends, family, and other social supports, or (in the United States) losing medical insurance. More common is the situation Hirschman refers to as that of a "lazy monopoly": limited competition enables the association to perform even more poorly than it would with a full monopoly. The availability of an exit option relieves the association of its more troublesome elements and saves its leaders from having to respond to the criticism or deal with the potential rebellion of its most vocal members. Hirschman notes that public schools in large metropolitan areas can be subject to this dynamic: parents most concerned about their children's education are often those who choose private schools, leaving public schools with less active, engaged, and committed parents.[18]

In short, the general rule is that the more nonvoluntary an association, the more important voice—but also (and this is key), the greater the likelihood that there will be pressures within the association for voice. Nonvoluntary associations lack the means to externalize politics through exit, and so voice is internally functional as a means of dealing with politics. When the costs of exit are high, voice within an association becomes relatively more attractive, as well as more important—not only for individuals, but for the health of the association as well.

So associations subject to nonvoluntary forces may be more likely to provide democratic experiences, assuming that they respond to their nonvoluntary nature by providing for voice.[19] All other things being equal, associations subject to nonvoluntary forces are less able to externalize conflict, and so must deal with it internally. There are, of course, many nondemocratic ways of dealing with internal conflict, and the presense of nonvoluntary factors can make authoritarian responses more likely. The point, however, is that nonvoluntary factors in association produce conflict from which it is costly to exit—and this is the very definition of politics.[20] "Democracy" has meaning primarily as a response to political conflict, so here is where we should look for the relationship between associations and developmental experiences—especially those relating to political and deliberative skills. Authoritarian responses are always possible and often effective when members have difficulty exiting. But within a modern culture that includes associative expectations, there are also limits to authoritarian responses: they damage allegiance to the association, and so reduce its performance. Michel's quasi-Weberian thesis—that there is an "iron law of oligarchy" within associations driven by its relative efficiency in the face of strategic demands—does not generalize beyond the age of deference.[21] When voice is suppressed in modern democratic cultures, it reappears as grumbling, whispers, resentment, uninspired and unresponsive performance, working-to-rule, and in other ways that can damage an association's capacities. So, it is likely that lack of opportunity for exit in the face of conflict will more often than not generate some demands for democratic procedure.[22]

Of course it is precisely within such associations that democracy has normative importance. Hirschman suggests (wrongly, in my view)[23] that political parties in the United States are an example: because there are only two parties, exit options are relatively limited for those seeking to have an impact on political representation. The limited options for exit tend to internalize political conflict, which necessitates organizational attention to political mechanisms for dealing with internal conflict. At the same time, because there is some provision for exit, parties have an incentive to combine within the same organization as many voices as possible. Likewise, the de facto compulsion in the workplace is what makes workplace democracy morally attractive.[24] Democracy within unions is important for the same reasons.[25] Similarly, this is why we usually think that companies that are granted monopolies ought to be required by law to submit their decisions to public bodies, and to make explicit provision for "voice" from their customers.[26] Because of the relatively compulsory nature of the family, especially for children, democracy (suitably interpreted!) is important here as well. Children—especially adolescents—know this, and when denied voice may threaten exit—a strategy that is powerful because, if serious, is destructive of the family and often self-destructive for the adolescent as well. The fallback is often a parental decision to negotiate—that is, provide for "voice."

The kinds of democratic functions associations serve, then, depend in part on the extent to which they are voluntary. All other things being equal (which they are not), voluntary associations will tend to externalize political conflict through exit, while compulsory associations are often under pressure to devise internal procedures and cultures for dealing with conflict. Voluntary associations may be able to attain a relative "purity" of purpose when compared to compulsory associations, which in turn may enable them to achieve higher degrees of solidarity, and to develop a distinctive voice in the public sphere, as well as higher capacities for subsidiarity, resistance, and representation. Under some circumstances, it may also be easier for voluntary associations to cultivate the pre-civic virtues of trust, reciprocity, and recognition, virtues that are sometimes hard to come by in conflictual atmospheres.[27] On the other hand, all other things being equal (which they are not), voluntary associations are likely to be impoverished in providing direct experiences of resolving political conflicts, especially when they involve conflicts over purposes. It is not unusual, for example, for a private school to split into two when groups of parents find they have differing educational philosophies. Nonvoluntary associations, in contrast, will find it difficult to externalize the conflicting purposes and characteristics of their members. Public schools, for example, usually lack the option of splitting and reconstituting themselves, and so must negotiate the conflicts within. We should expect nonvoluntary

TABLE 5.1
Potential impact of exit on democratic effects

Democratic effects	High exit	Constrained exit
Developmental effects		
Efficacy/ information	X	X
Political skills	—	X
Deliberative skills	—	X
Civic virtues	X	—
Public sphere effects		
Public deliberation	X	—
Representing commonalities	—	X
Representing differences	X	—
Institutional effects		
Subsidiarity	X	—
Coordination/cooperation	—	X
Resistance	X	—
Representation	X	—
Legitimation	—	X

associations to have more difficulty representing their members to external bodies and to find a clear public voice.[28] But because nonvoluntary associations must deal with internal conflict, members may be more likely to have the politically developmental experiences important for democracy, especially if the association's response to conflict is democratic in nature. Joshua Cohen appreciates this point in noting that associations established to govern functionally specific arenas—plant committees to monitor compliance with government occupational health and safety regulations, CDCs that seek to develop impoverished neighborhoods—are under *functional* pressures to perform (hence, there are nonvoluntary elements), and are more likely (because of their externally imposed performance criteria) to bring together people who may share a concrete concern but are very diverse in identities and backgrounds. These kinds of association are, other things being equal, more likely to serve as deliberative "schools of democracy."[29] In addition, nonvoluntary associations may be better at seeking and representing common purposes, coordinating among groups and individuals with conflicting purposes, and serving as the kinds of alternative political venues that can relieve legitimation pressures on the state. Table 5.1 provides a very rough summary of these expectations—rough because the table represents the (postulated) impact of only one of the many factors likely to affect associational contributions to democracy.

The Constitutive Media of Association

The developed liberal democracies are differentiated in their structure and composed of numerous institutions that specialize in their function. Associations are no different in this respect: they are differentially situated within society, in ways that not only affect exit costs, but sometimes alter the democratic effects of exit. While there are numerous trajectories along which differentiation occurs, among the most fundamental are the means through which collective decisions are made and collective actions organized—the "types of operational organization," to use the Parsonian term I introduced in chapter 2. Here I shall rely loosely on Habermas's revised version of Parsons's distinctions,[30] according to which there are three fundamental ways of making collective decisions and organizing collective actions. They can be organized through rules enforced by coercive power—the means that define the state. They can be organized by the unintended consequences of economic exchanges—that is, by markets. And they can be organized through the social resources of custom, traditions, norms, and (language-based) communication—that is, through associational relations. Thus, in the Parsonian/Habermasian terms I am using here, we can think of modern societies as having three media of integration and reproduction: power, money, and social resources (what Habermas and Parsons call "solidarity"), centered on the institutions of state, market, and association.

The distinction I made in chapter 2 between *associations* and *associational relations* becomes quite important in this context. I suggested that while associational *relations* are defined by the social resources, *associations* are differentially embedded in these three media so that associative relations have different impacts on democratic effects within different media-structured contexts. A reading group, bridge club, or drug rehabilitation support group operates purely through social media, while a professional association, union, or CDC combines social media with orientations toward markets and states. These locations in turn have much to do with the functional pressures that come to bear upon associations (which in turn has an impact upon their relative volunteerism) and upon the resources they can deploy. These influence the ways associations operate, reproduce their identities, negotiate conflicts among media, and pursue their goals—and thus their potential contributions to democracy.

TABLE 5.2
Associations distinguished by media location and reproduction

Medium	Nonvested	Vested
Social (norms and communication)	New Social Movements, activist churches	Schools, families, social groups, historical preservation societies, patriotic groups
Legal coercion	Public interest pressure groups, New Social Movements	Professional associations involved in regulation, business lobbies
Money	Firms, business consortiums	Unions, consumer groups using market tactics

The democratic effects of an association also are affected by whether it is embedded in its medium and serves to reproduce it or whether it seeks to alter the status quo, and in this sense is *oriented* toward the medium or its representative institutions and associations but does not participate directly in its existing configuration. We should therefore make a corollary distinction as to whether an association is *vested* or *nonvested* in its medium. A vested association is well situated within a medium's flow of resources. A business association or firm is ordinarily situated so as to benefit from the resource flows of markets; a civic booster association will benefit from a local hegemonic culture. Nonvested associations seek to alter flows of resources from without, as do anti–sweat shop activists or gay civil rights organizations. Table 5.2 represents these two dimensions and provides some examples. The boundaries between dimensions are, of course, theoretical: most actual associations have blurred entanglements. Unions, for example, seek to leverage markets to gain wage concessions; engage in social investing with pension funds (thus mixing political and economic activities); seek political influence through lobbying and campaign activities; sometimes serve as social clubs; and so on. Such associations have complex locations, often reflected in their internal organization (for example, as when unions set up legally distinct political action committees as required by law), but sometimes not.

The Media Embeddedness of Associations

Many kinds of associations are primarily embedded within and seek to reproduce the *social* media of norms, customs, traditions, and language-based communication. These associations rely almost entirely on associative relations for their reproduction. These include associations that engage in education and socialization, as well as groups that seek to alter the norms, traditions, or symbols that support social reproduction. Examples include families, schools, religious groups, social and sports clubs, hobby clubs, cultural groups supporting the arts, New Social Movements aimed at cultural transformations, and foundations that deal with cultural issues. If these groups have aims, they are cultural and social in nature, and their general effect is to reproduce or alter cultural systems.

Decisions and actions organized through *coercive power* usually take the form of rules backed by the powers of the state, that is, through law, administrative rules and regulations, and the like.[31] While the rules and laws themselves often evoke the social resources that give them legitimacy, they gain an organizational autonomy from social interactions.[32] This autonomy allows collective actions to be organized on a much broader scale than would be possible on the basis of everyday social resources alone. The relative autonomy of the political system is evident in the fact that it follows its own kinds of rationality—in positive law, in administrative rule making, in administrative decisions as to how rules are to be developed and applied, as well as in the fact that it can develop and apply universally binding policies and programs. Associations oriented toward or embedded within the medium of coercive (state) power include political parties, political pressure groups, economic lobbies seeking state-sanctioned benefits ("rent-seeking" interest groups), corporatist organizations, policy think tanks, groups devoted to political issues and discussion, often through the print and electronic media, professional associations that take on regulatory functions, groups organized to monitor compliance with laws, and groups that organize public sphere events (such as presidential debates) directly related to state-centered institutions.

Finally, collective decisions and actions organized through the medium of *money* work though the information and incentives provided by price mechanisms, or markets. Price mechanisms can aggregate vast numbers of relatively minor decisions over expanses of time and space, and can do so without planning, intentionality, face-to-face meetings, or any of the other mechanisms that characterize the other two media. The market is "impersonal" in the sense that it responds *only* to money, and is thus indifferent to individual needs and characteristics except insofar as they can be registered as demands in the market. Examples of associations embedded within or oriented toward markets include profit-making firms as well as certain kinds of nonprofits, unions, consumer groups, and even the increasingly active environmental and human rights groups that seek impact through market mechanisms.

What difference do these distinctions make? One central divide is between associations constituted by social media and those constituted by power or money. All other things being equal, a close relation to life-world reproduction enables high degrees of coordination but disables conflict resolution within the association, because nothing but social resources hold the association together. Associations based on social resources alone will tend to be robust in identity formation, subsidiarity, clearly articulated voice in public spheres, and perhaps the development of civic virtues, but they will be fragile with respect to conflict resolution. Every utterance in purely social situations tends to communicate cognitive content as well as numerous signals and reassurances that reproduce the social relation. For this reason, disagreements on the cognitive level are more likely to spill over into the reproduction of social relations. Most of us would be hard pressed to deny Russell Jacoby's observations in an op-ed piece about political talk: "Virtual strangers will passionately argue about last night's game," he writes,

> but try starting a discussion about the antagonism between Korean-American grocers and their customers, or the effects of affirmative action, or the desirability of immigration. That is, bring up urgent subjects about which almost everyone has opinions and ideas. You'll get funny looks. No one will say anything. People will inch away.
>
> Groups of friends are no better. The talk stays light and gossipy. Even discussion about politics is less a discussion than a general nodding of heads over that tragedy or this scandal. Everyone agrees, more or less; at least no one wants to spoil the good atmosphere. After all that's what friends are for: to concur and give support, not to challenge and argue.[33]

From a democratic perspective it might be a good thing to discuss religion and politics over dinner, but where there are real disagreements it takes very mature individuals not leave the dinner table feeling injured or angry. How much easier it is to be "well mannered" and not talk about such things! The point is that in the face of conflicts with political significance (unlike last night's game), social media often become overburdened, producing the equally antipolitical responses of exit (in the case of voluntary associations) or repression and self-censorship (in the case of nonvoluntary associations such as families).[34] To be sure, social groups can, and sometimes do, cultivate an ethic that makes it easier to argue and deliberate matters of importance, even "for fun." But such activities often require a conscious effort on the part of participants not to allow debates to damage social relations. The effect of embeddedness in social media is, I think, to challenge participants to be mature in ways we should not take for granted—at least for theoretical purposes.

The impersonality of money and the universality of law can, however, work to relieve social integration of the full burden of collective decision and action and to bracket conflicts so they are not tightly integrated with every aspect of an association's life. That is, it may be easier for associations that are *not* immediately involved in social reproduction to distance issues from identities, thus making process-oriented, discursive engagement of issues easier for members. Formal deliberative bodies embedded in political systems that include associative relations—parliaments, for example—combine rules of order with norms of courtesy in order to bracket conflict from social relations. Adversarial expectations make it the *norm* that there will be conflict and debate, which in turn makes politics easier, at least from a social-psychological perspective. The peculiar but politically innovative British notion that Her Majesty can and should have a "loyal opposition" is a case in point.

Nor is it accidental—to take a market-oriented example—that large corporations have often done a better job of addressing issues of race and gender than, say, universities (and a *much* better job than most voluntary associations). In the case of universities, race and gender issues immediately challenge the core ideals of intellectual freedom and inclusiveness, while the associative structures of universities can make it difficult to deal with the challenges. Institutional initiatives can seem to threaten academic freedom. Yet one who would raise such issues within the more intimate and social contexts of departments and programs can seem to be making personal accusations of racism, sexism, or hypocrisy, which can in turn damage one's ability to work within these contexts. The incentives favor the status quo. In contrast, many firms—especially larger, more impersonal ones—will have greater potential latitude in addressing such issues precisely because resolving them is instrumental to other goals. In most cases, the mission of the firm (the production of commodities or services) is related only indirectly to the reproduction of the identities of employees. Conflict over matters of race and gender distract from the business of making money. Because the goals of the association are impersonal and narrowly defined, issues of race and gender can also be narrowly defined, limited to issues of competence, equity, and other matters directly related to the institution's market-determined mission. In this context, a dialogue about race—essential to reproducing associative relations within the firm—may be easier for members because it is limited in its ramifications. Sometimes dialogue is easier and more productive if issues can be bracketed, the stakes lowered, and the significance not extended beyond the matters at hand. That is, media-imposed constraints can increase the probability that dialogue will occur by limiting its reach.

There is a dilemma here that deliberative democrats need to identify and address. Associations embedded in social media, precisely because of their relative freedom of systematic pressures, provide potential venues for *unrestricted* dialogue. Moreover, as Habermas rightly emphasizes, the normative guidance of "impersonal" systems can come only from the normative resources of associations constituted by *social* media, both through their internal "signaling" of normative issues and through the collective constitution of public spheres.

But it is not at all clear that, as Habermas claims, "public processes of communication can take place with less distortion the more they are left to the internal dynamic of a civil society that emerges from the lifeworld."[35] The connection between publics and life-worlds is, on Habermas's account, highly differentiated, not only by topic, but also by levels,

> according to the density of communication, organizational complexity, and the range—from the *episodic* publics found in taverns, coffee houses, or on the streets; through the *occasional* or "arranged" publics of particular presentations and events, such as theater performances, rock concerts, party assemblies, or church congresses; up to the *abstract* public sphere of isolated readers, listeners, and viewers scattered across large geographical areas, or even around the globe, and brought together only through the mass media. Despite these manifold differentiations, however, all the partial publics constituted by ordinary language remain porous to one another. . . . Because publics cannot harden into organizations or systems, there is no exclusion rule without a proviso for its abolishment.[36]

Public spheres are "spaces" constituted by public topics and public interactions, and in this sense they are not restricted by the characteristics of associations, which have organizational structure. As I suggested in chapter 4, however, associations may contribute to publics by developing the deliberative skills of individuals or by providing the voices that constitute public agendas and debates. What is not evident in Habermas's discussion is that the characteristics of association that enable these contributions are quite specific. On the one hand, associations reproduced by close social relations or through normative self-selection may become so overburdened with maintaining limited social purposes, affective empathy, or identity that they are unlikely to encourage discourse among members. By restricting internal dialogue, such associations gain a purity of voice and purpose that can help to constitute broader public conversations, but at the expense of political and deliberative experiences internal to the association. On the other hand, certain kinds of external (that is, media-imposed) restrictions on discourse may actually increase the capacities of associations to develop the deliberative skills of individuals. One cannot help but notice that some kinds of associations make dialogue more likely

TABLE 5.3
Structural conditions of deliberation

Distance of communication from the life-world	Structural situation encourages	
	Affective interaction	*Cognitive interaction*
Close (face-to-face)	**1** Discourse restricted by "social overburdening" (Friendship, family, small-group social life, churches)	**2** Discourse restricted by externally imposed goals (Pragmatic problem-solving in workplaces; formal deliberative bodies)
Distant	**3** Discourse restricted by affective, often one-way communication (Mass visual and aural media, advertising)	**4** Unrestricted discourse (Theoretical publics, mass print media, Internet)

just because dialogue is restricted by the fact that the institution reproduces itself in relation to goals determined by impersonal systems.

In contrast to Habermas, then, I would suggest that there is no direct and generalizable transmission belt from the associative venues that reproduce social relations to the "public processes of communication" that take place with "less distortion"—that is, less influence by power and money. But we can, perhaps, specify conditions under which we might expect such connections by distinguishing

- the distance of the association from the life-world, that is, abstraction from pragmatic contexts that tend to be saturated with the demands of social reproduction and action, and

- whether the structural location of the association encourages affective or cognitive forms of communication.

Combining these dimensions, as in table 5.3, suggests that we should expect "undistorted public discourse" of the sort that produces communicative power based on public argument and reasoning in spaces that are not directly mediated by associational relations. There are, however, important forms of *restricted* discourse that can have important democratic effects.

Presented in this schematic way, we can see that we should expect capacities for deliberative contributions of associations to depend on structural locations. Cell 4 represents Habermas's view that the more public spheres "detach themselves from the public's physical presence and extend to the virtual presence of scattered readers, listeners, or viewers linked by public media, the clearer becomes the abstraction that enters when the spatial structure of simple interactions is expanded into a public sphere. When generalized in this way, communication structures contract to informational content and points of view that are uncoupled from the thick contexts of simple interactions, from specific persons, and from practical obligations."[37] Such abstraction both enables and requires higher degrees of cognitive interaction, and would be supported by those kinds or dimensions of associations (including much of the written mass media) that specialize in this kind of interaction.

But although restrictions can suppress communication altogether, they are not *necessarily* bad; indeed, unrestricted discourse has its own kinds of limits. Thus, in the case of restrictions stemming from the "social overburdening" of communication (cell 1), the same restrictions that make deliberation difficult also provide the sensitivity to emerging problems and issues, suggesting that (ideally) conflicts experienced within these associations might be deliberated in others. Discourse restricted by imposed agendas or goals (cell 2: firms, formal deliberative bodies, scientific panels, etc.) can also focus the topic and relieve conversation of much of its social burden in ways that allow for sustained, face-to-face, cognitive debate. While the egoism and "discursive machismo"[38] that can derail deliberation will certainly exist in these contexts, they at least become problems subject to censorship when they derail discussions. Thus it is not always true that, as Habermas claims, "uncoupling communicated opinions from concrete practical obligations tends to have an *intellectualizing effect*."[39] Rather, it depends on the kinds of practical obligations—in particular, how closely they are tied to reproducing social relations.

Cell 3 represents communication abstracted from the life-world in the form of affectively powerful images, sounds, and symbols. This kind of communication has a high potential for manipulation, especially if it is one way, as it is in the mass media. Nonetheless, images that evoke the affective content of the life-world can play a crucial role in public debate, helping to balance the cool intellectualism of cognitive interaction with an affective empathy—a civic virtue in many contexts—that extends beyond everyday horizons of experience. Reports of the increasing body counts during the Vietnam War (even allowing for official deception) did not turn the public decisively against the war until the publication in *Life* magazine of the famous picture of a little girl, crying and naked, running from her burning village. Images of innocence and terror, not easily described in words alone, nonetheless "speak" across time, space, and culture with a power to give meaning to otherwise meaningless facts. Affective content can provide the motivation for what Arendt called the "enlarged perspectives" that encompass more than one's own immediate experiences. To become autonomous, however, political judgments following from affective messages need to be tested at the cognitive level of discourse. This is what separates visual presentations that are merely manipulative from democratically desirable forms of affective communication.

Vested versus Nonvested Associations

As suggested in table 5.2, it also makes a difference to democratic effects as to whether an association is functionally embedded within the system most closely associated with the medium (that is, civil society, state, or market) or whether it seeks to alter the workings of the system. Does the association reproduce the system from within? Or does it seek to alter it from without?[40] That is, is the association *vested* or *nonvested*?

By itself, however, the question of whether an association is vested or not does not tell us enough to draw conclusions about democratic effects. Ideally, we would want to look also at whether an association is able to marshal its resources in ways that allow it to avoid public accountability. Large corporations, for example, can often extract tax benefits from governments simply by offering to invest or threatening to leave. Wealth can enable associations to influence the decisions of representatives through campaign contributions. Vested associations with fewer resources, however, must often resort to more or less transparent bargaining and reason-giving through the "official" channels of democratic institutions. Thus we should ask:

- whether or not an association is vested in its medium and

- whether an association has sufficient power to work its will in nondemocratic ways.

These two distinctions—represented in table 5.4—need to be considered together because the democratic effects of vested associations are likely to be quite different depending upon power and money resources they can deploy. Clearly, both vested and nonvested associations can have democratic effects—although in different ways—as long as they work within distributional contexts that force issues onto democratic terrain (cells 1 and 2). Likewise, both vested and nonvested associations are bad for democracy when their power positions enable them to make collective decisions while escaping collective accountability. While the extrasystemic activities of organized crime, gangs, and some cults are clearly bad for democracy (cell 4), resource positions that enable some kinds of associations to bypass democratic accountability are, at least in the United States, more pervasively corrupting (cell 3).[41]

TABLE 5.4
Potential impact of media location and distribution of power on capacities for
collective action

Distribution of noncommunicative power	Vested associations	Nonvested associations
More egalitarian	**1** Associations that engage in bargaining, conflict resolution, and reason-giving. Capacities for collective action depend on achieving consensus.	**2** Associations seeking social change. By default, focused on influencing collective judgment through communicative power.
Less egalitarian	**3** Associations representing vested interests. Capacities for collective action depend upon hierarchical control of resources.	**4** Associations such as cults, gangs, organized crime that do not seek social change. Capacities for collective action depend on extrasystematic monopolies of power.

Not surprisingly given the attention he has paid to the ways social
actors are embedded within systems and how they impact on the public
sphere, Habermas makes such distinctions in attempting to identify more
precisely the kinds of groups that constitute the public sphere. We should

> distinguish, at least tentatively, the more loosely organized actors who "emerge
> from" the public, as it were [table 5.4, cell 2], from other actors merely "ap-
> pearing before" the public [cells 1 and 3]. The latter have organizational power,
> resources, and sanctions available *from the start*. Naturally, the actors who are
> more firmly anchored in civil society and participate in the reproduction of the
> public sphere also depend on the support of "sponsors" who supply the neces-
> sary resources of money, organization, knowledge, and social capital. But pa-
> trons or "like-minded" sponsors do not necessarily reduce the authenticity of
> the public actors they support. By contrast, the collective actors who merely
> enter the public sphere from, and utilize it for, a specific organization or func-
> tional system have *their own* basis of support. Among these political and social
> actors who do not have to obtain their resources from other spheres, I primarily
> include the large interest groups that enjoy social power, as well as the estab-
> lished parties that have largely become arms of the political system.[42]

Vested associations do not necessarily have to resort to public influence
to achieve their aims. In contrast, those nonvested associations that seek

change must, as it were, default to communicative power precisely because they lack other resources. Again, this is not to say that vested associations are necessarily bad for democracy: their effects depend upon whether their resource positions require them to openly bargain, negotiate, and offer justifications for their positions. What the distinction does point up, however, is that even when they work in democratic ways, vested associations will produce very different kinds of democratic effects than those of nonvested associations. All other things being equal, because vested kinds of associations are well placed to amass resources or because they benefit from the existing "mobilization of bias," they have high capacities for subsidiarity and coordination, as well as high capacities for representation and resistance. Such associations may be well placed for limited deliberation about internal problem-solving, and may serve other transformative and developmental functions as well. Having become entangled within a system, such associations may find they must negotiate and accommodate conflicts in order to retain their positions or serve their purposes. Indeed, it is possible to design institutions that push vested associations toward democracy, as suggested by European corporatist designs that bring all stakeholders onto the governing bodies of enterprises, including management, labor, and community leaders. When laws are used to "vest" those affected by corporate decisions, the effect can be to equalize the bargaining power of stakeholders, and thus to push decisions into forums that are more democratic than would otherwise be the case.

Whether or not the effects of vested associations are democratic, then, depends upon whether those affected by an association have the power to be represented in bargaining and other political processes.[43] It is when they do not that vested associations represent a threat to democracy, not so much because they fail to produce democratic effects, but because they undermine the democratic effects produced elsewhere. These are the groups represented in table 5.4, cell 3: typically, firms, associations of industries, and some kinds of professional associations. These are the groups that are able to make collective decisions in nonpublic ways because of their control over social resources—most often productive property or skills. They are the associations most likely, in Madison's words, to represent "conspiracies against the public interest." It is not the *fact* that associations control resources that is the problem; rather, by controlling resources they are often *also* able to avoid public procedures of justification for actions that affect the public. The issue here, in Michael Walzer's terms, is the convertibility of control over one resource (such as control over productive property) into another (the power to covertly influence public processes and policies). Yet even the most powerful vested interests are not self-sufficient in their power: they need the willing acquiescence and cooperation of those who labor and of governments that provide the public goods necessary to their activities. So given the combinations of privilege and vulnerability that characterize these kinds of associations, any resort to public argument and justification is a risk. It means that their privileged positions are subject to question, and no longer taken for granted. They must demonstrate that their privileges are, after all, justified in terms of the goods they return to society—and this is often a hard case to make. The results are often that their powers are circumscribed by labor law, environmental law, antitrust legislation, payments for some of the public goods they use to generate values, payments for past damages, and so on.

Even those vested associations that generate democratic effects are likely to have low capacities for contributing to public communication and debate.[44] In many cases, this will be because it is more difficult for these associations to purify their public voices: having a stake often implies higher costs of exit, which tends to internalize conflict. Public schools provide some of the most interesting examples of this kind of structural location: associative relations are central to their organization, although they are officially arms of the state, and at the same time serve the crucial economic function of training a workforce. They are "vested" in the sense that they borrow their authority from the state and are charged with socializing citizens and educating workers. Public schools are, in other words, vested in all three media. This unique combination of circumstances transforms public schools into lightning rods for public debate, but also limits their capacities to organize as a voice for education in the public sphere (in contrast, say, to teachers' unions or PTAs). In other cases associations become entangled in the broader enterprises of the state—as do professional associations that take on state-sanctioned regulatory functions, for example. Such associations cannot appear to be "political" without drawing into question the legitimacy they have borrowed, as it were, from the public, which can in turn endanger the powers they have acquired. Universities provide another interesting example. Like other associations with multiple attachments, their public voice is muted because they are entangled in so many different enterprises: not only do they socialize and educate students, but also support numerous kinds of research, engage in partnerships with industry, and contract for military development. But in addition, universities provide forums for ideas and debates: their public neutrality is a studied strategy that enables them to provide institutional shelter for multiple public sphere activities built around classroom debates, conferences and speakers, journals and newspapers, student and faculty associations, and research.

Externally oriented nonvested groups, in contrast, are better able to purify their goals and pursue them strategically, in part because they have few vested interests to compromise. When this circumstance is combined with high ease of exit, such groups can (all other things being equal) achieve a singularity of voice that functionally entangled associations—especially those that specialize in coordination—are less able to achieve. From the point of view of public debate and representation, these nonvested groups are suppliers of issues. But these associations will tend to face two kinds of difficulties not faced by functionally integrated associations. First, not being functionally integrated, these associations do not benefit from the established flow of resources. While this is obviously true (say) in the case of the relative power positions of unions and consumer groups with respect to firms, as well as the power of New Social Movements relative to established political parties, it is also true of those associations that wish to affect the flow of cultural symbols and social resources, as when a gay civil rights advocacy group seeks to disrupt the "natural" symbolic advantage of the traditional family or a religious movement seeks to reestablish "traditional" morality against the dominant media-driven images of decadence. Second, precisely because they are not functionally integrated, these associations must devote extra attention to maintaining the activism of their followings, thus reproducing identities that will, typically, constantly shift as groups shift missions, win or lose battles, find their initiatives co-opted, and the like. New Social Movements, for example, are faced with the double imperative of acting strategically, while doing so in a way that reproduces the identity of the association. Often these imperatives conflict, as when a group strategically compromises to gain a partial victory, but in doing so compromises the principles that animated its following—a dilemma with which, famously, the Greens in Germany and elsewhere have struggled. As Jane Mansbridge argues, the movement to approve an Equal Rights Amendment to the U.S. Constitution (the ERA) fell prey to a similar strategic dilemma. In order to organize sufficient strength within the feminist movement, advocates of the ERA exaggerated its potential impact on advancing the rights of women. But precisely because of these exaggerations, the ERA seemed dangerously radical to mainstream opinion, as well as irresponsible to the vested groups that would have to deal with its feared consequences, such as legally mandated co-ed restrooms.[45] The fears were mostly groundless, not least because a constitutional amendment requires enabling legislation that would presumably take appropriate distinctions into account. But the fears were provoked by the advocates themselves, seeking to energize support within the feminist movement by inflating the potential impact of the ERA. Such strategic dilemmas are typical of nonvested groups seeking change.

TABLE 5.5
Potential impact of media location on democratic effects

Democratic effects	Socially oriented associations		Politically (power) oriented associations		Market-oriented associations	
	Vested	Non-vested	Vested	Non-vested	Vested	Non-vested
Developmental effects						
Efficacy/information	X	X	X	X	X	X
Political skills	—	X	X	X	X	X
Deliberative skills	—	—	X	X	X	X
Civic virtues	X	—	—	—	—	—
Public sphere effects						
Public deliberation	—	X	X	X	—	X
Representing commonalities	X	—	X	—	—	X
Representing differences	—	X	—	X	—	X
Institutional effects						
Subsidarity	X	—	X	—	X	—
Coordination/ cooperation	X	—	X	—	X	—
Resistance	—	X	X	X	X	—
Representation	—	—	X	—	—	—
Legitimation	X	—	X	—	X	—

More generally, the division of democratic effects among vested and nonvested associations is bad for democracy only when vested associations can use their resources to avoid institutionalized bargaining and public accountability. At the extreme, nonvested groups can be driven from the political landscape unless their existence is provided for with some amount of money and protection. A healthy opposition within the associational landscape depends upon a state that provides for and enforces rights of political association, speech, petition, and due process, among others. Its members also require some degree of economic security, as suggested by the robust finding that the political activism that often accompanies membership in associations is distributed in much the same way as are income and education.[46] Thus, we should expect more egalitarian resource distribution to increase participation in groups oriented toward public influence.

Table 5.5 combines these considerations and provides a rough representation of kinds of democratic effects that we might expect to follow from different media locations. Again, these theoretical guesses should not be read onto actual associations, which are subject to other kinds of factors as well.

Constitutive Goods of Association

The final set of distinctions is perhaps more obvious. The manifest purposes of an association—the goods they seek to achieve—will have an impact on their democratic effects, independently of the effects accounted for by the factors I have just discussed. The purposes of an association can, as it were, produce a lean or bias toward specific democratic effects. Let me be clear about what I mean here: I am not suggesting that most associations have, or even should have, democratic purposes. Rather, the purposes that constitute an association—what I refer to as its *constitutive goods*—often have an impact on the democratic effects of association. Most associations do not exist for the sake of democracy, but rather for other reasons. Democracy may be served only incidentally to an association's purpose. This is why (as I noted in chapter 2) I have been using functionalist language, referring to democratic *effects* rather than democratic *purposes*. There are, of course, a few associations that explicitly define themselves in terms of democratic purposes. Associations such as the League of Women Voters, Common Cause, and the City Club of Portland (Oregon) devote themselves to making democracy work better by organizing debates, pushing for process transparency, and researching ballot measures, for example. But such purposes are merely one kind—although an important kind—among a vast array of possibilities.

Nor am I arguing that the democratic effects of an association are *determined* by its constitutive goods. Associational purposes are merely one set of factors. For example, of the goods I analyze below, I find that only one kind—public goods—involves an intrinsic lean toward cultivating deliberative skills. This does not mean that *only* those associations devoted to public goods are "schools of democracy" in this respect. The same effect might be the result of, say, low opportunities for exit within an association devoted to other kinds of goods. As I shall suggest in chapter 6, the democratic effects of any given kind of association will be the result of the combination of factors I detail in this chapter.

In the analysis below, I assume that in most cases associations can be distinguished by their constitutive goods. This assumption follows from the observation that in a differentiated society associations tend to specialize, so that they will tend to define themselves in terms of discrete purposes or related sets of purposes. As I argued in chapter 3, associations are not communities (although "greedy" associations may seek to be): they neither encompass the entire range of goods that constitute the lives of individuals nor do most seek to order these goods with respect to encompassing meanings and identities. For better or worse, in late-modern societies these tasks now fall to individuals who must shoulder these burdens of freedom. Associations today serve discrete and segmented goods, and they usually define their purposes (often with formal mission statements) in terms of a dominant good. To be sure, most associations draw other goods into the wake of their dominant good. The dominant good of the Sierra Club is the conservation of our natural heritage. This good defines its identity. But this same good—in part because it is subject to the collective action problems of public goods—drives the Sierra Club to become involved in organizing outdoor events for its members, raising money through calendar sales, and the like. Still, these other kinds of purposes support the Sierra Club's dominant purpose. Most kinds of associations, I am assuming, are like the Sierra Club in that they can be characterized in terms of a dominant constitutive good. There are important exceptions: public schools, for example, manifestly combine a number of goods—no doubt part of the reason that their purposes are continually being contested and redefined.

Distinguishing the Constitutive Goods of Association

Given the vast array of goods and purposes of associations, can we make distinctions that will not lead to an endless list? We can if we focus only on those features of goods that are important for their democratic effects. While the analysis I offer here is somewhat complex, in the end it reduces to a classification of six types of goods that make a difference for the democratic effects of association. The analysis is worth detailing, however, since it shows why we should make *these* distinctions rather than others, and why—for purposes of democratic theory—we can get by with a relatively small typology.[47]

I proceed by means of four dichotomies that, when combined, allow us to identify eight classes of goods, six of which have associational embodiments. Each dichotomy turns on a characteristic with consequences for democracy. First, we can distinguish between goods that can be enjoyed by *individuals* or small groups of individuals such as families and friends and goods that are inherently *social*, that is, goods such as a shared identity whose value depends on larger-scale social interaction and recognition. What distinguishes an individual good is that it loses value the more widely it is shared, even if possessing the good depends on complex social interdependencies. This is obviously the case with material goods (food, clothing, shelter). But it is also the case with nonmaterial goods that emerge from very small groups: love and friendship, for example. While love between two people will draw on widely shared social goods for, say, rituals of interaction, it cannot be expanded to love of a city or nation or humankind without becoming a different kind of sentiment. Social goods, on the other hand, depend on broad sharing for their value: many kinds of team sports and common social activities, citizenship, or identification with a people or community have value *only* because they are widely shared. Likewise with language: the more broadly shared its structures and conventions, the more value it has to individuals as a means of public communication and expression. Of course few if any activities are exclusively individual or social. For example, while the value of food in satisfying hunger is diminished as the same quantity of food is divided, the activity of eating almost always includes social goods that come into existence only through broad sharing, as is clear on occasions such as Thanksgiving or Seder. The point of this distinction is that social goods can be acquired by seeking them through common action, so that associations devoted to social goods will, all other things being equal, face an imperative to seek and enjoy goods together, with potential implications for the civic virtues of trust and empathy, as well as for cooperation. Individual goods involve no such imperatives, and lean instead toward bargaining.

Second, we can distinguish goods according to whether or not they are characterized by *excludability* or *jointness of supply* (nonexcludability). *Nonexcludable* goods, such as roads, parks, national security, aesthetically pleasing public spaces, and clean air, can be supplied to single individuals only if they are supplied to everyone. These goods usually require collective action for their provision. The significance of this distinction is that although nonexcludable goods may serve individual material interests, they require cooperation if they are to be provided. All other things being equal, associations seeking nonexcludable goods are more likely to induce democratic effects in the areas of civic virtues, political skills, critical skills, public sphere effects, cooperation, and subsidiarity.

Third, goods can be either *material* or *symbolic/psychological*. Material goods such as food, clothing, and shelter have physical presence and satisfy physical needs, although they rarely satisfy physical needs alone. Symbolic and psychological goods (which I consider a subset of symbolic goods) include recognition, self-identity, and symbolic resources such as language, culture, and lifestyle. Except in cases where these symbolic goods combine with excludability (as in sectarian identity-based associations), associations devoted to them are more likely to induce some civic virtues (such as empathy) and provide public representations of commonality, since the value of symbolic goods very often depends upon inclusion.

Finally, goods can be *scarce* or *nonscarce*. Scarce goods are those for which demand is greater than supply in ways that engender potential conflicts between individuals, whether the source of the scarcity is physical (as in the case of limited supplies of land) or social (as when an individual desires a royal title simply because it is scarce). Nonscarce goods are those for which there is a relatively unlimited supply, such as friendship, self-improvement, or language. There is, of course, a sense in which all goods are scarce because they are costly of time. Thus, pursuing friendships or improving one's ability to speak in public may mean that one cannot pursue other kinds of goods. This ontological scarcity has important ramifications for democratic organization: participating in deliberative decision making, for example, is costly of time and will trade off against other desirable goods—spending time with loved ones, for example.[48] The distinction I am making here, however, has to do with the potentials for political conflict inherent in the pursuit of goods: pursuing friendship or literacy, for example, may be costly of time but the supply of these goods is limited neither by physical scarcity nor by social scarcity, so we would not necessarily expect an increase of conflict were more people to pursue them. The significance of the scarce/nonscarce distinction is that associations devoted to nonscarce goods will tend to pursue cooperative and common strategies, while those devoted to scarce goods will often find themselves in conflictual situations. Cooperative relations are not ruled out, but—all other things being equal—associations devoted to scarce resources will pursue strategies aimed at changing allocations. Here, the operative term is *strategic*: scarce goods bias associations toward strategic bargaining. Strategic actions are antidemocratic only if associations can use their powers to avoid public accountability and (to use Habermas's term) the "official circulation of power." Indeed, strategic actions that are constrained by democratic processes can often carry over into discourse about distributive justice.

Combining these distinctions produces sixteen possible classes of goods, as suggested in table 5.6. Eight of these classes are empty of goods that are significant for democratic theory, while two others have no associational consequences, leaving a typology of six goods and their associated purposes.

Individual Material Goods

Goods that are individual, material, scarce, and excludable I refer to as *individual material* goods, and include food, clothing, shelter, and other material consumables enjoyable by individuals or small groups such as families. The significance of these goods is that while they are intrinsically scarce and conflicting, there is no *inherent* requirement for collective action to gain them, which is why they are often left to markets and generate

TABLE 5.6
Constitutive goods of association

	Goods that are excludable and material	
	Individual	Social
Scarce	1. Individual material goods	—
Nonscarce	2. Eclectic and plentiful material goods (no associational implications)	—

	Goods that are nonexcludable and material	
	Individual	Social
Scarce	3. Public material goods	—
Nonscarce	4. Nonexcludable natural goods (no associational implications)	—

	Goods that are excludable and symbolic	
	Individual	Social
Scarce	—	6. Status goods
Nonscarce	5. Interpersonal identity goods	7. Exclusive group identity goods

	Goods that are nonexcludable and symbolic	
	Individual	Social
Scarce	—	—
Nonscarce	—	8. Inclusive social goods

no contributions to state legitimacy. At the same time, because these goods are scarce, they often require cooperative efforts to produce them and generate political efforts to affect their distribution. Associations that pursue these goods by leveraging their power in the *market* (firms, consumer cooperatives, and unions when they pursue wage demands) may produce effects relevant to democracy within the association—such as developing a sense of agency, cultivating political skills, and developing capacities for subsidiarity.[49] But broader distributional effects, planning for futures, and so on, will be left to the markets. Associations that use *political* means to affect distribution (business lobbies, industrial networks, welfare advocacy groups, and unions when they act as social advocates) can stimulate debates about distributive issues, but only if they make their cases in public, and—in some sense—transform individual goods into public responsibilities. But here the association has to make the case that individual benefits also serve as public goods, and so its activities will follow the logic of public goods.

Eclectic and Plentiful Material Goods

Goods that are individual, material, nonscarce, and excludable I refer to as *eclectic* and *plentiful* material goods. Eclectic goods are those which so few individuals enjoy relative to supply that there is no scarcity—say, dandelions. Plentiful goods are in such great supply that there is no scarcity—say, fruit on a tropical island of natural abundance. These goods present no occasion or need for association, and so I do not retain them in the analysis.

Public Material Goods

Goods that are individual, material, scarce, and nonexcludable I refer to as *public material* goods. They include goods such as public radio and television, clean air and water, environmental integrity, and territorial security. Included in this category are rights to individual security, insofar as they are publicly guaranteed. As theories of collective action emphasize, public goods are open to free riders: because individuals may enjoy the good whether or not they pay, they must either be persuaded or coerced into paying.[50] And because these goods are inherently scarce, they bring with them a potential for conflict. The combination of these factors means that public goods must be achieved by collective action against the background potential for conflict. Thus, associations that pursue public goods must attend to common interests, and must persuade individuals they in fact have common interests.[51] For this reason, associations that pursue public goods through *social* media (for example, civic clubs that sponsor highway beautification or public park cleanup days) will attend closely to the civic dimensions of interests and take care to craft arguments that emphasize the benefits of public goods in contrast to the individual goods they often displace in the short term. With respect to the trade-offs between exit and voice, associations devoted to public goods are unique in that it is precisely the possibility of exit that stimulates voice: those who do not exit are stuck with the costs of seeking public goods, which can induce members to use the forces of moral persuasion against those who would exit. Associations that pursue public material goods through the *market* (such as groups that organize consumer boycotts or patronage to punish or reward firms for their environmental activities) are subject to a similar logic. Associations that pursue these goods through the *state* in order to stem exit (groups seeking environmental regulation or greater police presence in a community, for example) do not have a direct structural inducement toward voice. But because the compulsory nature of state solutions always draws the state's legitimacy into question, there remains an indirect inducement for justification. All other things being equal, associations that pursue public goods are the most likely to contribute to a broad range of democratic effects.

Nonexcludable Natural Goods

Goods that are individual, material, nonscarce, and nonexcludable I shall refer to as *natural* goods. These include attributes of our natural environment such as oxygen and sunlight that are normally in abundance. These goods likewise present no occasion or need for association, and so they drop out of the analysis. These goods can, of course, be spoiled: sunlight can be blocked by smog and tall buildings, and oxygen can be made less usable when combined with pollutants. But spoilage introduces scarcity, which transforms these goods into public material goods.

Interpersonal Identity Goods

Goods that are individual, symbolic, nonscarce, and excludable I refer to as *interpersonal identity* goods. These goods include the identities that emerge out of close interpersonal relations such as love, family, friendship, and primary group attachments. In principle, interpersonal identity goods are not scarce, since every new relationship brings new goods into being without this necessarily leading to conflict. They are, however, excludable, since each individual's constellation of interpersonal relations is unique and limited to a relatively small number of people. As Hannah Arendt emphasized, such goods tend to be antipolitical, in the sense that they neither demand nor lean toward collection action and can be degraded when exposed to publicity. These are *private* goods, in the sense that their inherent intimacy has an irreducibly private dimension. Nonetheless, it is within such intimate associations that individuals may learn empathy, develop the confidence necessary to political agency, or find relief from public adversity. Interpersonal identity goods are the closest of all goods to the background of psychological securities most individuals are able to take for granted. Their associational fabric ought to be, and usually is, jealously guarded—necessarily so, since intimate associations are all too easily disrupted by external political or economic pressures.

Status Goods

Goods that are social, symbolic, scarce, and excludable I shall refer to as *status* goods. Status goods are symbolic goods such as degrees, titles, exclusive club memberships, or material goods with an attached symbolic value such as expensive cars, houses, or vacation homes. The value of status goods depends upon their scarcity and excludability: the status of any good that is too widely available is degraded. Likewise, the value of a status good is inherently social: it is only when a good is widely recognized that ownership conveys status.[52] Associations that pursue these goods include, for example, gated residential communities, groups devoted to exclusive consumer goods, elite social and sporting clubs, elite prep schools, and to some extent highly selective colleges and universities. These associations can develop political skills and can often effectively represent their members' interests. But because these goods *are* exclusive and scarce, associations devoted to status goods are unlikely to take their cases public or even to risk public exposure through formal representative processes. All other things being equal, such goods must be covertly defended precisely because their possession cannot, by their very nature, be presented as an exclusive privilege in the common interest—or at least it is difficult to make such a case within a democratic culture. Nor—unlike individual material goods—can they be bargained as if they were equatable to other goods: they have value precisely because they are not equatable. For these reasons, associations pursuing these goods are unlikely to contribute to the public sphere or to democratic processes of representation, and they are more likely to reinforce uncivic attitudes than civic virtues. Whatever trust and empathy they generate will typically be of a particularistic nature, limited to those of a similar status.

Exclusive Group Identity Goods

Goods that are social, symbolic, nonscarce, and excludable I refer to as *exclusive group identity* goods. These goods depend on group distinctions (religion, language, ethnicity, race, age, or gender) or distinctive interests, hobbies, fads, and lifestyles. Unlike status goods, these goods are not *inherently* conflicting, since there is no shortage of such identities and their value does not depend on scarcity. Associations that pursue these goods can contribute to pluralism and diversity while providing individuals with a sense of agency, solidarity, and efficacy, especially if the group is marginalized by the dominant culture. In addition, such associations often sharpen public debate and political representation. But exclusive identity goods often militate against deliberation within the association, since disagreement will often seem a challenge to the identity. Moreover, for those identities given by biology and birth (race, sex, and generation, and to a lesser extent religion, ethnicity, and language) commonality is, as it were, pre-given. Nancy Rosenblum argues that under these circumstances, the possibility of discovering new interests or interests shared with those outside the group is precluded at the outset. Such groups may undermine civic virtue, reminding their members to trust only those like themselves and to distrust outsiders—a logic that is manifest in hate groups, but also has a long and ignoble history among religious and ethnic groups as well as within small towns and some neighborhoods in the United States and elsewhere. For the same reason, cooperative relations with other groups are not very likely: when a group defines itself in terms of identity-based distinctiveness, interests shared with others are submerged. Segments of the Christian Right in the United States, for example, speak in a rhetoric laden with the imagery of war against those who have not accepted their beliefs. Moreover, the representative qualities of (ascriptive) identity-based groups are often suspect: those who claim to speak for the group assume the group interests whether or not there exist processes within associations that might develop the voices of members.[53]

Of course exclusive group identities are often politically constructed from the outside rather than chosen, as when race is used as a pretext for denying voting rights, jobs, housing, schooling, and participation in clubs and associations. In the United States, as in most other countries, there is a long history of majority groups imposing exclusive group identities on minorities, forcing individuals who happen to be of a minority race or ethnicity into common cause with others who share the imposed identity. As I suggested above, these circumstances can produce associative ties by default (that is, there is a nonvoluntary factor that cannot be separated from identity), as in the case of Black churches, schools, and universities, which would not exist as "Black" except for the history of segregation in the United States. But when exclusive group identities are assumed in response to external domination, exploitation, or marginalization, they contribute to democracy something that no other kind of association can, namely, representation in public spheres for those who are subject to these injustices. For all of their troubling qualities, these kinds of exclusive identity-groups serve a critical function. They can serve as the conscience of a democracy, challenging public judgments and stretching the boundaries of public agendas.

Inclusive Social Goods

Goods that are social, symbolic, nonscarce, and nonexcludable I term *inclusive social* goods, and include common resources such as language, knowledge, and cultures, as well as the identities and recognitions that attach to the goals, ideals, activities, and dialogues that constitute membership in a society. Associations that seek such goods include those devoted to reforming political processes and securing rights of speech, association, and political participation, scientific and educational societies, public schools, debating societies, literary and cultural groups, and many kinds of charitable foundations. Associations devoted to social goods are essential to underwriting public spheres and political processes. In practice, of course, inclusive social goods are often attached to membership in political, economic, and social units in ways that introduce scarcity and excludability—as when membership in a public school is limited by the price of neighborhood real estate. But the goods themselves are nonscarce and nonexcludable, and are likely to emerge as distinct when venues exist within which they can be articulated and developed.

We should not expect inclusive social goods to encourage political and deliberative skills in any direct way, nor to introduce positions and agendas into the public sphere. These are effects that develop most fully in the face of conflict—and conflict will tend to be avoided by those who pursue social goods precisely because of their inclusive nature. The nonpartisan stance of the League of Women Voters, for example, is essential to its mission of providing a relatively inclusive forum for debate among candidates for political office. So, all other things being equal, inclusive social goods bias associations away from political conflicts, representations of differences, and direct deliberative involvements, except insofar as these are necessary to extending and securing these goods. But these goods can serve as conditions of these other democratic effects: the commonalities of recognitions, language, and some knowledge are conditions of public deliberation, bargaining, and other political processes. Associations that secure these social identity conditions of democracy can contribute indirectly to state legitimacy insofar as they help institutionalized politics to work better and provide cultural support for state-sanctioned inclusions.

I present a summary of the preceeding analysis in table 5.7, where I indicate how we might expect a constitutive good to bias an association toward a particular kind of democratic effect. Goods that bias associations toward the fewest democratic effects are in the left-hand columns of the table, while those with more are on the right. Again, the table is not predictive of the democratic effects of particular kinds of associations,

TABLE 5.7

Potential impacts of constitutive goods on democratic effects

Democratic effects	Types of purposes/goods					
	Status	Interpersonal identity	Individual material	Exclusive group identity	Inclusive social	Public material
Developmental effects						
Efficacy/information	X	X	X	X	X	X
Political skills	X	—	X	X	—	X
Deliberative skills	—	—	—	—	—	X
Civic virtues	—	X	—	—	X	X
Public-sphere effects						
Public deliberation	—	—	—	X	X	X
Representing commonalities	—	—	—	—	X	X
Representing differences	—	—	—	X	—	—
Institutional effects						
Subsidiarity	—	—	—	—	—	X
Coordination/ cooperation	—	—	X	—	X	X
Resistance	—	X	X	X	—	—
Representation	—	—	X	X	—	X
Legitimation	—	—	—	—	X	X

since the effects are also influenced by ease of exit and media embeddedness. But it does suggest a pattern that accords with the common view that groups with inclusively social and public purposes contribute quite broadly to democracy, whereas those with status orientations do not. And, as with the other distinctions, they will help identify the tendencies of particular combinations of qualities.

With these three sets of distinctions—ease of exit, constitutive media, and constitutive goods—we are now prepared to identify types of associations and relate them to their potential democratic effects.

Six

The Democratic Effects of Associational Types

THE DISTINCTIONS developed in the previous chapter begin to identity the democratic potentials of differently constituted and situated associations. The problem we are faced with, however, is the rather daunting complexity implied in these distinctions. Theory will not serve its purposes if it collapses into descriptive elaboration. Still, the reality is complex, and we do no favors to democracy if we oversimplify. From a theoretical perspective the point is to be precise enough to identify democratic potentials while general enough to see why associational kinds differ in these potentials. So what I attempt in this chapter is to strike a balance by developing a typology of associational kinds based on the differences that are important for democracy.

I proceed in two steps. In the first, I combine the distinctions from chapter 5 to produce a typology of associational types. In the second, more elaborate step, I relate these associational types to their potential democratic effects.

Dimensions of Associational Types

The first step is to combine the dimensions I developed in chapter 5 to generate possible associational types. With regard to the first dimension, ease of exit (which indicates the degree to which an association is voluntary), I rely on a somewhat limited range of possibilities, distinguishing whether ease of exit is relatively high, medium, or low. As I indicated in chapter 5, I am interested less in individuals' chosen attachments to an association—which can be very powerful indeed—than I am in the extent to which an association controls resources necessary for security, livelihood, or identity (that is, whether there is a potential power relation) or the degree to which individuals are associated on the basis of biological necessary (as children are with their parents). That is, to what degree are the voluntary qualities of purely associative relations mitigated by other kinds of forces and circumstances? As it turns out, constraints on exit are highly variable, and a good number of associations include enough constraints to have an impact on democratic effects without exit being so costly as to make the association involuntary. So, including a category of "medium" ease of exit may seem like too fine a distinction—especially from the point of view of limiting complexity—but, in fact, many associations have this quality.

From my discussion of media embeddedness in chapter 5, I carry two more dimensions into the typology: the nature of the medium in which associative relations are embedded—social resources, money, or state power—and whether or not an association is vested in its medium. The final dimension consists of the six kinds of goods or purposes that have differing consequences for democratic effects, which I also discussed in chapter 5.

Even with simplifications in each dimension, these distinctions generate a large number of hypothetical types—more than can be handled intelligibly by discursive means. Instead, I present the results in table 6.1, which indicates the full range of hypothetical types generated by combining variations in these four dimensions.

Although I provide examples, these types are not *descriptions of associations* but rather *ideal types generated by theoretical distinctions*. I mean the notion of *ideal type* to be understood in Max Weber's sense: as a theoretical construction generated for reasons of normative significance. Ideal types involve a selective accounting of those facets of reality that are significant according to some set of normative criteria—here, the dimensions of democracy I discussed in chapter 4. At the same time, ideal types presuppose a close relationship to structures of social action and reproduction—which I sought to accomplish by developing the ideal types according to the constraints and possibilities typical of the developed liberal democracies (chapters 3 and 5). Ideal types are not, however, causal claims, and therefore not directly explanatory. What they provide are theoretical expectations that relate to abstracted dimensions of associational relations. These expectations should, however, enable explanatory hypotheses that focus empirical investigations into causes. So what the typology does provide is a conceptual infrastructure that potentially relates these causes to normatively significant effects.

I emphasize this point because, in fact, there is no neat relationship between the types I present here and actual associations. Nonetheless, the typology is sufficiently detailed so that we can ask: Do associations exist that approximate these specific combinations of characteristics? Do they combine in ways that produce distinctive democratic possibilities or dangers? For this reason, I provide examples in table 6.1 of associations that might approximate these characteristics. My examples are simply illustrative, and they do not even begin to be exhaustive. Nor do I provide the empirical analysis that would be necessary to bridge the theory to actual cases—a project would go far beyond the purely theoretical aims of the analysis. The examples do, however, begin to show what a bridge between democratic theory and the terrain of association might look like.

TABLE 6.1
Defining the characteristics of associations

Ease of exit	Medium of social reproduction	Orientation toward medium	Constitutive goods					
			Status	Interpersonal identity	Individual material	Exclusive group identity	Inclusive social	Public material
High	Social	Vested	Elite social clubs	Social clubs, recreational groups	—	Groups dedicated to cultural tradition; fraternal orders	Cultural, knowledge oriented, educational & recreational groups	Civic & environmental groups
High	Social	Nonvested	—	—	—	Counter hegemonic life style groups & New Social Movements	—	—
Medium	Social	Vested	Gated neighborhoods, private schools	—	—	Parochial schools, churches	Universities, academic research institutes	—
Medium	Social	Nonvested	—	—	—	—	—	—
Low	Social	Vested	—	Families, neighborhoods, public schools	Families, small group mutual aid	Ethnic and racial identity groups	Public schools	—
Low	Social	Nonvested	—	—	—	—	—	—
High	Political (Legal coercion)	Vested	Elite political & professional groups	—	Business lobbies, unions, prof. assocs.	Patriotic groups	Mainstream mass media & foundations	—
High	Political	Nonvested	—	—	Welfare rights & child health advocacy groups	New Social Movements, ethnic, racial, & religious advocacy groups, militia movements	Public knowledge, political process, rights advocacy, oppositional mass media, & foundations	Environmental, public transportation, & public health advocacy groups

TABLE 6.1 (*continued*)
Defining the characteristics of associations

Ease of exit	Medium of social reproduction	Orientation toward medium	Status	Interpersonal identity	Individual material	Exclusive group identity	Inclusive social	Public material
						Constitutive goods		
Medium	Political	Vested	—	—	Political parties, corporatist bodies	—	Political parties, corporatist bodies	Political parties, corporatist bodies RCAs
Medium	Political	Nonvested	—	—	—	—	—	—
Low	Political	Vested	—	—	—	—	—	—
Low	Political	Nonvested	—	—	Organized crime	Organized crime, secret revolutionary cells	Secret revolutionary cells	—
High	Economic	Vested	Connoisseur's assocs.	—	Self-help economic networks, consumer cooperatives	Ethnic, religious, or life style separatist economic networks	—	—
High	Economic	Nonvested	—	—	—	—	—	Market-oriented environmental groups, public interest NGOs.
Medium	Economic	Vested	—	—	Firms, Unions, Industrial research institutes & networks; professional assocs,; nonprofit gov't contractors	—	Unions engaged in social investing	Quasi-public market-oriented NGOs, gov't corporations, nonprofit gov't contractors
Medium	Economic	Nonvested	—	—	—	—	—	—
Low	Ecomonic	Vested	—	—	—	—	—	—
Low	Economic	Nonvested	—	—	—	—	—	—

Of the many hypothetical possibilities that exist, I can think of examples for fewer than one-third, or thirty-four types. In many cases, the empty locations represent theoretical impossibilities. For example, the cells representing membership in *economic associations with low exit* are empty because economic association can be made compulsory only through the use of directly coercive means, as in slavery or peonage. But in such cases, the medium of association would be political (in the sense of requiring direct coercion) rather than economic, where coercion may be present but mediated through market structures in ways that provide, on average, chances for exit. The most important example of this kind of relationship in the United States today is not slavery, but organized crime, although there remain cases in which workers—usually illegal immigrants—are subject to slavelike conditions.

There are other instances of theoretical improbability in table 6.1. Most of the *nonvested social* cells, for example, are empty because individuals usually regard the life into which they are socialized from an internal (that is, "vested") point of view: they reproduce their culture, language, identity, and social relations by participating within them. The one important exception occurs when groups cultivate an oppositional consciousness among their members toward the culture that has defined them—as in gay and lesbian cultural groups, the Black Pride movement, and feminist consciousness-raising groups.

In still other cases, the dimensions are theoretically overdetermined, leaving some cells empty. Thus, the cells representing *nonvested political associations with medium opportunities for exit* are empty because the fact of nonvesting leaves associations with few resources for controlling exit up to the point of using extralegal violence. But such means of limiting exit also tends to make it relatively absolute, meaning chances for exit are low, as in the case of organized crime and some secret revolutionary cells.

In some cases, cells are left empty not because of theoretical impossibility, but because of arbitrary judgments about circumstances inherent in theoretical exercises such as this. For example, does the fact that residential community associations (RCAs) draw on residential investments that make exit difficult but not impossible mean that exit options are "medium" or "low"? There is, of course, no general answer, since the difficulties of exit depend upon the circumstances of individual homeowners. I am guessing, however, that for most home owners the financial difficulties involved in moving count as a significant but not overwhelming (that is, "medium") constraint on exit. Thus, depending on background circumstances, particular associations might be better characterized by cells other than the ones in which I have located them.

In many cases there are also overlapping purposes. Often these overlaps occur when exit is constrained and associations are fully entangled in social reproduction. Public schools, for example, exemplify two cells, representing the fact that they serve at least two kinds of goods—interpersonal identity goods insofar as they are involved in socialization and inclusive social goods insofar as they are involved in reproducing knowledge as well as citizens. Large, politically vested associations such as political parties and corporatist bodies are called upon to represent a large number of goods—from the highly symbolic to issues concerning distribution of material goods.

In addition, some kinds of associations may stretch between media, so that they will exemplify two types of locations. New Social Movements, for example, typically combine social purposes and political purposes. The social purposes show up in, for example, consciousness-raising groups and shared social activities. The political purposes show up in issue-based coalitions, writings, endorsements, and other political activities. But since the forces that structure these complementary activities are distinct, I distinguish New Social Movements as *social* movements from New Social Movements as *political* movements. Often this distinction corresponds to internal differentiations: within the women's movement, for example, the National Organization for Women (NOW) is structured as a political group, whereas feminist consciousness-raising groups are distinct and structured as social groups. Both, however, will identify themselves as part of "the women's movement." The relationship between evangelical churches (which are socially reproduced) and the Christian Coalition (which is politically oriented) is similar.[1]

Still other examples may seem contradictory, but in fact help to illustrate qualities of associations that often go unnoticed. Thus, ethnic and racial identity–based groups have *low* possibilities for exit with respect to the internal, *social* reproduction of groups. Individuals are born into these groups (one cannot choose not to be African American, nor, more significantly, to escape the imposed identity "African American") or socialized into an ethnicity at such an early age that membership is virtually compulsory. It is a different question, however, as to how one bears this identity with respect to political media: one can try to avoid making a political issue of one's identity, thus introducing an element of voluntarism into identity-based *political* associations.

Other locations reflect specific kinds of associational strategies: thus, *nonvested economic* groups—groups that certify products as environmentally friendly, for example—work through markets, but operate externally to them by altering the parameters of consumer demand.

There are two kinds of associations I list in table 6.1 that I shall not carry over into my analysis: the two types that are politically organized, nonvested, and have low possibilities for exit. These groups include organized crime, gangs, and secret revolutionary cells. Such groups challenge the state's monopoly over the means of legitimate violence, and must therefore organize themselves through coercion—even if members initially make the voluntary choice to join. And both are easy cases in terms of their potential democratic effects: they have few, if any. This is because their very means of constitution defy a democratic relationship between coercion and legitimacy. These characteristics in turn sever any possible relationship between democratic institutions or democratic public. Nor can I think of any way in which such groups cultivate democratic dispositions and capacities among their members. Nonetheless, there have been and still are circumstances in which secret revolutionary cells are necessary means of waging struggles for democracy, namely, under totalitarian or quasi-totalitarian regimes in which secrecy is an absolute strategic necessity—for example, in Romania under the dictatorship of Nicolae Ceauşescu, or in Germany under Hitler. This is why secret revolutionary cells are distinct from organized crime. Although they may have similar group structures, they are distinguished by purpose: revolutionary cells intend their activities to benefit society through institutional change, while organized crime seeks only to empower and enrich the members of the association. Still, secret revolutionary cells are always in danger of mirroring the antidemocratic effects of the regimes they oppose, the dilemmas of which Albert Camus keenly portrayed in *The Just Assassins*.[2] Where they push a closed society toward democracy we should thank them—for members often make heroic sacrifices for the sake of democratic causes. In the end, however, we should regard such groups as strategic necessities under bad circumstances, but not as part of the associational fabric of democracy.

More generally, the locations indicated in table 6.1 indicate the kinds of democratic effects we should look for, given associations with distinct characteristics with respect to exit, media location, and purposes. Rather than discuss each type of association separately, however, I group them according to their potential democratic contributions or dangers, the second and final step in the analysis. Proceeding in this way should help to retain the normative focus of democratic theory, which is all too easily lost within the myriad of associational kinds.

More Points on the Logic of the Analysis

Before speculating about the relationships between associational types and their democratic effects, I should like to underscore a few more points on the logic of the analysis. In what follows, I am making summary judgments about the extent to which particular factors might bear on the democratic effect in question. Again, because of their complexity, I present these judgments in a series of tables; in each I sort out the kinds of associations that might contribute to each kind of democratic effect. In chapter 5, I made some guesses about the potential democratic effects of single factors, *all other things being equal*. Here, however, I am considering the factors together, since it is their conjunction that conditions the potential democratic effects of each associational type. But this means that the factors will vary in importance and effect, depending upon how they combine with other factors. In the abstract, there are several considerations that affect how the factors might be weighed.

Key Factors

Not every factor is important in determining the effect in question: in some cases, a single factor may be the most important characteristic determining the democratic effect in question. For example, even if an association has a high potential for exit—and hence for depoliticization of internal conflict—if it is devoted to public material goods, it will have an incentive to attend to internal conflicts and resolve them through deliberation. The reason is that public goods can be gained only through extensive cooperation. Where the state may rely on law to assure cooperation, associations must rely on the normative force of agreement. In such cases, the democratic effects of gaining political and critical skills will be caused by the association's purpose, which is likely to override the effects of easy exit. In the tables that follow, *I have emphasized the key factors with boldface type*, so that they contrast with factors whose effects are overridden by key factors or are simply less relevant.

Functionally Equivalent Factors

Some factors are likely to serve as functional equivalents in producing a given democratic effect. Thus, as in the above example, associations with low possibilities for exit will internalize politics, just as will associations that pursue public goods, since the logic of collective action fails unless conflicting individual interests can be bridged. That is, associations may produce similar effects for different reasons.

Mitigating Factors

It can also be the case that factors pull in opposite directions so that some function to produce an effect, while others dampen it. Not surprisingly, in many cases it is difficult to predict democratic effects on the basis of theory alone. Social groups based on racial or ethnic identity, for example, have constrained exit, which would lead us to predict that conflict is internalized. At the same time, whenever a group's purpose includes an exclusive group identity, there are often subtle and sometimes not-so-subtle pressures for group solidarity that will tend to dampen internal politics: questioning a group's strategies, motives, or principles is all too easily read by members as evidence of disloyalty. Because many associational kinds are subject to mitigating factors, I separate judgments of each kind of democratic potential into three categories: "high" and "low" for types in which key factors lean in the same direction and "mixed" for types in which key factors mitigate one another.

Developmental Effects

Efficacy and Information

The first two effects of association I discussed in chapter 4—that associations may develop a sense of political efficacy among their members and serve as conduits of information—are key contributions to democracy. From a theoretical perspective, however, they are among the least problematic. There are no reasons as a general matter to think that voluntary associations will decrease efficacy. People join associations as one expression and manifestation of their agency, and these effects should be reinforced by experiences of belonging and acting together. In fact, the relationship between participation in voluntary associations and political efficacy has been studied more than other effects. Verba, Schlozman, and Brady, for example, suggest that efficacy is enhanced by all the forms of association they studied, especially when compared to the nonassociative act of voting.[3] In the case of more compulsory associations with internally authoritarian structures, efficacy certainly may be reduced or even replaced by inefficacy—in authoritarian families and workplaces, for example. But this effect stems from the displacement of associative relations by coercion and economic dependency.

Likewise, the impact of associational life on the amount of information individuals have about the world is likely to be positive, simply because associations bring people into contact with one another.[4] To be sure, many associations—primarily political pressure groups and those devoted to educating the public about causes—specialize in information. Associations such as the Nature Conservancy and Human Rights Watch gather data, sue for government files, document industrial abuses, monitor human rights abuses, and so on. Through these activities associations can help individuals to master much more information than they could *as* individuals by searching out and summarizing information related to causes and issues. But these "information specialized" associations differ in their informational effects only in degree from those not explicitly oriented toward providing information—families and hobby clubs, for example. The only situation in which an association might reduce individuals' access to information would be those that seek to envelop individuals within a community (such as cults), exclusive of all other associational ties.

The difficult issues, then, will not be found here. We can safely generalize that, with few exceptions, associational life provides individuals with the efficacy and information necessary (although not sufficient) for democratic citizenship.

Political Skills

Unfortunately, the democratic effects of information and efficacy are the only ones that are unambiguous. When we turn to the question of whether and how associational life develops political skills, we find a more varied picture. *Political skills*, as I have been using the term, include skills in speaking and self-presentation, negotiation and bargaining, coalition building, imagining solutions that will bridge conflicts, knowing when to compromise and when not to, and having the sophistication to know when one is being pressured, threatened, or manipulated.

Not all associations will not provide opportunities to cultivate these capacities. When political skills are useful and needed, opportunities to cultivate them are likely to emerge. What we should look for, then, are associational types likely to be involved in conflicts in ways that affect their purposes and their abilities to act upon them—whether among their own members, with other groups, or in negotiating conflicts with governments. When associations are so constituted or situated, then the opportunities for developing political skills are likely to present themselves.

Accordingly, associational types likely to be poor at cultivating political skills are those listed in table 6.2a. What three of these four kinds of associations have in common is a high ease of exit combined with an internally generated social solidarity. Within such groups—social clubs formed to generate social activity, recreational groups, lifestyle groups, historical associations, even groups devoted to patriotic or nationalist goals—conflict will often be experienced as a threat to group solidarity and will tend to be externalized rather than resolved.

In the case of groups devoted to interpersonal goods, conflict is an inappropriate intrusion into interpersonal solidarity. Conflicts of interest and identity will tend to be resolved by mobility: if an individual feels uncomfortable with the mission or identity of the group, she will often leave

TABLE 6.2a
Associational kinds with low potentials for developing political skills

Examples of associational types	Ease of exit	Medium of social reproduction	Orientation toward medium	Goods of association
Social clubs, recreational & sports assocs.	**High**	**Social**	Vested	Interpersonal identity
Groups dedicated to cultural traditions, fraternal orders	**High**	**Social**	Vested	**Exclusive group identity**
Elite social clubs	**High**	**Social**	Vested	Status
Patriotic and nationalist groups	**High**	Political	Vested	**Exclusive group identity**

rather than fight. These effects are replicated and strengthened within groups devoted exclusively to group identities of the sort that are chosen—fraternal orders, patriotic groups, and the like—for such identities reach deeply into the constitution of persons, and so conflict over associational identities and activities too easily shade into interpersonal conflicts. These combinations of factors produce situations in which high mobility combines with social fragility to externalize conflict. Opportunities to hone political skills will, under these circumstances, be the exception rather than the rule. Groups that are primarily expressive of identity—often nationalist, patriotic, and racist groups—will, of course, come into conflict with other groups, and sometimes with the law. However, expressive associations of these kinds often experience conflict with other groups as affirming their identity—so much so that negotiations and bargains will dull the effects such conflict can have in solidifying group identity. Instead, these kinds of associations will often display distinctions precisely for the purposes of evoking the conflicts, and not for the purpose of forming broader ties.[5] Absent such purposes, expressive groups will do little to cultivate political skills. Indeed, to these groups, *politics* is itself a dirty word, denoting lack of principle, "selling out," opportunism, and similar vices.

Nonetheless, some of the more benign of these groups—fraternal orders, for example—may cultivate some pre-political skills. Ritualized speeches where agreement is predetermined and the atmosphere supportive and safe may develop speaking skills that might subsequently be put to political uses. These may be important to the overall complexion of a democracy if these are (as they are often likely to be) the only places individuals can safely present themselves to others. Moreover, such associations may find themselves in situations that demand a political response. No association is an island. Fraternal orders may find themselves under attack for excluding women or African Americans, or they may not be replicating themselves because the very rigidity of their identity fails to speak to new generations molded by different experiences—the current situation for fraternal orders such as the Elks and the Moose. External circumstances may provoke soul searching. Still, the characteristics of these associational kinds—high exit, social reproduction, and exclusive group identity—are likely to limit the political experiences of members.

The group of associations with high potentials to cultivate political skills presents a more complex picture, mostly owing to a number of functionally equivalent factors (table 6.2b). Still, four patterns of association emerge as significant.

First, the most obvious are associations that are politically oriented or embedded within political processes. Clearly, advocacy groups, political parties, RCAs, public educational groups, CDCs, and similar political groups will all provide opportunities to cultivate political skills, just because they are oriented toward political media. Of course, we should not expect to find these effects unless members are actually active in the association—making calls to potential supporters, negotiating cooperative agreements with businesses for neighborhood development, and so on. Passive members—those who simply write checks, for example—will have little opportunity for politically formative experiences through their association.

Second, and more interesting, are associational types that possess the delicate and volatile combination of low exit and embeddedness in social media of reproduction. Families, neighborhoods, and public schools combine internal reproduction of social media, interpersonal and social goods, and low (or costly) opportunities for exit. These kinds of association are likely to confront the most difficult kinds of issues—moral and ethical issues that touch directly on socialization and identity. But they do so within structural environments that internalize political conflict. For this reason, they are also likely to be demanding as well as promising associational environments for developing political skills. Political sociologists, for example, have long noted the influence of family on the political identities of children, as well as the influence of parental example on association membership and volunteerism. What is important here, however, is that the family is a primary association in which low-level conflict is pervasive and routine, and exit is difficult. Thus, the family is the kind of association—maybe *the* association—that provides children not only with their first "political" experiences, but also with experiences that demand continual conflict resolution. Child psychologists have, of course, long been interested in these dynamics from the perspective of developmental psychology. Some families resolve conflicts through listening, dialogue, and negotiation (albeit within the limits imposed by parental responsibility and children's immaturity) in ways that produce confident,

TABLE 6.2b
Associational kinds with high potentials for developing political skills

Examples of associational types	Ease of exit	Medium of social reproduction	Orientation toward medium	Goods of association
Families, neighborhoods, public schools	Low	Social	Vested	Interpersonal identity
Families, small group mutual aid	Low	Social	Vested	Individual material
Public schools	Low	Social	Vested	**Inclusive Social**
Universities, academic research institutes	Medium	Social	Vested	**Inclusive Social**
Plotical parties, corporatist bodies	Medium	**Political**	Vested	Individual material
Political parties, corporatist bodies, RCAs	Medium	**Political**	Vested	**Public material**
Political parties, corporatist bodies	Medium	**Political**	Vested	**Inclusive Social**
Welfare rights & child health advocacy groups	High	**Political**	Nonvested	Individual material
New Social Movements, ethnic, racial, & religious advocacy, militia movements	High	**Political**	Nonvested	Exclusive group identity
Mainstream mass media & foundations	High	**Political**	Vested	**Inclusive social**
Public knowledge, political process, & human rights advocacy, oppositional mass media & foundations	High	**Political**	Nonvested	**Inclusive social**
Environmental advocacy groups	High	**Political**	Nonvested	**Public material**
Quasi-public, market-oriented NGOs, gov't corporations, nonprofit gov't contractors	Medium	Economic	Vested	**Public material**
Unions engaged in social investing	Medium	Economic	Vested	**Inclusive social**
Civic & environmental groups	High	Social	Vested	**Public material**
Market-oriented environmental groups, public interest NGOs	High	Economic	Nonvested	**Public material**
Self-help economic networks, cooperatives	**High**	**Economic**	Vested	**Individual material**
Ethnic, religious, or lifestyle separatist economic networks	**High**	**Economic**	Vested	**Exclusive group identity**

flexible, and socially skillful children. Other families resolve conflict by demanding rigid obedience and backing it up with deprivations or violence, with outcomes that are less satisfactory from a democratic perspective. Public schools have come to attend very closely to the dynamics of conflict resolution: in seeking to stem violence, they increasingly teach the political skills of de-escalation of conflict, negotiation, listening, and dialogue.

A third interesting class are those associations concerned with public material goods and inclusive social goods—public schools, universities, public interest foundations, international nongovernmental organizations devoted to hunger, human rights, and disease prevention, civic associations, environmental groups, and so on. These associations cultivate political skills *even* when they have high opportunities for exit. The reason has to do with special qualities of public goods and the inclusive qualities of social goods. In the case of public goods, individuals can "free ride." Thus, those who do belong to associations devoted to public goods have reason to attract potential members and to resolve conflicts with existing members—highly political activities. Inclusive social goods such as knowledge and human rights do not possess the same collective action problems, but they do require extensive cooperation. Consistent with this hypothesis, Carmen Sirianni has documented the "social learning" that has taken place within the environmental movement over the last several decades. Groups devoted to environmrntal causes have learned to collaborate, find common ground with adversaries, and engage in experimental forms of community problem solving, often with results that are more satisfactory than would have been the case had these groups worked in isolation or simply sought solutions based on state regulation.[6]

Finally, two categories of groups combine unique circumstances, the two that associate on a cooperative basis for economic purposes. These include consumer cooperatives, ethnic self-help networks (such as the rotating credit associations developed by new immigrants to the United States), religious economic networks (which are prominent in the United States today but extend back to the days of the frontier), gay and lesbian business networks, and the like. Because these associations seek to bring people together in a high-exit economic environment, one would predict that politics would be externalized through exit. But precisely because of this potential fluidity, such associations must be highly persuasive to maintain members. These associations have incentives similar to those of groups devoted to public goods to keep members within a network, simply because members can move outside the network when it is convenient, which then degrades the network's capacities to provide individual material benefits to members. In the case of consumer cooperatives, associations must convince a sufficient number of people to retain their associa-

TABLE 6.2c
Associational kinds with mixed potentials for developing political skills

Examples of associational types	Ease of exit	Medium of social reproduction	Orientation toward medium	Goods of association
Cultural, knowledge-oriented, & educational groups, recreational groups	High	Social	Vested	Inclusive social
Counter-hegemonic lifestyle groups & New Social Movements	High	Social	Nonvested	Exclusive group identity
Elilte political & professional associations	High	Political	Vested	Status
Business lobbies, unions, professional associations	High	Political	Vested	Individual material
Connoisseurs' associations	High	Economic	Vested	Status
Gated neighborhoods, private schools	Medium	Social	Vested	Status
Parochial schools, churches	Medium	Social	Vested	Exclusive group identity
Firms, unions, industrial research institutes & networks, professional associations, nonprofit gov't contractors	Medium	Economic	Vested	Individual material
Ethnic & racial identity groups	Low	Social	Vested	Exclusive group identity

tion for a sufficiently long period of time that individual material benefits begin to accrue. Identity-based economic networks should prove to be somewhat more stable, since they are often formed out of adversity and can provide an identity-based sense of belonging for which individuals may be willing to pay an economic cost.

Associations have *mixed* potentials for cultivating political skills (table 6.2c) when possibilities for conflict combine with one or more characteristics that limit, without eliminating, an association's ability to handle conflict. No neat patterns emerge here, except those of mitigating factors. Thus, cultural and educational groups that pursue social goods via the close ties of social organization (for example, smaller groups devoted to literacy or increasing art appreciation in local schools) are induced to attend to conflicts by the inclusive nature of social goods. But their ability to do so is dampened by easy exit and their reproduction through social means. Social groups based on ethnic or religious identities have a lower potential for exit (since an individual is often strongly identified with a religion or born into an ethnicity), and so will tend to internalize conflicts. At the same time, the fact that such groups are reproduced through social media means that conflict will be limited by the close link between solidarity and identity. Similarly, some churches and parochial schools have constrained exit, but whatever political conflict is internalized is dampened by prior agreements about identity and the social means of reproduction. Conflicts will often be coded in terms of the identity: Who is the more devout? Who is the more faithful to the heritage? Status goods also impose some constraints on political conflict: although individuals may aggressively pursue these goods through association, they also serve as a basis for self-selection and prior agreement. In addition, status goods are difficult to defend publicly *as* status goods. The ethos of many status-based associations may even forbid discussion: position and status are often damaged if their purposes must be spoken rather than simply "known." Yet such goods also occasion strategic political maneuvering for precisely the same reasons. Especially when combined with other factors such as close social reproduction of the group (a factor that suppresses conflict) or a political orientation (which works to evoke conflict), the picture is mixed at best. Likewise, associations of connoisseurs have a high potential for exit from economic producers, but are also more likely to protest when the quality of a producer's goods declines.[7] Firms, unions, professional associations, and business networks with economic purposes tend to have some constraints on exit, which will tend to internalize conflict. But at the same time, since their economic goals are imposed by market location, the domain of conflict is usually limited to strategic issues. In short, a democratic theory should probably not look to these kinds of associations for environments that will unambiguously cultivate the political skills of their members, but neither should it dismiss them.

Civic Virtues

As I noted in chapter 4, the term *civic virtues* is beset with ambiguities, in part because it is often used to include a number of distinct dispositions that underwrite democratic processes, including a willingness to play by the rules, attend to the common good, trust others, empathize with others, tolerate differences, respect rights, and deliberate and listen in good faith. I also noted that these are high expectations and probably unrealizable— although unrealizability in itself is not an argument against ideals toward which we should strive. But there is, of course, a weakness in any strategy that stipulates the presence (or absence) of civic virtue: people's motivations and commitments are often conditioned by the very social and political processes that the stipulations are supposed to explain. The weaknesses I am concerned about here are specific forms of this more common deficiency: they have to do with overly general expectations that associations will develop civic virtues. On the face of it, such expectations are implausible. At best, some kinds of associations may cultivate some of these virtues.

In chapter 4, I developed a suggestion by Nancy Rosenblum that instead of focusing on a long list of demanding civic virtues, we should ask whether virtues relevant to democracy might accompany experiences of cooperative collective action. This approach makes the case somewhat easier by asking whether associations cultivate "pre-civic virtues" or *civil virtues* as a consequence of cooperative experiences—in particular, reciprocity, trust, and recognition.

While these virtues are not uniquely democratic, democracies can work better if they build upon them. The problem, of course, is that democracy is a way of dealing with conflict in the face of pressures for collective action. Conflict often fractures the same civil dispositions that underwrite democratic responses. The conditions of reciprocity are thrown into question by the strategic maneuverings and threats endemic to politics. And if trust were generalized we would hardly need democracy: there would be no need to monitor representatives and officials.[8] Recognition of others in political settings—respecting them as persons, responding to their arguments, and trusting them to follow through on agreements—is much easier when broadly shared norms, understandings, and activities already exist.

Yet background experiences of "civil" cooperation—the "democracy of everyday life," as it were—may educate about commonalities and provide empathetic connections in ways that may make democracy easier, deliberation more likely, and bargaining and compromise less threatening. A virtue of the most mundane of associations—school-based soccer leagues, for example—is that they limit the purpose of association to public and inclusive social goods that are already agreed upon. But in so doing, they join people together who may be radically different in every respect except their enthusiasm for their children's sporting activities. Democrats, I think, will have to hope that virtues cultivated within more agreeable arenas will temper the more fractious arenas of politics in such a way that people can respond to conflicts in democratic ways.

I am suggesting, then, that the most promising associative venues for cultivating civil virtues will tend to be less political in the sense that their characteristics bias them against conflict and toward inclusive goods. There is, in short, a political price to be paid for civility—which is why democracy cannot build on civility alone. Nonetheless, if civility is a key piece of a democratic associational ecology, then we should look to associational types in which political conflict is buried and where there are so-

TABLE 6.3a
Associational kinds with low potentials for developing civic virtues

Examples of associational types	Ease of exit	Medium of social reproduction	Orientation toward medium	Goods of association
Groups dedicated to cultural traditions, fraternal orders	High	Social	Vested	**Exclusive group identity**
Elite social clubs	High	Social	Vested	**Status**
Counter hegemonic life-style groups & New Social Movements	High	Social	Nonvested	**Exclusive group identity**
Gated neighborhoods, private schools	Medium	Social	Vested	**Status**
Parochial schools, churches	Medium	Social	Vested	**Exclusive group identity**
Ethnic & racial identity groups	Low	Social	Vested	**Exclusive group identity**
Patriotic groups	High	**Political**	Vested	**Exclusive group identity**
New Social Movements, ethnic, racial, & religious advocacy, militia movements	High	**Political**	Nonvested	**Exclusive group identity**
Elilte political & professional associations	High	**Political**	Vested	**Status**
Ethnic, religious, or life-style separatist economic networks	High	Economic	Vested	**Exclusive group identity**
Connoisseurs' associations	High	Economic	Vested	**Status**

cial bonds that enable people to pull together.[9] We should look for characteristics that emphasize commonalities—associations devoted to public goods or inclusive social goods, for example. In addition, we should look to venues in which cooperation is based on social reproduction of the sort that can lead to easy agreements to pursue common goods, even if individuals find they must bracket the disagreements they might pursue in more politicized venues.

If these speculations have any validity, then table 6.3a indicates the associational venues we should *not* look to for civil virtues. There is a clear pattern here: associations that pursue goods defined in opposition to others—emphasizing zero-sum boundaries and distinctions—are not likely to cultivate civil virtues. This is clearly the case with status goods and with exclusive group identity goods. When these goods combine with social and political media of reproduction, their uncivilness is often reinforced. Social reproduction carries the weight of group or status distinction into everyday interchanges, producing in-group bonding in opposition to out-groups who are subject to invidious evaluations. A particularized form of trust may develop among members of in-groups, but at the expense of out-groups—thus reinforcing whatever intolerance might have characterized members upon joining. This logic is exemplified in some kinds of organized religion.[10] Christian fundamentalists in the United States, for example, are more intolerant than nonfundamentalists.[11] And historically Catholic countries have populations characterized by lower generalized trust (that is, the disposition to trust strangers) than their northern European and Asian counterparts.[12] As a general matter, associations based on exclusive identity goods make issues out of distinctions that cannot be bridged, owing to the exclusive nature of the goods. While associations devoted to status goods ordinarily prefer not to work their will in public ways (one does not argue about status—its nonreciprocal nature is merely possessed and displayed), associations based on exclusive group identities often seek affirmation of their identity by asserting their superiority to other races, ethnicities, or faiths. Because identity cannot be compromised, members of such associations often see the politics as a zero-sum game, even as war—a rhetoric often heard from the religious right in the United States. To be sure, such public postures are not always bad from the perspective of other democratic effects. They can challenge oppressive hegemonies and can pry open public agendas. But they do not produce civil effects.

In contrast, the clear pattern in table 6.3b is that associations devoted to public material and inclusive social goods are most likely to cultivate civil virtues. These are goods that require extensive cooperation and are broadly beneficial.[13] Associations with characteristics such as these are likely to produce the classic Tocquevillian effect of reminding their members of their dependence upon others, drawing them out of their individual forgetfulness of common goods and collective dependencies. Moreover, these effects should be the strongest when associations devoted to inclusive purposes are reproduced through purely social media: the manner of reproduction inscribes the ethos of the association into the everyday relations that constitute it. At the same time, social reproduction tends to suppress political conflict while emphasizing commonalities. The effect is strengthened when the possibilities for exit are high, since no one feels coerced to give of their time and resources. To a greater or lesser degree these circumstances can be found in social and recreational clubs, civic

TABLE 6.3b
Associational kinds with high potentials for developing civic virtues

Examples of associational types	Ease of exit	Medium of social reproduction	Orientation toward medium	Goods of association
Social clubs, recreational & sports assocs.	**High**	**Social**	Vested	Interpersonal identity
Cultural, knowledge-oriented, & educational groups, recreational groups	**High**	**Social**	Vested	**Inclusive social**
Civic & environmental groups	**High**	**Social**	Vested	**Public material**
Universities, academic research institutes	Medium	**Social**	Vested	**Inclusive social**
Public schools	Low	**Social**	Vested	**Inclusive social**
Market-oriented environ-mental groups, public interest NGOs	**High**	Economic	**Nonvested**	**Public material**
Quasi-public, market-oriented NGOs, gov't corporations, nonprofit gov't contractors	Medium	Economic	Vested	**Public material**
Unions engaged in social investing	Medium	Economic	Vested	**Inclusive social**
Welfare rights & child health advocacy groups	**High**	Political	**Nonvested**	Individual material

groups, environmental and conservation groups devoted to keeping up and protecting public lands, and so on. Associations devoted to organizing recreational sporting events turn out to be especially interesting: Eric Uslaner has found that these kinds of associational ties have an independent effect in creating generalized trust.[14] From the standpoint of democratic processes, the interesting point is that team sports require that individuals compete within a framework of rules they trust their opponents to follow—a social situation that mirrors, as it were, democratic politics, but with lower stakes.

There are some exceptional cases in table 6.3b. Public schools tend to internalize conflict owing to low ease of exit. But often the shared commitments to the goal of education can work against the politicizing effects of low ease of exit. Indeed, it is the very vulnerability of public schools that leads supporters to emphasize common goods, to develop inclusive activities, and to bridge to parents via PTAs. When public schools include diverse populations, they can often create new civic bonds based on common concerns for children's education and socialization. Universities, while less interesting, possess some of these same characteristics primarily because of their defining commitments to inclusive knowledge. Economic associations such as unions that use their pension funds for social investing and market-oriented environmental groups can have similar effects owing to their commitments to inclusive goods, and thus their need to portray a civil and inclusive image. The pressures to "go public" with civic commitments is intensified when economic groups are nonvested: they must influence markets by convincing people to use their economic resources to common benefit. Finally, it is worth commenting on the one "political/individual material" example in table 6.3b, welfare advocacy groups. It is *only* by cultivating civil virtues, especially those of recognition and empathy with the life-chances of others, that nonvested groups such as these can affect patterns and principles of distribution. Such groups are directly political, but have a structural incentive to cultivate civil virtues within the political processes on behalf of the material deprivations of others.

The groups in the table 6.3c are characterized by conflicting attributes and mitigating factors, which—as in all the cases of mixed potentials—make it difficult to generalize about their potential contributions to civil virtues. Associations in which social reproduction is devoted to interpersonal and individual material goods—families, for example—connect people for cooperative purposes, but narrowly and without inducements to reach beyond the primary association. Associations that are "political" in their orientation have incentives to fight for their causes: conflict is inscribed in the nature of their activities, tending to dampen civil virtues. And when exit is constrained, as it is for several of these types, conflict will be internalized into the association as well, again straining civil virtues. At the same time, these effects can be mitigated by commitments to inclusive goods. Economic associations are quite distinctive in their effects: Trust over space and time is essential to economic cooperation, but it is unclear as to whether or how trust and cooperation generalize beyond economic exchanges. So in each case, factors exist that mitigate one another, suggesting that these associations may not detract from civil virtues, but neither are they likely to be robust "schools of civic virtue."

Critical Skills

Although deliberative capacities and dispositions are often lumped together with other kinds of civic virtues, the associational venues likely to cultivate them are distinct. Nor is it necessary—as I suggested in chapter

TABLE 6.3c

Associational kinds with mixed potentials for developing civic virtues

Examples of associational types	Ease of exit	Medium of social reproduction	Orientation toward medium	Goods of association
Families, neighborhoods, public schools	Low	Social	Vested	Interpersonal identity
Families, small group mutual aid	Low	Social	Vested	Individual material
Political parties, corporatist bodies	Medium	Political	Vested	Individual material
Political parties, corporatist bodies, RCAs	Medium	Political	Vested	Public material
Political parties, corporatist bodies	Medium	Political	Vested	Inclusive social
Firms, unions, industrial research institutes & networks, prof. assocs., nonprofit gov't contractors	Medium	Economic	Vested	Individual material
Business lobbies, unions, professional associations	High	Political	Vested	Individual material
Environmental advocacy groups	High	Political	Nonvested	Public material
Mainstream mass media & foundations	High	Political	Vested	Inclusive social
Public knowledge, political process, & human rights advocacy, oppositional mass media & foundations	High	Political	Nonvested	Inclusive social
Self-help economic networks, cooperatives	High	Economic	Vested	Individual material

4—that the associations likely to cultivate individuals' deliberative capacities also contribute to constituting public spheres. The qualities of an association that enable it to develop the deliberative capacities of its members may, for that very reason, make it difficult for the association to develop the strong, consistent public positions often necessary to bring issues before the public. Here I am concerned only with the effects associations may have on individuals' capacities for making cognitively based judgments and for subjecting judgments to critical scrutiny—what I am referring to simply as the *critical skills* that underwrite deliberation and that constitute a key aspect of individual autonomy.

As with the development of political skills, I am assuming that associations are more likely to provide their members with political experiences if they are constituted in ways that they are (*a*) induced to resolve internal conflicts rather than externalizing them or (*b*) induced to deal with other groups, governments, or organized powers to achieve their goals. Such associations are more likely to provide members with political experiences, and thus with opportunities to develop political skills. But while political skills may be honed by a variety of circumstances, those that induce *deliberative* political skills are somewhat more specific. Deliberation is, after all, only one among many ways of responding to conflict. Thus, we should look for structural features that induce an association to seek plus-sum resolutions to conflict, which typically require deliberation. In addition, we should look for circumstances that encourage members to develop what Hannah Arendt referred to as "enlarged perspectives"—that is, the capacity to distance the objects of judgment from immediate identities and interests. As I suggested in chapter 5, this distancing makes it easier—psychologically speaking—for individuals to respond to the cognitive content of claims, as well as to be able to discuss issues without fear that the discussion will also threaten friendships, identities, and solidarities (see table 5.3 and discussion). Alternatively, the purposes of an association can provide functional equivalents of structural inducements for deliberation if they involve public material or inclusive social goods. Likewise, it will help if associations are committed by their mission to deliberation, as are public schools and universities.

Table 6.4a represents the combination of factors especially lethal to critical skills: high ease of exit combined with direct social reproduction of exclusive group identity or status goods. When individuals can easily leave an association rather than question its policies, strategies, purposes, or identity, conflict will tend to be externalized. Over time, there is little to deliberate, since self-selection assures agreement. In addition, if an association is reproduced primarily through social relations, it is often difficult for members to distance discussion of issues from the many other dimensions of communication that cement social relations—a circumstance I discussed in chapter 5 (see table 5.3). Cognitive disputes spill over into social disputes that threaten social relations—the glue that holds together associations embedded in social media. Thus, social clubs, hobby clubs, recreational associations, and the like are built on subtle pressures to agree rather than disagree, to support rather than oppose, and to "go with the flow." These effects become even more pronounced in associations based on exclusive group identities or on status goods: these purposes tend to be defining of persons, so any challenge to the shape of the identity or its associated goods is easily interpreted by members as a sign of disloyalty and betrayal. The constitutive forces of these associational

TABLE 6.4a
Associational kinds with low potentials for developing critical skills

Examples of associational types	Ease of exit	Medium of social reproduction	Orientation toward medium	Goods of association
Social clubs, recreational & sports assocs.	High	Social	Vested	Interpersonal identity
Groups dedicated to cultural traditions, fraternal orders	High	Social	Vested	Exclusive group identity
Elite social clubs	High	Social	Vested	Status
Patriotic groups	High	Political	Vested	Exclusive group identity
New Social Movements, ethnic, racial, & religious advocacy, militia movements	High	Political	Nonvested	Exclusive group identity
Ethnic, religious, or lifestyle separatist economic networks	High	Economic	Vested	Exclusive group identity
Connoisseurs' associations	High	Economic	Vested	Status

types combine to make the personality of the challenger the issue—not the issue itself. Cognitive skills tend to be stunted when they cannot be distanced from the social reproduction of identities—a situation conducive to dogmatism. Groups that build on ideological or religious dogmatism reinforce the effect: in the minds of dogmatists, principles do not need to be deliberated because they are self-evidently true. Indeed, critical discussion can only devitalize principles by sowing the seeds of doubt and demonstrating a lack of faith or conviction.

Sometimes the medium toward which a group is oriented can also dampen critical discussion. Political groups that are nonvested, for example, are better able to act strategically if they are highly solidaristic. They cannot afford, as it were, ongoing deliberation without providing fuel for opponents or becoming so internally fragmented that they cannot effectively push their message. There are, of course, exceptions that prove the rule. The German Green Party is ideologically committed to an egalitarian deliberative democracy, and was better able to practice democracy as a nonvested group. But this same commitment sometimes hampered its ability to act strategically, and so was easier to maintain precisely because the party worked from without. But the incorporation of the Greens into the new ruling coalition in Germany in November 1998 dramatically re-

TABLE 6.4b
Associational kinds with high potentials for developing critical skills

Examples of associational types	Ease of exit	Medium of social reproduction	Orientation toward medium	Goods of association
Families, small group mutual aid	Low	Social	Vested	Individual material
Families, neighborhoods, public schools	Low	Social	Vested	Interpersonal identity
Public schools	Low	Social	Vested	Inclusive Social
Universities, academic research institutes	Medium	Social	Vested	Inclusive Social
Political parties, corporatist bodies	Medium	Political	Vested	Individual material
Political parties, corporatist bodies, RCAs	Medium	Political	Vested	Public material
Political parties, corporatist bodies	Medium	Political	Vested	Inclusive Social
Quasi-public, market-oriented NGOs, gov't corporations, nonprofit gov't contractors	Medium	Economic	Vested	Public material
Unions engaged in social investing	Medium	Economic	Vested	Inclusive social
Civic & environmental groups	High	Social	Vested	Public material
Public knowledge, political process, & human rights advocacy, oppositional mass media & foundations	High	Political	Nonvested	Inclusive social

duced its internal democracy. Now that the party is vested with power in a strategic environment, there is a functional pressure for a leadership that can "stay on message." But such cases are, I think, limited to situations in which an association's identity is defined by its democratic commitments. Finally, in the case of the two economically oriented kinds of groups, there exist no inducements within the association for anything but exit in case of conflict, an antipolitical factor that will militate against deliberative experiences.

Table 6.4b represents groups that are more likely to favor deliberative approaches to conflict, but the reasons are varied. In general, low possibilities for exit combined with a vested position will tend to internalize conflict and induce voice. Individuals have stakes, and they cannot easily remove themselves from the association. In contrast, a nonvested position allows issues and goals to be purified of their practical consequences—a situation that is often good for public voice but can combine with dogmatisms to dampen deliberative experiences. Vested associations, especially where ease of exit is low, are less able to afford dogmatists: stakeholders are likely to remain within the association and push for their positions, and the members of the association must figure out how to carry out their purposes while negotiating conflict. These pressures can move an association toward deliberative mechanisms. This can be true even of low-exit primary groups such as families. In so-called traditional families the father makes decisions, presumably repressing conflict with his authority. In the past, however, this kind of family structure depended to some significant degree upon the father's legally sanctioned control over family property, as well as over the body of his wife. These structures are changing, however, in favor of more equal power relations as women gain in independence and children become aware of their capacities for disruption. Under these circumstances, low ease of exit and equalizing power positions combine to make deliberative means of resolving issues more necessary. At the limits of dysfunction, deliberation shades into therapy, which proceeds by encouraging individuals to resolve affective issues by disentangling them from minor practical issues that can be more easily resolved. That is, issues are raised to a cognitive status, a process that can be formative of critical capacities for all involved.

The goods of association can also produce deliberative inducements. Here again, families, neighborhoods, and public schools emerge as especially interesting (and potentially fractious) because interpersonal identity goods combine with low ease of exit to produce difficult conflicts. These circumstances place a high premium on deliberative resolutions. Public schools (where ease of exit depends upon income) are especially volatile, owing to the fact that they are often called upon to provide and negotiate identity goods (citizenship and moral character) as well as education. Yet precisely because public schools are committed to the inclusive social good of education (with its highly cognitive content), they may seek deliberative resolutions to conflicts, making use of PTAs, public hearings, consultations with activists, and so on. Needless to say, there is nothing necessary here: entrenched public school bureaucracies and even teachers' unions often fortify themselves against parents and other stakeholders who seek a voice. Nonetheless, the deliberative potentials remain because of the unique characteristics of public schools and the associations that build around them.

Public material and inclusive social goods can also drive deliberative judgments even without the added structural pressures of low opportunities for exit and an internal orientation toward media. Public material goods by their very nature call people out of their narrow horizons. In the case of social goods, political process-oriented groups like the League of Women Voters often pursue these goods out of cognitively defended commitments, which will in turn will tend to produce an atmosphere conducive to deliberation, even when there are high opportunities for exit.

The large number of associational types in table 6.4c represent mixed cases in which some kinds of pressures or goods tend toward deliberative conflict resolution, while others limit the topic of discussion. Although again there are no neat patterns, some are worth comment. The associations with constrained (low or medium) exit internalize conflict—which should be good for deliberation, as will their "vested" status. But when they also combine with exclusive identity or status goods, the effect will be to dampen deliberation.

When constrained exit combines with individual material goods—in the case of firms and unions bargaining for wage and benefit packages—there are inducements for bargaining and sometimes for deliberation about social or identity issues that limit the functioning of the organization. At the same time, the fact that purposes of such associations are limited to making money means that there are few inducements to discuss broader topics. It is worth noting, however, that associations such as workplaces may induce limited deliberative skills *precisely because they restrict discourse* in ways that enable cognitive distancing from identity issues, a possibility I discussed in chapter 5 (see table 5.3).[15] Individuals may develop critical skills in such situations, but they are likely to be limited in their substantive scope. Nonetheless, workplace-based forms of association are worth close attention just because they are the most consuming and inclusive forms of association for the majority of people.

The associative types characterized by high ease of exit in table 6.4c can, of course, externalize conflict, which is not good for deliberative experiences. Nonetheless, the types listed here each combine high ease of exit with other characteristics that may also induce deliberation. In many cases, their vested status is important: it means that although individuals *can* exit, they are also stakeholders who benefit from remaining within the association, which provides inducements to deliberate rather than exit. Likewise, the incentives attached to public material or inclusive social goods will incline associations to reach out to others, using deliberative means.

In this class we also have the apparent contradiction that vested as well as nonvested locations are important for deliberative effects. But the problem is only apparent: the vested/nonvested status of each type produces

TABLE 6.4c
Associational kinds with mixed potentials for developing critical skills

Examples of associational types	Ease of exit	Medium of social reproduction	Orientation toward medium	Goods of association
Ethnic & racial identity groups	Low	Social	Vested	Exclusive group identity
Parochial schools, churches	Medium	Social	Vested	Exclusive group identity
Gated neighborhoods, private schools	Medium	Social	Vested	Status
Firms, unions, industrial research institutes & networks, prof. assocs., nonprofit gov't contractors	Medium	Economic	Vested	Individual material
Counter-hegemonic lifestyle groups & New Social Movements	High	Social	Nonvested	Exclusive group identity
Cultural, knowledge-oriented, & educational groups, recreational groups	High	Social	Vested	Inclusive social
Business lobbies, unions, professional associations	High	Political	Vested	Individual material
Elilte political & professional associations	High	Political	Vested	Status
Welfare rights & child health advocacy groups	High	Political	Nonvested	Individual material
Mainstream mass media & foundations	High	Political	Vested	Inclusive social
Environmental advocacy groups	High	Political	Nonvested	Public material
Self-help economic networks, cooperatives	High	Economic	Vested	Individual material
Market-oriented environmental groups, public interest NGOs	High	Economic	Nonvested	Public material

different effects because of the ways they combine with other characteristics. A vested status can induce people to remain within the association, and thus serves to internalize conflict even when the opportunities for exit are high. But in the case of counterhegemonic lifestyle groups and many New Social Movements, it is their *nonvested* status relative to the dominant culture that can provoke deliberative experiences. These groups are typically involved in consciousness-raising of one sort or another. They question the ways in which they themselves carry a dominant identity, and subject these elements of their own self-definitions to critical scrutiny. The two other kinds of nonvested groups—including welfare rights advocacy and market-oriented environmental advocacy groups—are subject to slightly different logics. Because of their nonvested status, they are driven to provide reasons to themselves and others for their purposes. That is, they depend upon communicative power—the power of arguments about distributive justice, for example—more than do vested groups. Such groups, however, are subject to high ease of exit and thus to the kind of self-selection that inhibits internal deliberative conflict resolution.

Public Sphere Effects

Political autonomy, as I introduced the term in chapter 4, refers to the capacity of a society to collectively decide its futures. Decisions are politically autonomous when people give due consideration to what they want for the collectivity, usually by participating in some kind of public reasoning process—listening and responding to the reasons that others offer for their positions. When public judgments are made under the influence of public reasoning, and when these judgments motivate just because people accept the reasoning, then they amount to *communicative power*. In a democracy, communicative power ought to replace other forms of force in collective decisions—a bit of common sense indelicately attested to by a White House spokesman who characterized their approach to Congress as it was considering impeachment of President Clinton: "We seek to bend ears, not break arms." More generally, in a democracy political conflicts are resolved through communicative power rather than displaced into markets or resolved through coercive imposition, even if the result is a (coercively enforced) law or a decision to leave the conflict to markets.

The term *public sphere* names the social spaces constituted by networks of communication, and which generate communicative power (see chapter 4). Public spheres have a number of conditions, including protection by the state by means of rights that individuals can deploy not only against the state, but also against uses of power and money within society that threaten communicative power. Likewise, highly unequal distributions of economic power can produce vulnerabilities—within and between locales, in workplaces, and among individuals—that can dampen or exclude communicative power. Corporate concentration may enable a handful of businesses to dominate the mass media through saturation, thus undermining the autonomy of public judgments. These conditions of public spheres are fairly well understood and studied.

Less well understood are the associative conditions of public spheres. It is now commonplace that public spheres emerge from and are supported by associations and associative networks. We know, of course, that public spheres thrive on a variety of active, outspoken advocates, on associative venues that bring together people with different interests and identities, and on means of communication that are not dominated by the state or by commercial interests. But what, more exactly, are the kinds of associations most likely to generate public spheres and the political autonomy they enable? Or, in the terms I use here, what kinds of public sphere effects should we expect from what kinds of associations? As I suggested in chapter 4, we can begin to address the question by recognizing that there are at least three distinct although overlapping features of democratic public spheres: public communication and deliberation, representations of difference, and representations of commonality. These aspects of public spheres are distinct primarily from the perspective of association: while many associational types will produce few if any of these public-sphere effects, those that do will be distinctive in their contributions.

Public Communication and Deliberation

Public communication and deliberation are the activities that constitute public spheres and the communicative power they generate. The sources of these activities are, very often, associations that provide the connections between individuals' needs and problems and their articulated public voice by working to bring issues before the public and providing arguments for positions—constituting issue-agendas and discussions that extend over time and space. Associations connect public spaces to individual life-worlds. If public spheres are in constant danger of being hijacked by what Max Horkheimer and Theodor Adorno famously referred to as the "culture industry," associational connections can, at least in principle, provide experiential counterweights.

But not every kind of association has the capacity or the incentive to "go public" in ways that keep public communication and deliberation vital and autonomous. Indeed, most associations prefer to do their work quietly—if not behind the scenes. Some, especially those that are primarily social, do not need publicity to achieve their purposes. Others, such as scientific and technical associations, are locked into specialized languages in ways that make it difficult for them to enter public discussions without skillful translators. Still others develop sheltered working relations among groups that could easily be disrupted by the rough-and-tumble of public advocacy and argument. Some groups—social service providers, for example—seek to base their legitimacy upon their expertise, which will cause them to be very cautious about taking any public stand that could be construed as "political."[16] The appearance of partisanship can erode the legitimacy of expert authority. And there are associations that actively seek to avoid public exposure because they can better work their wills through power and money. Finally, U.S. tax law encourages associations to keep a low public profile by providing tax advantages to "nonpolitical" associations. Elizabeth Boris estimates that only 5.5 percent of tax-exempt organizations have advocacy as any part of their mission, and these tend to be the smaller rather than larger organizations.[17] To be sure, contributions to the public sphere do not require advocacy as such: studies of public policies, surveys, and other such activities can promote public sphere dialogue without appearing to be "political." Nonetheless, even if we take these activities into account, a relatively small proportion of associations are involved in public sphere activities of any description.

The kinds of associations that are likely to keep the public sphere vital are those that have something to gain by going public, and are so constituted that they can "stay on message"—that is, they must have the capacity to project their voice over time and space. In addition, a few kinds of associations—often foundations such as the Pew Charitable Trusts, the Kettering Foundation, and the Kaiser Family Foundation—are devoted to provoking and enhancing the quality of public dialogue. As I have suggested, however, the associations most active and important in constituting public communication and dialogue may not be the same as those that cultivate the critical skills of members. There may even be an inverse relationship: the groups that can present the most sharply defined and closely argued public positions often have memberships that self-select for the issue, producing an internal atmosphere in which debate is limited to strategic issues of how best to gain public influence.

Compared to other democratic effects, the logic that drives contributions to public communication and deliberation is relatively straightforward. One key factor has to do with whether an association is oriented toward political media. The importance of this factor is clear: if associations are politically embedded or oriented, their purposes are, for this same reason, contestable and thus become potential elements in public debates. In contrast, in the case of economic media, communication is—to use Habermas's terms—"delinguistified." Markets "communicate," but not publicly, and not in any way that can constitute deliberation. Even groups that form within markets, such as ethnic self-help networks (rotating credit associations, for example) and identity-based economic networks (networks of Christian businesses and consumers, for example), operate with means they can control—solidarity and pooled economic resources—and do not need public exposure to achieve their purposes. Nor do associations that reproduce through social media (civic groups, hobby clubs, and sporting clubs, for example) need public exposure to achieve their purposes. Rather, they thrive on background consensus, which they will tend to maintain through self-selection and exit rather than by going public with their conflicts. So if we are interested in public sphere effects, we should first look to those associations that are directly oriented toward politics.

A second key factor is whether or not an association is vested in its medium, since this will affect its motivations to go public. All other things being equal, associations that are *not vested* in the medium they are trying to effect will be motivated to make use of communicative power—that is, to go public and attempt to press their cause by persuasion. Associations that are *vested* in their medium of reproduction are more likely to avoid the unpredictability of public exposure and justification, preferring to exercise influence through money, power, or the mobilization of bias. Vested associations will seek to justify publicly their positions and activities only when they are threatened with public criticism, demonstrations, legislative proposals, work stoppages, and the like. Business lobbies and trade associations, for example, prefer to exercise political influence through large campaign contributions or threats of capital flight rather than by attempts to publicly justify demands for favorable public policies. For these kinds of associations, public controversy is anathema, and we are likely to hear of them only when they launch ad campaigns to increase the markets for their products—as when we are exhorted to drink more milk or eat more beef. In contrast, because *nonvested* groups seek change and do not benefit from established flows of resources, they will seek to communicate their positions and to stimulate public debate. Communicative power is the only power that nonvested groups can exercise.

A third key factor is ease of exit. When associations cannot externalize political conflict, they have an incentive *not* to insert themselves into public debates—not just because it is often difficult to find a clear, consistent, and effective public voice when there are many voices within the association, but also because a low public profile is often necessary to maintain a balance of voices and forces within. If leadership should nonetheless take a strong public stand on an issue without a broad consensus within the association, this amounts to declaring war on those who disagree. In contrast, when exit is easy, associations can purify their public voice and maintain the internal consensus necessary to "stay on message" over the long periods of time it takes to constitute and affect public debates. Alternatively, an association may externalize conflict not through exit, but rather by seeking to decouple issues. Amnesty International, for example, focuses only on the evils of political imprisonment, torture, and execu-

TABLE 6.5a

Associational kinds with low potentials for constituting public communication and deliberation

Examples of associational types	Ease of exit	Medium of social reproduction	Orientation toward medium	Goods of association
Families, small group mutual aid	Low	Social	Vested	Individual material
Families, neighborhoods, public schools	Low	Social	Vested	Interpersonal identity
Ethnic & racial identity groups	Low	Social	Vested	Exclusive group identity
Parochial schools, churches	Medium	Social	Vested	Exclusive group identity
Gated neighborhoods, private schools	Medium	Social	Vested	Status
Social clubs, recreational & sports assocs.	High	Social	Vested	Interpersonal identity
Groups dedicated to cultural traditions, fraternal orders	High	Social	Vested	Exclusive group identity
Elite social clubs	High	Social	Vested	Status
Civic & environmental groups	High	Social	Vested	Public material
Firms, unions, industrial research institutes & networks, prof. assocs., nonprofit gov't contractors	Medium	Economic	Vested	Individual material
Quasi-public, market-oriented NGOs, gov't corporations, nonprofit gov't contractors	Medium	Economic	Vested	Public material
Self-help economic networks, cooperatives	High	Economic	Vested	Individual material
Ethnic, religious, or lifestyle separatist economic networks	High	Economic	Vested	Exclusive group identity
Connoisseurs' associations	High	Economic	Vested	Status

tion, and not on the ideologies of the victims or other policies, processes, and practices of the governments. This is a strategic choice, based on the assumption that their public influence depends upon constructing a broad consensus about these issues from among people of widely varying political views.

These logics are illustrated in table 6.5a, which lists the kinds of associations we should expect to contribute little to constituting public spheres.

TABLE 6.5b

Associational kinds with high potentials for constituting public communication and deliberation

Examples of associational types	Ease of exit	Medium of social reproduction	Orientation toward medium	Goods of association
Mainstream mass media & foundations	High	Political	Vested	**Inclusive social**
Welfare rights & child health advocacy groups	High	Political	Nonvested	Individual material
New Social Movements, ethnic, racial, & religious advocacy, militia movements (as public groups)	High	Political	Nonvested	Exclusive group identity
Public knowledge, political process, & human rights advocacy, oppositional mass media & foundations	High	Political	Nonvested	Inclusive social
Environmental advocacy groups	High	Political	Nonvested	Public material
Market-oriented environmental groups, public interest NGOs	High	Economic	Nonvested	**Public material**
Unions engaged in social investing	Medium	Economic	Vested	**Inclusive social**

Because these groups are vested in their media and have other means to achieve their purposes, they lack the incentives to go public. Because they are embedded in social and economic media, making "public issues" of things is inappropriate, ineffective, or disruptive. And for the associative types with constrained exit, the imperatives of managing internal conflict will undermine any incentives these groups might have to become actors in the public arenas. So, although associational life may provide the infrastructure of public spheres, a very large number of associational types will make few contributions to public communication and deliberation.

With a couple of exceptions, table 6.5b mirrors the reasoning displayed in table 6.5a. What New Social Movements, identity-based advocacy groups, rights advocacy groups, oppositional media, and groups that specialize in gathering and communicating information about the nonpublic activities of governments, businesses, and other associations have in common is that they are not vested, and so must rely on communicative power—information, argument, rhetoric, and demonstration—to achieve their objectives.[18] When combined with easy exit, these groups can clarify their messages and "go public," effects that are strengthened if the groups are politically oriented. Groups such as Common Cause (specializing in exposing the illegitimate influence of money within political processes) operate primarily by gathering information about the financing of political campaigns and making it public. Groups such as the League of Women Voters sponsor candidate debates and publicize candidate responses to questionnaires in an attempt to enhance the relationship between elections and good public judgments. The two economically oriented types in this table—unions engaged in social investing and conservation groups that achieve their objectives by buying and preserving land, for example— benefit from high public profiles because they must use persuasion to interest people in diverting their money to their causes. In both cases, commitments to inclusive goods strengthen the incentives to go public.

The established media—the only vested kind of association in table 6.5b—also function to constitute publics. It is the professional business of newspapers, television, and news magazines to provoke public discussion and to justify media displays of public issues in terms of their broad social contributions. The danger from a democratic perspective, of course, is that because the established media is business, it is primarily responsive to the powers of money rather than to the life-worlds of mostly passive media consumers. Nonetheless, even if only interested in market share, the mass media can often push issues onto the public agenda that had, perhaps, been relegated to the margins of debate by a mainstream consensus about what should and should not be discussed. Surely it counts as a provocation to public debate when Ellen DeGeneres declares herself a lesbian on her sitcom *Ellen*, or when former Vice President Dan Quayle finds himself debating a fictitious sitcom character, Murphy Brown, on the morality of single motherhood. Moreover, in the world of journalism, issues sell—especially new ones—so that it is in the interests of media professionals to look for that which may have been overlooked. An established newspaper, the *Washington Post*, uncovered the Watergate scandal. Television programs such as CBS's *60 Minutes* look for problems and issues that have yet to be exposed, often focusing on fraudulent business practices. In these ways, whatever their motivations, the mass media continually provoke attention to issues. To be sure, such provocations to public communication and deliberation are displayed before passive viewers. Whether this is a problem for democracy, however, depends upon whether and how these provocations to be taken up, deepened, and acted upon by associations that have more than a vicarious connection to individuals' life-worlds. That is, the democratic effects of the mass media depend upon its associational complements.

The associational types represented in table 6.5c make limited contributions to public communication and deliberation. The predominant pattern is that the vested positions of these types bias against public exposure

TABLE 6.5c
Associational kinds with mixed potentials for constituting public communication and deliberation

Examples of associational types	Ease of exit	Medium of social reproduction	Orientation toward medium	Goods of association
Public schools	Low	Social	Vested	Inclusive Social
Universities, academic research institutes	Medium	Social	Vested	Inclusive Social
Political parties, corporatist bodies	Medium	Political	Vested	Individual material
Political parties, corporatist bodies, RCAs	Medium	Political	Vested	Public material
Political parties, corporatist bodies	Medium	Political	Vested	Inclusive Social
Counter-hegemonic lifestyle groups & New Social Movements	High	Social	Nonvested	Exclusive group identity
Cultural, knowledge-oriented, & educational groups, recreational groups	High	Social	Vested	Inclusive social
Business lobbies, unions, professional associations	High	Political	Vested	Individual material
Patriotic groups	High	Political	Vested	Exclusive group identity
Elilte political & professional associations	High	Political	Vested	Status

and activities, while other factors tend to provoke activity. Political parties in the U.S. two-party system, for example, constantly seek to develop strategic agendas "in house." They often fail, however, owing to the existence of factions that appeal to publics in order to move the party in their direction. In spite of the strategic intentions of leaders, American parties are increasingly providing forums for public debates rather than guiding and forming public debates. But parties are not well placed to push the margins of public debate. In the United States, the electoral dynamics of the two-party system limit the distance either party can move from mainstream consensus. Moreover, parties are limited by the strategic problems of gaining power, and they are usually close to the many institutions of government.

Institutions such as universities are committed by purpose and design to public communication, discourse, and judgment, and they provide important forums for public discussions. However, because universities are reproduced in large part through social consensus, they find themselves constrained by the need to maintain civility, which may in turn lead to rather awkward speech codes, newspaper censorship, and other constraints on public discourse combined with symbolic commitments to "diversity." Likewise, because universities are full of people with strongly held opinions, they cannot afford to take public stands on most major issues. Instead, they are likely to act much as any other interest group, keeping a low profile while lobbying legislatures and businesses for more money, a goal that will unite virtually all constituencies within the university. Similarly, social groups that are committed to public education or the arts as well as cultural groups often find they are most effective at retaining members and achieving their purposes if they narrowly circumscribe their issues and avoid taking overtly "political" stands.

I have counted business lobbies, professional associations, unions, and other vested groups with political orientations among the "mixed" cases because of the peculiar ways in which these groups enter public arenas. Such groups have an incentive to avoid public exposure even when they seek political influence. But because capitalist economic systems place most important social decisions in private hands, groups such as these often find themselves forced to confront the problems—or "externalities"—they generate in the process. The American Medical Association belatedly decided to enter the public debate on the availability of health care because it became clear that the privileged positions of doctors were being eroded by new financial realities, falling public confidence, and increasing awareness that one externality of market-based medical care is that large numbers of people go without any care at all. The tobacco lobby cynically raised issues of principle—free speech and individual liberties—when confronted with possible bans on tobacco advertising, limited bans on smoking, and possible Food and Drug Administration regulatory authority. Cynical or not, the tobacco groups helped clarify the meanings of these principles—although the clumsiness of their public campaigns exposed their inexperience in the use of communicative power. More generally, every *vested* group that works through political media risks public exposure and can find itself forced to become a public actor.

Representing Differences

Those theories of democracy that emphasize the desirability of deliberative judgments often seem biased toward groups that have deliberative intentions. Deliberation, however, is only one facet of the public sphere, and comes, as it were, at a relatively late stage in the life of political issues. After all, the conditions of deliberative engagement are stringent and exceptional: bargaining positions must be equal enough to force issues in a deliberative direction, and individuals must recognize others as speakers and respond to their claims. Democracies work when potential conflicts, rooted in injustices and marginalizations, find their place in public discourse and move toward resolutions, whether through the discovery of shared interests and consensus or through bargained compromises. The idea of a public is broader than that of deliberative engagement and judgment. Publics come into being where there are issues and agendas, and more often than not, these are placed before the public by groups using communicative but nondeliberative means. Their focus is often representational and symbolic rather than directly deliberative, because they have yet to gain a seat at the table. They must *represent* their existence, as it were, prior to being *recognized*; and such representations often draw on symbolic tactics: demonstrations, protests, boycotts, civil disobedience, street theater, and the like. When there are tough issues, more often than not deliberation is itself forced as the last, best alternative to the disruption that can be caused by any group sufficiently committed to a cause. In contrast, groups that are privileged and vested have much to lose when they emphasize difference, precisely because the differences represented by their privilege can become an issue. All other things being equal, vested groups will emphasize commonality—in particular, the shared benefits of the status quo. For these reasons, groups committed to maintaining differences are essential to democracy and public deliberation. Without them, deliberation will be limited to the agendas of those who already have a seat at the table, and whatever consensus emerges will be exclusive.

So public spheres depend upon associations with the capacities and incentives to represent differences and resist hegemonic commonalities. Some kinds of associations specialize in putting topics on the agenda by seeking to demonstrate the exclusivity of a mainstream consensus. By representing differences, they alter the parameters of public spheres. Often groups that specialize in mischief set the stage for groups that deliberate.[19] Would the Sierra Club and Greenpeace look as relatively moderate as they do without the guerrilla tactics of Earth First!? Earth First! may not achieve public acclaim, but it has provided one motive for the lumber industry to negotiate and perhaps even deliberate with mainstream environmental groups over the environmental costs of clear-cut logging. In this way, uncivil groups like Earth First! can create the conditions for a deliberative public sphere—although obviously, there is nothing necessary about this particular outcome.

There are, of course, limits to the kinds of nondeliberative symbolic tactics that are functional for democracies. Violence against persons, even when the intent is to "send a message"—as in racist, ethnic, or homophobic violence—never has a place in the democratic expansion of the parameters of public debate. Violence against persons so damages even the minimal trust parties need for deliberative engagement that it tends to exclude future deliberative engagements rather than expand agendas. One cannot be sure that the perpetrator will not revert to violence in the future, nor that the aggrieved will not harbor memories that will be avenged in kind. Talk, under these circumstances, seems pointless and even dangerous.

It is a different matter in the case of symbolic mischief, including demonstrations, guerrilla theater, and civil disobedience of various kinds. Such tactics amount to modes of communication aimed at focusing public attention on issues that have no place within mainstream publics and are unrepresented within formal institutions. Certainly such tactics are politically risky: groups engaging in mischief are just as likely to draw public censure as they are to enhance the legitimacy of their cause. In the last several decades, for example, symbolic mischief by hate groups—cross burnings and racist graffiti, for example—has helped to solidify public judgment against racism, at least of the overt sort. In other cases, however, mischief on the margins has moved issues quickly and dramatically into mainstream deliberation. In the late 1950s and early 1960s, for example, the civil rights movement in the United States had no other way of placing civil rights on the public agenda than by resorting to civil disobedience—civil rights issues having virtually no presence in local politics, state politics, Congress, or the executive branch and only a very limited presence in the federal courts. Likewise, one of the questionable tactics of Earth First! has been "tree spiking" in the national forests of the western United States—that is, driving spikes into trees in tracts marked for cutting so that loggers and mill workers face the dangers of broken saws should they cut the trees. The tactic would certainly be less justifiable had the U.S. Forest Service not allowed and even encouraged environmentally destructive logging practices in the national forests, in violation of federal law. Nor would the tactics be justifiable if Earth First! failed to announce each instance of tree spiking—for then it would count as random endangerment of persons. Clearly, deciding what kinds of mischief count as contributions to democratic public spheres is contextual: the case is much better when political institutions fail to respond.

Of course, not all differences are important for constituting public agendas in these highly political ways. Some differences are politically benign but socially valuable contributions to pluralism. Ethnic groups who display their customs, music, and food in urban street fairs are, for the most part, important reminders of the richness of a diverse society and culture. But often differences of race, culture, ethnicity, region, religion, gender, identity, or lifestyle combine with differences in control over the resources that determine life-chances—access to education, housing, jobs, and wealth and income. These conjunctions cause differences to become politically volatile, and in a democracy the injustices attached to differences ought to be represented in public discourses.

As table 6.6a suggests, the logic of difference is relatively simple. The key factor is whether a group is vested in its medium of reproduction. Groups with vested interests cannot take up oppositional roles without sacrificing existing interests and established working relations. Nor do they have an incentive to make public issues out of benefits that flow to their members. Those who benefit from the status quo will, if anything, mobilize to keep issues out of the public sphere; when they enter the public sphere, they are more likely to emphasize commonalities than differences—a trait that may be good for deliberation, but not so good for establishing broad public agendas that are sensitive to suppressed issues and injustices.

Instead, the representations of differences that serve to expand the parameters of public deliberation are likely to come from groups that are *nonvested* in the medium they seek to change, as suggested in table 6.6b. These groups are often oppositional and counterhegemonic in style. They must often engage in tactics that circumvent mainstream political and economic institutions, precisely because their voices and interests are not represented within them. Such groups help to expand the boundaries of public deliberation by reminding us of issues, injustices, and needs that are not addressed within the mainstream.

Most of the groups represented in table 6.6c contribute to representations of differences because they reproduce exclusive identity goods. But these are social groups, and they tend to be inward looking, focused on reproducing distinctive lifestyles and identities. Their contributions to representing differences thus stem mostly from the fact of their existence rather than from their political intentions: they are exemplars rather than advocates of differences. In other cases, an economic orientation dampens the oppositional effects of being nonvested. One economically oriented kind of association—environmental groups that use information and advocacy to change people's market decisions—must constantly encourage those with assets to alter their uses by showing them the benefits of doing so. But because these groups must, as it were, beg and persuade to achieve their objectives, there are limits to how oppositional they can be. Another economic kind—unions engaged in social investing, for example—works to change criteria of investment, highlighting the extent to which markets fail to match needs. But because unions have constrained exit while aiming at inclusive goods, they are limited in their capacities to represent differences. And in both cases, the logic of economic bargaining means that oppositional goals tend to be balanced with a rhetoric of shared and common interests. Finally, one political class of associations—patriotic groups, English-only groups, and the like—mobilizes exclusive national

TABLE 6.6a
Associational kinds with low potentials for representing differences

Examples of associational types	Ease of exit	Medium of social reproduction	Orientation toward medium	Goods of association
Families, small group mutual aid	Low	Social	**Vested**	Individual material
Families, neighborhoods, public schools	Low	Social	**Vested**	Interpersonal identity
Public schools	Low	Social	**Vested**	Inclusive Social
Gated neighborhoods, private schools	Medium	Social	**Vested**	Status
Universities, academic research institutes	Medium	Social	**Vested**	Inclusive Social
Social clubs, recreational & sports assocs.	High	Social	**Vested**	Interpersonal identity
Elite social clubs	High	Social	**Vested**	Status
Civic & environmental groups	High	Social	**Vested**	Public material
Cultural, knowledge-oriented, & educational groups, recreational groups	High	Social	**Vested**	Inclusive social
Political parties, corporatist bodies	Medium	Political	**Vested**	Individual material
Political parties, corporatist bodies, RCAs	Medium	Political	**Vested**	Public material
Political parties, corporatist bodies	Medium	Political	**Vested**	Inclusive Social
Business lobbies, unions, professional associations	High	Political	**Vested**	Individual material
Elilte political & professional associations	High	Political	**Vested**	Status
Mainstream mass media & foundations	High	Political	**Vested**	Inclusive social
Firms, unions, industrial research institutes & networks, prof. assocs., nonprofit gov't contractors	Medium	Economic	**Vested**	Individual material
Quasi-public, market-oriented NGOs, gov't corporations, nonprofit gov't contractors	Medium	Economic	**Vested**	Public material
Self-help economic networks, cooperatives	High	Economic	**Vested**	Individual material
Connoisseurs' associations	High	Economic	**Vested**	Status

TABLE 6.6b
Associational kinds with high potentials for representing differences

Examples of associational types	Ease of exit	Medium of social reproduction	Orientation toward medium	Goods of association
Welfare rights & child health advocacy groups	**High**	Political	**Nonvested**	Individual material
New Social Movements, ethnic, racial, & religious advocacy, militia movements (as public groups)	**High**	Political	**Nonvested**	Exclusive group identity
Environmental advocacy groups	**High**	Political	**Nonvested**	Public material
Public knowledge, political process, & human rights advocacy, oppositional mass media & foundations	**High**	Political	**Nonvested**	Inclusive social

TABLE 6.6c
Associational kinds with mixed potentials for representing differences

Examples of associational types	Ease of exit	Medium of social reproduction	Orientation toward medium	Goods of association
Ethnic & racial identity groups	Low	Social	Vested	**Exclusive group identity**
Parochial schools, churches	Medium	Social	Vested	**Exclusive group identity**
Groups dedicated to cultural traditions, fraternal orders	High	Social	Vested	**Exclusive group identity**
Counter-hegemonic life-style groups & New Social Movements	High	Social	Nonvested	**Exclusive group identity**
Patriotic groups	High	**Political**	Vested	**Exclusive group identity**
Unions engaged in social investing	Medium	Economic	Vested	**Inclusive social**
Market-oriented environmental groups, public interest NGOs	High	Economic	**Nonvested**	**Public material**
Ethnic, religious, or life-style separatist economic networks	High	Economic	Vested	**Exclusive group identity**

identities by emphasizing differences, indeed, by mobilizing resentment against Spanish speakers and recent immigrants, welfare recipients, and other vulnerable minorities. These groups undoubtedly emphasize differences in the name of a nativist commonality, but their contributions are far from democratic. Whereas most nonvested groups emphasize differences in order to expand the inclusiveness of public agendas, these groups are exclusionary. At best, such groups provoke public airings of injustices and exclusions by helping to focus and mobilize opposition to their aims.

Representing Commonalities

It is common to emphasize the political dangers of the rhetoric of difference; after all, the legitimacy of collective actions depends on some degree of consensus. The kind of consensus necessary to legitimatize a collective action does not have to be based on common interests, but it does require a convergence of interests or a legitimate compromise. Even bargains depend on common understandings of promises as well as the trust that they will be upheld. And if opposition is totalized rather than segmented by issue, the cleavages may become so extensive that there are not enough commonalities to underwrite future bargains. When this happens, politics looks more and more like war. One might argue, then, that associations devoted to representing commonalities can underwrite and even enable differences to be segmented and bracketed sufficiently for them to be democratically negotiated. This would be a distinctive democratic effect, and we should expect the kinds of associations that specialize in commonality to differ from those that are more overtly politicized and oppositional.

There may even exist complementarities between representations of commonality and difference. Most representations of differences imply, counterfactually, universal ethics of recognition, justice, and inclusive citizenship. Often, public rhetorics of difference draw attention to what is not, in fact, common, even though it ought to be. So some associations that get high marks for representing difference can also represent commonalities. Welfare advocacy groups, for example, may simultaneously point to discriminations and exclusions while arguing that, after all, we owe the conditions of opportunity and dignity to other people by virtue of the fact that we share the commections of citizenship with them or simply because they too are human.

Yet representations of commonality are more susceptible to ideological dangers than are other representational strategies. An association's appeals to commonality may mask conditions and interests that are not, in fact, common. Certainly most vested groups have incentives to justify their activities, privileges, or demands as contributing to the common good, whether through appeal to ethical principles (distributive justice, merit, or dessert), efficiency, or the coincidence of particular and public interests. Even so, ideological commonalties often generate dynamics that tear at ideological masks and clarify ideological dissimulations. Attempts to shroud particular interests in the common good invite people to measure these interests in terms of common goods—and they may very well find them lacking. So while a group's assertions about commonalities may not be convincing, they can nonetheless induce principled deliberation about an issue where it had been absent. American tobacco companies, for example, have done their best to keep issues about the health implications of smoking out of the public arena, preferring to rely on the influence of money to protect tobacco products from regulation. When pushed into the public arena, the companies could not, of course, argue that their profits were more important than health—and so they argued principled cases that appealed to common interests, from those involving questions about the certainty of scientific evidence to those having to do with the freedoms of choice and speech, the dangers of government regulation, and even the principles of distributive justice with reference to the regressive effects of tobacco taxes. The tobacco companies have been losing the public debate, but they are losing in part because their own practices are being measured against the principles of common interest they hold in public. The risk that vested interests take in resorting to rhetorics of commonality is that others might take them seriously and measure their activities and privileges against their own rhetoric. The rhetoric of commonality can, under democratic circumstances that empower deliberative challenges, undermine its ideological uses.

There exist, of course, many associations that seek public and shared goods directly, without needing to dissimulate or to argue for the correspondence between particular and common interests. For some groups (for example, environmental groups), the commitment to principle is essential to pursuing the association's purpose, since public goods are subject to free riders. Such groups are induced by the public goods they seek to emphasize a common cause. Public interest groups will emphasize the inclusive qualities of the goods they advocate against special interests, thus emphasizing the potential for common interests against the reality of division.

The two key factors that drive associations toward representations of commonality are the extent to which they are politically embedded or oriented and their constitutive goods. Associations that are low in their potential contributions (see table 6.7a) include status-based groups that seek to avoid public exposure, in part because these goods cannot (by definition) be justified in common terms. Groups devoted to exclusive group identities define themselves as distinct from others, and so are un-

TABLE 6.7a
Associational kinds with low potentials for representing commonalities

Examples of associational types	Ease of exit	Medium of social reproduction	Orientation toward medium	Goods of association
Ethnic & racial identity groups	Low	Social	Vested	**Exclusive group identity**
Parochial schools, churches	Medium	Social	Vested	**Exclusive group identity**
Gated neighborhoods, private schools	Medium	Social	Vested	**Status**
Elite social clubs	High	Social	Vested	**Status**
Groups dedicated to cultural traditions, fraternal orders	High	Social	Vested	**Exclusive group identity**
Counter-hegemonic lifestyle groups & New Social Movements	**High**	Social	Nonvested	**Exclusive group identity**
Elilte political & professional associations	High	Political	Vested	**Status**
New Social Movements, ethnic, racial, & religious advocacy, militia movements (as public groups)	High	Political	Nonvested	**Exclusive group identity**
Patriotic groups	High	Political	Vested	**Exclusive group identity**
Firms, unions, industrial research institutes & networks, prof. assocs., nonprofit gov't contractors	Medium	**Economic**	Vested	Individual material
Connoisseurs' associations	High	**Economic**	Vested	Status
Ethnic, religious, or lifestyle separatist economic networks	High	**Economic**	Vested	Exclusive group identity
Self-help economic networks, cooperatives	High	**Economic**	Vested	Individual material

likely to invoke commonality. The two political types of association that seek exclusive identities are unique: their identities often depend on public evocations of threats and conspiracies against their members, such that their public rhetoric does not include, even counterfactually, an evocation of commonality. Finally, economically oriented groups that seek individual, status, and exclusive identity goods are not, for the most part, oriented toward the public sphere at all, and contribute little unless their activities are contested.

Groups likely to evoke commonality (represented in table 6.7b) are likewise distinguished by specific combinations of the goods they seek, and the media within which they are embedded. Politically oriented groups will tend to couch their public rhetoric in terms of common interests. Groups seeking individual material goods must often invoke broad distributional claims or claims about the ways in which private benefits produce common goods—as when the American Pharmaceutical Association seeks to justify the extraordinary profit margins of their member companies by arguing for the common health benefits of high-cost research and development. Groups that seek public or social goods are likewise driven by the nature of the good toward common justifications. But even in the absence of a political orientation, groups that seek public and inclusive goods have incentives for representing commonalities built into their purposes.

The groups represented in table 6.7c—families, neighborhoods, social clubs, and some dimensions of public schools—are ambiguous in their location. Their social media cause them to be inward looking, and their dynamics can often lead toward a protective stance against the world at large. On the other hand, they can also cultivate appreciation for common interests that cut across other kinds of divides.

It is worth noting that once we look at the many kinds of groups with incentives to represent commonalities, and once we note their relative weight in the spectrum of associations in, say, the United States, the neoconservative complaint that "multiculturalism" and the "politics of difference" are taking over the political landscape and represent a threat to national "community" seems suspect on the face of it. To be sure, associations with very particular concerns and interests have exploded in numbers within the last couple of decades. But most of these associations are so constituted that they have strong incentives to represent commonalities. In contrast, only a few kinds of groups have incentives to represent differences, and these are among the weakest kinds. They may seem noisy, but this indicates their nonvested status rather than their power. They lack noncommunicative means of influence. The dangers to democracy are, I think, elsewhere: there are so many kinds of associations with incentives to cloak their interests within the rhetoric of commonality that there is a danger of inauthentic consensus on any given issue. Or—perhaps more likely—there is a danger that so many associations attempt to mask their particular interests with a rhetoric of the common good that individuals become cynical about any claim to commonality.

TABLE 6.7b
Associational kinds with high potentials for representing commonalities

Examples of associational types	Ease of exit	Medium of social reproduction	Orientation toward medium	Goods of association
Public schools	Low	Social	Vested	**Inclusive Social**
Universities, academic research institutes	Medium	Social	Vested	**Inclusive social**
Civic & environmental groups	High	Social	Vested	**Public material**
Cultural, knowledge-oriented, & educational groups, recreational groups	High	Social	Vested	**Inclusive social**
Political parties, corporatist bodies	Medium	**Political**	Vested	Individual material
Political parties, corporatist bodies, RCAs	Medium	**Political**	Vested	**Public material**
Political parties, corporatist bodies	Medium	**Political**	Vested	**Inclusive social**
Business lobbies, unions, professional associations	High	**Political**	Vested	Individual material
Welfare rights & child health advocacy groups	High	**Political**	Nonvested	Individual material
Environmental advocacy groups	High	**Political**	Nonvested	**Public material**
Mainstream mass media & foundations	High	**Political**	Vested	**Inclusive social**
Public knowledge, political process, & human rights advocacy, oppositional mass media & foundations	High	**Political**	Nonvested	**Inclusive social**
Quasi-public, market-oriented NGOs, gov't corporations, nonprofit gov't contractors	Medium	Economic	Vested	**Public material**
Market-oriented environmental groups, public interest NGOs	High	Economic	Nonvested	**Public material**
Unions engaged in social investing	Medium	Economic	Vested	**Inclusive social**

TABLE 6.7c
Associational kinds with mixed potentials for representing commonalities

Examples of associational types	Ease of exit	Medium of social reproduction	Orientation toward medium	Goods of association
Families, small group mutual aid	Low	Social	Vested	Individual material
Families, neighborhoods, public schools	Low	Social	Vested	Interpersonal identity
Social clubs, recreational & sports assocs.	High	Social	Vested	Interpersonal identity

Institutional Effects

The final class of democratic effects are those that associations have on democratic institutions—not only as complements to the familiar institutions of representational government, but also as democratic institutions in their own right. These effects are, of course, distinguishable from individual and public sphere effects only for analytic purposes; in reality, the institutional effects are intertwined with the others. Political representation and democratic legitimacy, for example, both depend on public judgment, while subsidiarity—when associations function as devolved venues of collective action—depends on and develops the political efficacy of its members. Still, here as elsewhere, the fact that democratic effects are often complementary does not mean they originate in the same kinds of associational milieus or that all associations have similar capacities to affect democratic institutions.

Political Representation

Although democratic theorists typically emphasize the importance of secondary associations in making representative political institutions work, there are a relatively few associational kinds that have capacities for effective political representation; the conditions of effective representation, while straightforward, are demanding. First, an association must have political representation as a purpose, and structure itself so that it can represent its members. Second, an association must be able to develop a message, advocate it, and combine the message with inducements such as money, votes, or public arguments that will cause decision makers to enter the message into their deliberations and negotiations. All other things being equal, associations that are vested in their medium of reproduction will have higher capacities to make their messages stick. Third, whether

TABLE 6.8a
Associational kinds with low potentials for representation

Examples of associational types	Ease of exit	Medium of social reproduction	Orientation toward medium	Goods of association
Families, neighborhoods, public schools	Low	**Social**	Vested	Interpersonal identity
Ethnic & racial identity groups	Low	**Social**	Vested	Exclusive group identity
Parochial schools, churches	Medium	**Social**	Vested	Exclusive group identity
Gated neighborhoods, private schools	Medium	**Social**	Vested	Status
Social clubs, recreational & sports assocs.	High	**Social**	Vested	Interpersonal identity
Groups dedicated to cultural traditions, fraternal orders	High	**Social**	Vested	Exclusive group identity
Elite social clubs	High	**Social**	Vested	Status
Counter-hegemonic lifestyle groups & New Social Movements	High	**Social**	Nonvested	Exclusive group identity
Universities, academic research institutes	Medium	**Social**	Vested	Inclusive Social
Civic & environmental groups	High	**Social**	Vested	Public material
Cultural, knowledge-oriented, & educational groups, recreational groups	High	**Social**	Vested	Inclusive social

or not an association relies upon public argument for its effect, it must be able to speak with one voice; it must be able to connect its inducements to a message. For this reason, easy exit will help to purify the message as well as to align the membership behind the purpose of the association.[20]

Thus, types of association represented in table 6.8a have low potentials for political representation because they are not oriented toward political media. The old observation that bankers are too busy making money to bother with politics has more than a little truth to it. This does not mean, of course, that the American Bankers Association is ineffective at representing bankers—but its purposes are explicitly political. Likewise in the case of socially reproduced associations: political representation is not what they do, even though they may find themselves (defensively) arguing a political case, as might happen when a soccer league loses playing space to a baseball league or a city government seeks to shut down a gay club.

TABLE 6.8a *(continued)*
Associational kinds with low potentials for representation

Examples of associational types	Ease of exit	Medium of social reproduction	Orientation toward medium	Goods of association
Families, small group mutual aid	Low	**Social**	Vested	Individual material
Public schools	Low	**Social**	Vested	Inclusive Social
Ethnic, religious, or lifestyle separatist economic networks	High	**Economic**	Vested	Exclusive group identity
Connoisseurs' associations	High	**Economic**	Vested	Status
Firms, unions, industrial research institutes & networks, prof. assocs., nonprofit gov't contractors	Medium	**Economic**	Vested	Individual material
Quasi-public, market-oriented NGOs, gov't corporations, nonprofit gov't contractors	Medium	**Economic**	Vested	Public material
Self-help economic networks, cooperatives	High	**Economic**	Vested	Individual material
Market-oriented environmental groups, public interest NGOs	High	**Economic**	Nonvested	Public material
Unions engaged in social investing	Medium	**Economic**	Vested	Inclusive social

The associations with high capacities for representation (table 6.8b) combine an internal relation to political media—meaning that they have established representative channels of influence—with high opportunities for exit, allowing a singularity of purpose. Associations such as business lobbies, unions, and professional associations with close links to economic media are also able to channel money into their political endeavors, either directly by supporting public officials in elections and fighting for their interests through the courts or indirectly through public media campaigns designed to put pressure on public officials. In addition, those business lobbies with members who can credibly threaten to move their businesses to new locations are often highly effective at influencing political decisions. Such power can be used more effectively by sector-specific business associations because interests of members converge in ways they do not in the big umbrella business groups such as the National Association of Manufacturers. Likewise, business associations can wield economic

TABLE 6.8b
Associational kinds with high potentials for representation

Examples of associational types	Ease of exit	Medium of social reproduction	Orientation toward medium	Goods of association
Patriotic groups	High	Political	Vested	Exclusive group identity
Elilte political & professional associations	High	Political	Vested	Status
Business lobbies, unions, professional associations	High	Political	Vested	Individual material
Mainstream mass media & foundations	High	Political	Vested	Inclusive social

power more effectively if they represent sectors with mobile capital—manufacturers rather than, say, public utilities or service-based businesses that depend on highly skilled labor.

In addition, think tanks such as the American Enterprise Institute are effective at translating financial support into ideas that are then used both directly and indirectly to influence public officials. The mainstream media can also have high capacities for representation, although the logic is different: they "select" their "members" (who are usually passive but can be mobilized by media focus on an issue) according to the issues they think will attract readers, viewers, and advertising. The mass media have extraordinary capacities to stay on message through successive news stories, issue programming, and talk shows in ways that can often (although not always predictably) generate multiple pressures upon representatives. Likewise, patriotic groups such as veterans' associations can keep up steady pressures, benefiting from a "mobilization of bias" in favor of patriotic themes and the singularity of their members' commitment. It is certainly not accidental that politicians court the Veterans of Foreign Wars but not, say, associations representing mothers on welfare, in spite of the fact that the veteran and the mother each have one vote.

Associational types with mixed capacities for representation (table 6.8c) are "political" in their orientation, but work against two kinds of limiting factors. Associations with low exit, such as political parties (in the United States) and corporatist bodies, often find they must negotiate conflict within, which makes their message more difficult to convey. This was perhaps the key lesson of Newt Gingrich's "Contract with America," which was an effective tactic to rally conservative Republican activists during the 1994 congressional elections, but a liability when it came to building legislative majorities. On the other hand, high-exit nonvested groups are weakened by the fact that they do not have established chan-

TABLE 6.8c
Associational kinds with mixed potentials for reprsentation

Examples of associational types	Ease of exit	Medium of social reproduction	Orientation toward medium	Goods of association
Welfare rights & child health advocacy groups	High	**Political**	**Nonvested**	Individual material
New Social Movements, ethnic, racial, & religious advocacy, militia movements (as public groups)	High	**Political**	**Nonvested**	Exclusive group identity
Environmental advocacy groups	High	**Political**	**Nonvested**	Public material
Public knowledge, political process, & human rights advocacy, oppositional mass media & foundations	High	**Political**	**Nonvested**	Inclusive social
Political parties, corporatist bodies	**Medium**	**Political**	Vested	Individual material
Political parties, corporatist bodies, RCAs	**Medium**	**Political**	Vested	Public material
Political parties, corporatist bodies	**Medium**	**Political**	Vested	Inclusive social

nels of representation and must seek representation indirectly through public opinion. Still, political groups that are linked to their social equivalents—churches and New Social Movements, for example—have the advantage of being able to mobilize the votes and energies of their members by reaching into established social circles, a power discovered by the Christian Right in the United States during the 1980s.

There are really no surprises here: groups that can mobilize resources and target specific issues and policies do better at developing representative linkages to state powers and policies than do groups with low resources or diffuse messages. This structural analysis simply shows, once more, that the groups with the highest capacities for political representation also tend to be the wealthy, the powerful, and the organized, and they know what they want.

Resistance

Insofar as representative institutions are structured by and respond to power, the capacity to resist is implied in representation. Representation is effective when groups are able to empower their message. The converse does not hold, however: capacities to resist do not necessarily imply the more demanding capacities of representation. Resistance can be passive, as when people fail to file income tax returns or refuse to obey a law they perceive to be unfair or unjust. It can be undemanding: the vote provides a non-message-specific means of resistance, as does the refusal to vote by those who are alienated from the political system. It can be unorganized, as when middle- and upper-class urban dwellers withdraw their children from public schools or move to the suburbs. State and sometimes corporate decision makers must often anticipate resistance even if there is no representative voice to complement it, simply because even passive and unorganized resistance can make policies unworkable. In workplaces, most of which remain authoritarian, passive resistance to policies may be the only form of voice available. But it can often be effective, as workers who are "unmotivated" can cause an entire corporate organization to perform poorly in a competitive environment.

Because associations often control resources—from capital to votes to the power to organize and communicate—they also possess means of resistance, even if they lack representative capacities. As I noted in chapter 4, whether this is good or bad for democracy depends upon how various kinds of power are distributed within this system, and the purposes for which it is deployed. The capacity to resist accumulated powers—of states or corporations, for example—can make democracy effective. But capacities to resist can also disenable collective actions, democratic or otherwise. If power is widely distributed, collective actions can fall victim to gridlock; if not, then collective actions are subject to veto by the powerful, wealthy, or organized minorities. Ideally, widely distributed capacities to resist are matched with the public spheres and representative structures through which interests can be mediated, transformed into public judgments, and translated into collective action. We can also see, however, that there are structural asymmetries: association-based capacities to resist are easier to come by than capacities for representation and deliberation. The United States political system exaggerates this bias toward gridlock: its single-member district system of representation sets a high threshold for representation, in this way magnifying the asymmetry between representation and resistance. Theoretically, a system based on multimember districts reduces this asymmetry because it allows a greater degree of formal representation for a broader range of groups and interests.

Many groups have some capacities for resistance, but not all do. The associational types grouped in table 6.9a tend to have low capacities for resistance for several reasons. First, and perhaps most importantly, groups that pursue public and inclusive social goods are limited by the fact that they cannot exclude nonmembers from enjoying the goods they achieve,

TABLE 6.9a
Associational kinds with low potentials for resistance

Examples of associational types	Ease of exit	Medium of social reproduction	Orientation toward medium	Goods of association
Families, neighborhoods, public schools	**Low**	**Social**	Vested	**Interpersonal identity**
Public schools	**Low**	Social	Vested	**Inclusive social**
Universities, academic research institutes	**Medium**	Social	Vested	**Inclusive social**
Civic & environmental groups	High	Social	Vested	**Public material**
Cultural, knowledge-oriented, & educational groups, recreational groups	High	Social	Vested	**Inclusive social**
Political parties, corporatist bodies	**Medium**	Political	Vested	**Individual material**
Political parties, corporatist bodies, RCAs	**Medium**	Political	Vested	**Public material**
Political parties, corporatist bodies	**Medium**	Political	Vested	**Inclusive social**
Welfare rights & child health advocacy groups	High	Political	**Nonvested**	**Individual material**
Environmental advocacy groups	High	Political	**Nonvested**	**Public material**
Mainstream mass media & foundations	High	Political	Vested	**Inclusive social**
Public knowledge, political process, & human rights advocacy, oppositional mass media & foundations	High	Political	**Nonvested**	**Inclusive social**
Quasi-public, market-oriented NGOs, gov't corporations, nonprofit gov't contractors	**Medium**	Economic	Vested	**Public material**
Market-oriented environmental groups, public interest NGOs	High	Economic	**Nonvested**	**Public material**

and thus cannot withhold them for strategic reasons. Whatever capacities these associational types have for resistance are communicative: they can seek to affect only public debates and judgments, affecting state or corporate policies only indirectly by addressing their legitimacy within public spheres. To be sure, there are some apparent exceptions. When public goods such as watersheds in national forests are protected by law and threatened with spoilage, environmental groups can resist the spoilage through the courts. In such cases, however, collective action problems have already been resolved through law. In other cases, environmental groups can take direct action against those who would spoil public goods, as does Earth First! In these cases, however, the aims of resistance are symbolic: camping in trees and blocking logging roads are tactics designed to bring public attention to the spoilage. Then again, associations that provide public goods under a political grant of monopoly, such as government corporations, cannot appear to be using their resources to resist influences they do not like without endangering their monopoly. A somewhat different logic afflicts associations such as political parties and public schools that have constrained exit. Because constraints on exit usually produce a diversity of interests within the association, and because the diversity of interests itself makes collective decisions and actions more difficult, the ability of the association to withhold resources in any given instance is weak. Finally, associations such as welfare advocacy groups that operate as external pressure groups but also control few resources have few means of resistance.

There are two logics that explain high potentials for resistance, represented in table 6.9b. The first is exemplified by types of associations that combine exclusive identity goods with high possibilities for exit—activist religious movements and some New Social Movements, for example, as well as those associations that can mobilize existing cultural biases against change. This combination of key factors produces a relatively "pure" identity basis for mobilization, which can serve as a basis for disruption, demonstration, and the like. The second logic is economic, and even more powerful: groups that are vested in essential productive resources have immediate, effective, and sometimes overwhelming capacities for resistance through capital flight, skills flight, withholding labor (strikes), and so on. Clearly, where these kinds of resources are unevenly distributed, as they always are in a capitalist society, the ability to affect public policy will also be unevenly distributed—a point so well developed I need not belabor it here.[21]

The associational kinds with mixed potentials for resistance (table 6.9c) control important resources (often "social capital" and legitimacy), which can be withheld or transformed into active resistance, but are constrained

TABLE 6.9b
Associational kinds with high potentials for resistance

Examples of associational types	Ease of exit	Medium of social reproduction	Orientation toward medium	Goods of association
Groups dedicated to cultural traditions, fraternal orders	High	Social	Vested	Exclusive group identity
Counter-hegemonic lifestyle groups & New Social Movements	High	Social	Nonvested	Exclusive group identity
Business lobbies, unions, professional associations	High	Political	Vested	Individual material
Patriotic groups	High	Political	Vested	Exclusive group identity
New Social Movements, ethnic, racial, & religious advocacy, militia movements (as public groups)	High	Political	Nonvested	Exclusive group identity
Elilte political & professional associations	High	Political	Vested	Status
Self-help economic networks, cooperatives	High	Economic	Vested	Individual material
Ethnic, religious, or lifestyle separatist economic networks	High	Economic	Vested	Exclusive group identity
Firms, unions, industrial research institutes & networks, prof. assocs., nonprofit gov't contractors	Medium	Economic	Vested	Individual material

in other respects. Groups that are socially reproduced have, as it were, direct control over social capital, a resource that can be intensified by exclusive identity goods. But where exit is constrained, conflict is internalized and the group's capacities to act strategically are also constrained. In addition, some kinds of purposes limit strategic capacities for resistance. Interpersonal identity goods tend to be indifferent to strategic action—except, perhaps, defensively. Status goods do not thrive with public exposure because it is difficult to justify their exclusions, making all but passive resistance risky. The one exceptional case includes groups such as unions engaged in social investing. Although unions cannot withhold social benefits, they can threaten to withdraw investments when corporations engage in practices with antisocial consequences.

TABLE 6.9c
Associational kinds with mixed potentials for resistance

Examples of associational types	Ease of exit	Medium of social reproduction	Orientation toward medium	Goods of association
Families, Small group mutual aid	Low	Social	Vested	Individual material
Ethnic & racial identity groups	Low	Social	Vested	Exclusive group identity
Parochial schools, churches	Medium	Social	Vested	Exclusive group identity
Gated neighborhoods, private schools	Medium	Social	Vested	Status
Social clubs, recreational & sports assocs.	High	Social	Vested	Interpersonal identity
Elite social clubs	High	Social	Vested	Status
Connoisseurs' associations	High	Economic	Vested	Status
Unions engaged in social investing	Medium	Economic	Vested	Inclusive social

Subsidiarity

Subsidiarity refers to the possibility that associations can themselves be-come venues of collective actions in ways that are more appropriate or efficient or democratic than would be the case if they were organized by governments or markets. I am considering this effect separately from the more "political" work of coordinating among groups or between groups, governments, and firms—which requires different kinds of associational capacities. The notion of subsidiarity brings into focus associations that are designed to do things (for example, civic service organizations, famine relief NGOs, and associations that provide social services under govern-ment contract), in contrast to more political forms of association that specialize in coordinating, pressuring, guiding, and affecting other locuses of collective action—for example, advocacy groups, groups that monitor corporate practices, and CDCs.

As I noted in chapter 4, we cannot treat capacities for subsidiarity as if they are a priori good for democracy. Whether they are good, bad, or indifferent depends upon the purposes of the association, the resources it deploys, and the extent to which it is accountable to those affected by its actions. Certainly subsidiarity is a good thing if it means bringing collec-tive actions closer to the people who seek and are affected by them. Subsidiarity can shorten the distance, as it were, between self-governance and collective action. Especially in the United States, governments pursue subsidiarity through associations on the assumption that associations can deal with the issues they specialize in better than governments, which are often overly encumbered by bureaucratic structures in the ways they deliver services, especially social services.[22] The assumption is also that associations are sensitive to local circumstances in ways that governments are not likely to be, given their rule-based and procedural natures. The recent explosion of nonprofit associations that gain large parts of their income from government contracts indicates the pervasiveness and political effectiveness of these assumptions. Where these assumptions hold, associational capacities for subsidiarity can be good for democracy.

But associations can also monopolize resources and behave like factions, deploying them—as Madison feared—"as conspiracies against the public interest." Clearly, whether or not subsidiarity is good or bad for democracy will depend on the powers inherent in subsidiarity, the uses to which they are put, and the degree to which associations are accountable to those affected.[23] Thus, we need to ask not only about what kinds of associations have capacities of subsidiarity, but also about whether and how they are democratically accountable.

With regard to the first question, the key factors are clear: we should expect capacities for subsidiarity to be greater when the purposes of an association are uncontested (an attribute enhanced by easy exit) *and* when an association is sufficiently vested in its medium to marshal the resources necessary for collective action. In the case of *social* media, such vesting involves a high degree of agreement, trust, and other features of "social capital." In the case of *market-oriented* associations such as firms, vesting implies control over productive resources. Nonprofit associations that serve as government contractors, especially in the areas of health care and social services, exemplify the logic of subsidiarity as it is being practiced in the United States. Most of these associations, however, behave very much like for-profit firms competing for government business, and so could just as well count as market-oriented types. Most *politically* oriented associations—advocacy groups, for example—will tend to be low in capacities for subsidiarity. Their political orientation implies they are seeking to influence collective actions via the capacities of the state rather than directly organizing collective actions through their own resources. Some apparent exceptions underscore the rule: many industry-group associations borrow, as it were, legal-regulatory powers from the state in order to regulate the economic activities of members (as in the case of state bar associations). Sometimes an association does so under threat of direct regulation: an industry group will persuade a government that it can regulate its members better than the government would be able to do, while

TABLE 6.10a
Associational kinds with low potentials for subsidiarity

Examples of associational types	Ease of exit	Medium of social reproduction	Orientation toward medium	Goods of association
Business lobbies, unions, professional associations	High	Political	Vested	Individual material
Patriotic groups	High	Political	Vested	Exclusive group identity
Elite political & professional associations	High	Political	Vested	Status
Mainstream mass media & foundations	High	Political	Vested	Inclusive social
Welfare rights & child health advocacy groups	High	Political	Nonvested	Individual material
New Social Movements, ethnic, racial, & religious advocacy, militia movements (as public groups)	High	Political	Nonvested	Exclusive group identity
Environmental advocacy groups	High	Political	Nonvested	Public material
Public knowledge, political process, & human rights advocacy, oppositional mass media & foundations	High	Political	Nonvested	Inclusive social
Political parties, corporatist bodies	Medium	Political	Vested	Individual material
Political parties, corporatist bodies, RCAs	Medium	Political	Vested	Public material
Political parties, corporatist bodies	Medium	Political	Vested	Inclusive social

pointing out to its members that they ought to accept regulation by the association as the lesser evil. Sometimes the relationship is corrupt: an association gains access to government regulation in order to secure a monopoly position. But in each such case, capacities of subsidiarity depend upon state powers combining with those of association.

Thus, the associational types represented in table 6.10a have low potentials for subsidiarity primarily because of their orientation toward state powers: they seek influence over powers they do not directly control. Political groups that are not vested in political media are especially unlikely

TABLE 6.10b
Associational kinds with high potentials for subsidiarity

Examples of associational types	Ease of exit	Medium of social reproduction	Orientation toward medium	Goods of association
Elite social clubs	High	Social	Vested	Status
Groups dedicated to cultural traditions, fraternal orders	High	Social	Vested	Exclusive group identity
Civic & environmental groups	High	Social	Vested	Public material
Cultural, knowledge-oriented, & educational groups, recreational groups	High	Social	Vested	Inclusive social
Social clubs, recreational & sports assocs.	High	Social	Vested	Interpersonal identity
Connoisseurs' associations	High	Economic	Vested	Status
Ethnic, religious, or lifestyle separatist economic networks	High	Economic	Vested	Exclusive group identity
Self-help economic networks, cooperatives	High	Economic	Vested	Individual material
Quasi-public, market-oriented NGOs, gov't corporations, nonprofit gov't contractors	Medium	Economic	Vested	Public material
Firms, unions, industrial research institutes & networks, prof. assocs., nonprofit gov't contractors	Medium	Economic	Vested	Individual material

to have capacities for subsidiarity: they neither intend to undertake collective projects, nor do they have the resources to do so.

In contrast, associational types that should have high potentials for subsidiarity—represented in table 6.10b—combine high ease of exit (which helps to produce internal consensus about goals and purposes) with a vested position in social or economic media, giving them the resources they need to undertake collective actions. Socially oriented groups can, under these circumstances, build and rely upon common identities, trust, and interpersonal relations. Civic groups that organize cleanup days or soccer leagues that organize teams and tournaments need only to draw on the social relations that align people's wills and enlist their energies and talents. Economically oriented associations typically pursue goals determined by the market (or government contracts) and, when successful, gain the returns from the market (or government contracts) that reenable the association. Although exit from firms is constrained for most employees, the purposes imposed by markets and contracts limit internal conflict over goals. In market economies, "economic subsidiarity" simply means that most capacities for organizing production and services are in the hands of "private" associations.

Portrayed in these ways, we can begin to see where the antidemocratic potentials of subsidiarity lie. In the case of economic associations, the dangers lie in the fact that control over economic resources can be translated into the unaccountable power to shape the architecture of neighborhoods and cities; to determine the fortunes of workers and employees; to mold public spaces through advertising and sponsored programming; and to externalize onto others the costs of production such as pollution, education and training of workers, infrastructure, hazards of work, and a flexible and disciplined workforce (including a "necessary" level of unemployment). In the last couple of decades in the United States subsidiarity has often been pursued in highly irresponsible ways from a democratic perspective: public functions have been "privatized" simply to reduce government spending and employment, an action motivated by the simplistic creed that less government is always more efficient. Often the results are antidemocratic: opportunities for patronage-based corruption are increased while public accountability is reduced. These points are not, of course, arguments against subsidiarity, but rather against farming out socially necessary functions to associations without the institutions that can check their capacities for harm and direct their activities toward collectively decided goals. The problem here is not subsidiarity per se, but rather the sort of subsidiarity that moves the powers of collective actions into venues that escape democratic accountability and reduce the chances that those affected will have a voice in directing these powers. The democratic response should not involve opposing subsidiarity in principle. Subsidiarity is necessary if the advantages of a complex and differentiated society are to be maintained. But it may involve tracking devolutions of power with democratic devices such as worker-owned and -managed firms or management that includes stakeholder representation, in addition to the more familiar means of enforcing accountability, by means of audits, oversight, redirections of investments through tax policy, and cost recovery through taxation. In addition, as I suggest in chapter 7, with the right mix of kinds, associations will check and balance one another—as various "watch" groups now do with many corporations and the mass media. Each of these devices can be a way of holding associations accountable for the effects of their activities.

TABLE 6.10c
Associational kinds with mixed potentials for subsidiarity

Examples of associational types	Ease of exit	Medium of social reproduction	Orientation toward medium	Goods of association
Families, small group mutual aid	Low	Social	Vested	Individual material
Families, neighborhoods, public schools	Low	Social	Vested	Interpersonal identity
Ethnic & racial identity groups	Low	Social	Vested	Exclusive group identity
Public schools	Low	Social	Vested	Inclusive social
Universities, academic research institutes	Medium	Social	Vested	Inclusive social
Parochial schools, churches	Medium	Social	Vested	Exclusive group identity
Gated neighborhoods, private schools	Medium	Social	Vested	Status
Counter-hegemonic lifestyle groups & New Social Movements	High	Social	Nonvested	Exclusive group identity
Unions engaged in social investing	Medium	Economic	Vested	Inclusive social
Market-oriented environmental groups, public interest NGOs	High	Economic	Nonvested	Public material

The antidemocratic potentials of social subsidiarity are more subtle and certainly do not require the heavy hand of the state to remedy. The dangers here are distributional: socially evolved capacities for subsidiarity ("social capital") are more prevalent among the better educated, wealthier strata of society. Because social capacities for subsidiarity spill over into other domains—in particular, into economic success and political influence—democrats should be concerned about this maldistribution. This form of inequality might be (and sometimes is) addressed through incentives to build associations among those who lack them—municipally sponsored sports leagues, CDCs, public housing associations, associations armed with low-interest loans that devote themselves to renovating housing, and so on.

The logic of the mixed cases (table 6.10c) is likewise straightforward. Vested social groups should be able to generate capacities for subsidiarity.

However, constrained exit means that the background consensus necessary for subsidiarity will often be lacking. In other cases, nonvested associations lack resources for subsidiarity. But these influences are countered by high exit and purposes that evoke identity-based or moral commitment. In the one economic case of constrained exit—unions engaged in social investing—the legal powers of unions to control pension funds and membership dues enable them to leverage markets from without. Here constraints on exit (borrowed from state-sanctioned labor law) generate capacities for subsidiarity that would not otherwise exist.

Coordination and Cooperation

Although coordination and cooperation are closely related to subsidiarity, they are not the same thing. As I am conceiving these effects, coordination and cooperation refer to associations' capacities to function as venues of democratic political devolution. I suggested in chapter 4 that associations can, potentially, lead to greater overall inclusiveness in collective decisions and actions than would be the case were collective matters organized only by the state and markets. This is so, I think, when devolution of politics into associational venues is paired with three further conditions.

- Associations that carry out these political functions are open to public scrutiny and subject to the same kinds of standards for publicity that govern, or ought to govern, the public sphere.[24] Secret cooperation is often indistinguishable from conspiracy.

- Those affected have ways and means to enter the processes when they so choose. Devolution is not democratic when it amounts to a venue shift with the effect of cutting legitimate participants out of political processes. Patronage, for example, excludes political losers from the right to enjoy public benefits to which they have contributed or to which they are entitled as members of a collectivity.

- Associational representatives have legitimate claim to speak for their members. There should be mechanisms, either through exit or internal democracy, that align the interests of members with those who represent the association.

These are, of course, tough tests. But they are necessary to distinguish those modes of coordination and cooperation that work to supplement democratic institutions from those that undermine them.

Whatever the possibilities and dangers, not all associations have the capacities for cooperation and coordination. The key factors here are likely to be ease of exit, the status of an association as vested or nonvested, and the purposes of association. Easy exit helps to clarify purposes so

TABLE 6.11a
Associational kinds with low potentials for coordination and cooperation

Examples of associational types	Ease of exit	Medium of social reproduction	Orientation toward medium	Goods of association
Families, neighborhoods, public schools	Low	Social	Vested	Interpersonal identity
Ethnic & racial identity groups	Low	Social	Vested	Exclusive group identity
Parochial schools, churches	Medium	Social	Vested	Exclusive group identity
Gated neighborhoods, private schools	Medium	Social	Vested	Status
Social clubs, recreational & sports assocs.	High	Social	Vested	Interpersonal identity
Groups dedicated to cultural traditions, fraternal orders	High	Social	Vested	Exclusive group identity
Elite social clubs	High	Social	Vested	Status
Counter-hegemonic lifestyle groups & New Social Movements	High	Social	Nonvested	Exclusive group identity
Patriotic groups	High	Political	Vested	Exclusive group identity
Elite political & professional associations	High	Political	Vested	Status
New Social Movements, ethnic, racial, & religious advocacy, militia movements (as public groups)	High	Political	Nonvested	Exclusive group identity
Ethnic, religious, or lifestyle separatist economic networks	High	Economic	Vested	Exclusive group identity
Connoisseurs' associations	High	Economic	Vested	Status

that officials or agents of the association can speak for the association in its external relations. Vested associations are likely to have something to cooperate about and the resources to negotiate with. And purposes will influence an association's incentives to reach beyond its boundaries.

The associational types listed in table 6.11a have low capacities for coordination and cooperation primarily owing to the kinds of goods they seek. Associations that seek exclusive identity goods will be unlikely to be able to develop close working ties with other groups, mostly because identity goods cannot be bargained and compromised in the ways that, say, material goods can be. For this reason there are few incentives and many disincentives to reach out to other associations. Members will often regard cooperation across identities as a betrayal of principle. Such groups may, of course, develop working alliances with groups with similar identities—alliances of militias and white power groups, for example, or as in the case of the Christian Coalition, a political alliance of conservative Protestant sects. But these alliances often reflect the coincidence of identities, not the capacities of associations to negotiate conflicts with other groups.

Groups that pursue status goods will often wish to remain exclusive, and to do so in ways that are within the public eye (status is not status if it is not so recognized), but not within the public sphere. No doubt these groups have capacities for coordination and cooperation among like-minded groups, but—as with exclusive identities—these goods do not lend themselves to bargaining, negotiation, and compromise. It is, again, precisely their exclusivity that gives them their value.

Associational types that pursue interpersonal identity goods—families, recreational groups, and the like—have low capacities for coordination and cooperation because these goods do not demand or lend themselves to extensive networks that require negotiation in ways that are significant for democracy. Friendship, love, teaching, commitments to care, and guiding by example cannot be bargained or negotiated without compromising the goods themselves. There are, of course, many situations in which interpersonal identity goods become attached to material goods, which then require cooperation and coordination. Recreational associations may have demands for land and facilities controlled by municipalities. And families must get along with their neighbors. These kinds of incentives to cooperate, however, stem from material entanglements (see table 6.11c) rather than from interpersonal identity goods.

The associational types we might expect to have high capacities for coordination and cooperation—represented in table 6.11b—are distinguished by the kinds of goods they seek and their vested positions. Purposes make a difference: groups seeking public material goods have built-in inducements toward coordination and cooperation, while groups seeking inclusive social goods have principled reasons to reach out to other groups. In the United States, for example, environmental groups have learned to move beyond gridlock and achieve results by exploring plus-sum options with former adversaries.[25] Groups seeking individual material goods—firms, unions, business lobbies, and the like—have incentives to cooperate for mutual gain. The dangers to democracy here attach primarily to cooperative arrangements among associations pursuing individual material goods in the market (or, using money to influence politics), since there are no

TABLE 6.11b
Associational kinds with high potentials for coordination and cooperation

Examples of associational types	Ease of exit	Medium of social reproduction	Orientation toward medium	Goods of association
Universities, academic research institutes	Medium	Social	**Vested**	**Inclusive Social**
Civic & environmental groups	**High**	Social	**Vested**	**Public material**
Cultural, knowledge-oriented, & educational groups, recreational groups	**High**	Social	**Vested**	**Inclusive social**
Business lobbies, unions, professional associations	**High**	Political	**Vested**	**Individual material**
Mainstream mass media & foundations	**High**	Political	**Vested**	**Inclusive social**
Firms, unions, industrial research institutes & networks, prof. assocs., non-profit gov't contractors	Medium	Economic	**Vested**	**Individual material**
Quasi-public, market-oriented NGOs, gov't corporations, nonprofit gov't contractors	Medium	Economic	**Vested**	**Public material**
Unions engaged in social investing	Medium	Economic	**Vested**	**Inclusive social**
Self-help economic networks, cooperatives	**High**	Economic	**Vested**	**Individual material**

built-in incentives for publicity, whereas there are for secrecy. Cooperative efforts are aided by easy exit, which helps to solidify purposes and cement relations between an association's members and its activists and leaders, although a high degree of internal deliberative democracy in associations with constrained exit may achieve the same effect.

The modes of association represented table 6.11c are the mixed cases in which one kind of factor mitigates the effects of other kinds. In all cases, the purposes of these kinds of associations provide incentives for them to reach out to other groups or to governments. In the cases of vested groups with constrained exit, the resulting internalization of con-flict means that external relations must be handled so as to accommodate internal diversity. Political parties, for example, may avoid public cooper-ation with other associations that could produce the appearance of en-

TABLE 6.11c
Associational kinds with mixed potentials for coordination and cooperation

Examples of associational types	Ease of exit	Medium of social reproduction	Orientation toward medium	Goods of association
Families, small group mutual aid	Low	Social	Vested	Individual material
Public schools	Low	Social	Vested	Inclusive Social
Political parties, corporatist bodies	Medium	Political	Vested	Individual material
Political parties, corporatist bodies, RCAs	Medium	Political	Vested	Public material
Political parties, corporatist bodies	Medium	Political	Vested	Inclusive Social
Market-oriented environmental groups, public interest NGOs	High	Economic	Nonvested	Public material
Welfare rights & child health advocacy groups	High	Political	Nonvested	Individual material
Environmental advocacy groups	High	Political	Nonvested	Public material
Public knowledge, political process, & human rights advocacy, oppositional mass media & foundations	High	Political	Nonvested	Inclusive social

dorsing purposes with which one or another group within the party might disagree. At the same time, parties have difficulty marshaling electoral resources without the involvement of other associations.

The associational types that are not vested but seek public and inclusive goods likewise occupy contradictory locations. On the one hand, nonvested groups lack the resources that might cause other groups or governments to seek them out for cooperative ventures. On the other hand, they cannot achieve their purposes without extensive cooperation. Human rights groups, for example, require the cooperation of governments, but typically lack any resources but publicity and persuasion. At best, they can threaten the legitimacy of governments with poor rights records—which is often low in any case. Environmental groups that use strategies based on market pressure (boycotts, consumer education, and showing industries how to do well by doing good, for example) have incentives to cooperate because they pursue public goods, but their abilities to do so are limited by the fact that they do not have control over productive resources. Like human rights groups, their cooperative powers are limited by the fact that they must persuade those who often have few incentives to be persuaded.

Democratic Legitimation

As Habermas pointedly noted, "There is no administrative production of meaning."[26] The state cannot directly produce its own legitimacy. The state can live off of the symbolic resources that attach to nationality and citizenship, although these are rarely sufficient to legitimacy in postconventional societies. And it can help to construct processes that provide legitimacy—for example, by enabling public debate in legislatures, providing for public hearings, and structuring other venues of communicative power. But for the most part, legitimacy is borrowed from those venues that generate the moral authority and informed consent implied in political autonomy. This is why associations, especially those that underwrite public sphere activities, figure importantly into the legitimacy of the state. This is also why totalitarian and authoritarian states always seek to destroy autonomous associations—especially student groups, the media, independent unions, think tanks, cultural groups, segments of universities, dissident churches, and other sources of autonomous political judgment.

Not all legitimacy is democratic. Even when associations are legally autonomous (as they are not under nonliberal regimes), some modes of legitimacy are expressive and evocative rather than autonomous. Patriotic and nationalistic groups, veterans associations, and the like produce these kinds of legitimacy. *Democratic* legitimacy, however, is more specific, and follows from the three possibilities to which I referred in chapter 4.

- Associations may engender broad public discussions about public issues. Legitimacy is a *direct* and *substantive* outcome of state decisions made with the guidance of public opinion.

- Associations may underwrite *process* legitimacy—that is, if associations provide their members with effective voice in public affairs, those members may judge political processes to be legitimate even if they disagree with outcomes.

- Associations may *devolve* the locuses of decisions and thus the locuses of legitimation—an increasingly common and likely possibility given the differentiation of forms of moral discourse and norms appropriate to different spheres of activity, as well as the increasing difficulties of global planning and coordination of policies. Devolution can provide indirect contributions to the democratic legitimacy of the state by relocating collective actions and the expectations that accompany them. Devolutions count as contributions to

TABLE 6.12a
Associational kinds with low potentials for producing democratic legitimacy

Examples of associational types	Ease of exit	Medium of social reproduction	Orientation toward medium	Goods of association
Ethnic & racial identity groups	Low	Social	Vested	Exclusive group identity
Parochial schools, churches	Medium	Social	Vested	Exclusive group identity
Gated neighborhoods, private schools	Medium	Social	Vested	Status
Social clubs, recreational & sports assocs.	High	Social	Vested	Interpersonal identity
Groups dedicated to cultural traditions, fraternal orders	High	Social	Vested	Exclusive group identity
Counter-hegemonic lifestyle groups & New Social Movements	High	Social	Nonvested	Exclusive group identity
Elite social clubs	High	Social	Vested	Status
Patriotic groups	High	Political	Vested	Exclusive group identity
New Social Movements, ethnic, racial, & religious advocacy, militia movements (as public groups)	High	Political	Nonvested	Exclusive group identity
Elite political & professional associations	High	Political	Vested	Status
Ethnic, religious, or lifestyle separatist economic networks	High	Economic	Vested	Exclusive group identity
Connoisseurs' associations	High	Economic	Vested	Status

democratic legitimacy if, in fact, the effect is to connect collective actions to collective justifications for all those affected, even if the connection bypasses the state altogether.

The groups we should expect to have low potentials for democratic legitimation (table 6.12a) are those constituted by exclusive group identity goods and status goods. Exclusive identity goods may provoke public deliberation, but because identities cannot be compromised, associations devoted to exclusive identity goods will find little that is legitimate either in most political decisions or in the processes of compromise usually nec-

essary to produce them. From the identity-based perspective, only decisions that express identity are legitimate. But when identities are exclusive, any *expressive* collective decision is also exclusive—and therefore
not democratic. Status-based associations are no more promising, but the
reasons are different: their purposes bias them toward withdrawal from
the processes that generate democratic legitimation. When these groups
are reproduced in relation to social and economic media, there is little
to draw them into public debate. Although some of these groups have
potentials for subsidiarity, the mode of subsidiarity will be exclusive, and
so cannot enhance *democratic* legitimacy. To be sure, members of such
associations may lower the expectations they place on the state because
they can rely (say) on the charity of the association when they have needs.
But because groups committed to exclusive goods cannot be inclusive,
legitimacy is (as it were) privatized rather than democratically devolved.

Constitutive goods are also a key factor for some of the associational
kinds we might expect to be high in their potentials for generating democratic legitimacy, as indicated in table 6.12b. Inclusive social and public
material goods are outward looking in ways that support broadly normative deliberation and legitimation. Associations such as welfare advocacy
groups have principled reasons to go public with normative arguments
about distributive justice and to connect these reasons directly to public
decisions. When public judgments influence government policies, the policies gain in democratic legitimacy. Among those groups with capacities
for subsidiarity—vested social and economic groups—constrained exit
can often produce democratic structures internal to the association. These
groups are well positioned to devolve the thresholds of democratic legitimacy. Political associations such as parties and corporatist bodies combine constrained exit with a political orientation in ways that can encourage process legitimacy. In addition, politically oriented groups that have
high capacities for coordination and cooperation, can—if combined with
pressures for normative argument—potentially connect decision making
and legitimacy.

Finally, the groups with mixed potentials for contributing to democratic legitimacy are listed in table 6.12c. The patterns here are varied.
Groups that are socially reproduced tend to be inward looking, and so
are not directly involved in generating democratic legitimacy. They may
produce indirect effects, however, when capacities for subsidiarity combine with low exit to generate democratic subsidiarity. In addition, groups
dedicated to inclusive social and public material goods with high exit will
generate democratic forms of subsidiarity often essential to maintaining
the commitments necessary for inclusive goods. Groups that are politically oriented and seek individual material goods may generate democratic legitimacy when they go public with their cases. But they are also

TABLE 6.12b

Associational kinds with high potentials for producing democratic legitimacy

Examples of associational types	Ease of exit	Medium of social reproduction	Orientation toward medium	Goods of association
Public schools	Low	Social	Vested	**Inclusive Social**
Universities, academic research institutes	Medium	Social	Vested	**Inclusive Social**
Political parties, corporatist bodies	Medium	**Political**	Vested	Individual material
Political parties, corporatist bodies, RCAs	Medium	**Political**	Vested	**Public material**
Political parties, corporatist bodies	Medium	Political	Vested	Inclusive social
Welfare rights & child health advocacy groups	High	**Political**	Nonvested	Individual material
Environmental advocacy groups	High	**Political**	Nonvested	**Public material**
Mainstream mass media & foundations	High	**Political**	Vested	Inclusive social
Public knowledge, political process, & human rights advocacy, oppositional mass media & foundations	High	**Political**	Nonvested	Inclusive social
Quasi-public, market-oriented NGOs, gov't corporations, nonprofit gov't contractors	**Medium**	Economic	Vested	**Public material**
Unions engaged in social investing	**Medium**	Economic	Vested	Inclusive social
Market-oriented environmental groups, public interest NGOs	High	Economic	Nonvested	**Public material**

limited by the fact that individual material goods lend themselves to bargaining, thus circumventing broadly normative discussions about the legitimacy of distribution. Finally, vested economic groups constituted by individual material goods lack structural incentives to contribute directly to democratic legitimacy. However, they may make indirect contributions if their capacities for subsidiarity are linked to democratic decision making. Thus, worker-owned and -managed firms and democratically struc-

TABLE 6.12c
Associational kinds with mixed potentials for producing democratic legitimacy

Examples of associational types	Ease of exit	Medium of social reproduction	Orientation toward medium	Goods of association
Families, small group mutual aid	Low	Social	Vested	Individual material
Families, neighborhoods, public schools	Low	Social	Vested	Interpersonal identity
Civic & environmental groups	High	Social	Vested	Public material
Cultural, knowledge-oriented, & educational groups, recreational groups	High	Social	Vested	Inclusive social
Business lobbies, unions, professional associations	High	Political	Vested	Individual material
Firms, unions, industrial research institutes & networks, prof. assocs., nonprofit gov't contractors	Medium	Economic	Vested	Individual material
Self-help economic networks, cooperatives	High	Economic	Vested	Individual material

tured unions can devolve democratic legitimacy within their limited spheres of activities.

Taken as a whole, these judgments about the democratic effects of associations begin to provide a picture of what democractic associational ecologies should look like. These judgments are, I hasten to emphasize once again, purely theoretical and summary. They are not predictive of what particular associations will contribute, nor of what their effects might be when viewed within the broad associational ecologies of the advanced liberal democracies. Rather, they provide a set of ideal types that, taken as a whole, tell us what we should look for if we are interested in the democratic effects of associational life. I do not venture beyond theory here: my aim has been to push theory up to the point that it can do no more without looking at the cases and their combined effects. What I can provide in conclusion, however, are a few general observations about the kinds of associational terrains that will tend to enhance or endanger democracy.

Seven

Conclusion: Democratic Associational Ecologies

DEVELOPED liberal democracies today are complex and differentiated in their structure, postconventional and pluralist in their social landscape, and embedded within increasingly globalized markets, political regimes, and cultures. Liberal-democratic states remain central and often dominant players within this emerging political landscape, and the project of democratizing even established liberal-democratic states continues to demand the vigilance of democrats. But today's liberal-democratic states provide one kind of venue for collective action among many, and their powers are increasingly dependent upon venues of collective action they do not control. As venues of collective action become differentiated, pluralized, and extraterritorial, so does politics. Wherever there is politics, there are opportunities for democracy.

Under these circumstances it is entirely appropriate that democrats should turn their attention to associational life, and not just because the migration of politics demands it. Here radically democratic possibilities are conceivable and achievable in ways that can only seem utopian within the context of large-scale state venues. Not only does the close relationship between collective decision, action, and self-rule remain intact in many associational kinds, but associations are replete with new possibilities as the limits of state and market-organized collective actions become clear. And, as deliberative democrats emphasize, public spheres supported by vigorous associational contexts are the incubators and anchors of the normative dimensions of political life. Nor do changes in the political landscape trade off against the more familiar liberal-democratic expectations of associations. Associations still leverage and counterbalance state powers, while providing much of the substance of representative institutions.

The analysis I have offered here is both critical and reconstructive of these democratic hopes and expectations. On the critical side, I have sought to show that broad generalizations about the contributions of associations to democratic purposes are virtually meaningless, undercut by the large variety of associational capacities, locations, and purposes. On the reconstructive side, however, I have hoped to show that more discrete, lower-level generalizations can provide, as it were, a preface to a democratic theory of association. Although general accounts may be meaningless, it is not only possible but necessary for democratic theorists to provide more modest, "second-level" accounts of the democratic potentials of associational life.

By way of conclusion, I discuss two further issues that are key to judging the democratic potentials of associations. Although these issues follow naturally from the theoretical considerations presented so far, a thorough consideration of them extends beyond what can be accomplished by theory alone. The first has to do with the necessity of judging the democratic effects of associational kinds within their broader contexts. The second has to do with locating agents of democratization.

Democratic Associational Ecologies

In the last chapter I developed a number of schematics to help guide judgments about the democratic effects of associational life. Although my mode of analysis—disaggregation—was necessary to these judgments, it is not sufficient. There, I looked at associational kinds effect by effect. While my aim was to identify discrete democratic effects in order to distinguish among the pluralism of possibilities, the very means of analysis undermined an equally important point: the democratic potentials of particular associational kinds depend upon their contexts. The question of what kinds of *potential* democratic effects associations have is only one part of the problem. The other crucial question is what kinds of contexts would evoke and develop these democratic potentials. That is, democracy describes an ecology of effects flowing from a multiplicity of forms of collective decision and action.

It follows that there are very few associational kinds that are bad for democracy *in themselves*. Rather, potential democratic effects are either realized or—sometimes—function in antidemocratic ways depending on the mix of associations, their relative weights in the mix, and their relations to state powers and market structures. To be sure, there are a few associational kinds with few if any democratic potentials, even when viewed within the greater ecology of democracy. These include organized crime, hate groups, and associations that pursue goods that by their nature are exclusive and scarce. But within the right associational ecology, even hate groups may provide something of an inverse democratic function: they can mobilize publics against the corrosive effects of hate, producing progressive coalitions that might not otherwise form. Their dangers develop as they become more common and less marginal within an associational ecology.

It goes far beyond what I can offer here to provide accounts of what democratic associational ecologies might look like. What I can do, however, is suggest some general considerations that should guide more detailed accounts.

Associational Mixes

As is clear from the preceding analyses, because of their varying locations, capacities, and purposes, no single kind of association can provide all of the effects necessary for a democratic ecology of associations. From a democratic perspective, it is best to have an associational mix that underwrites, in aggregate, the full range of democratic effects and their norms—individual autonomy, political autonomy, and institutional democracy.

Associational Balances

If no associational kind can serve every effect, it is also the case that effects potentially trade off against one another. An associational ecology is democratic when no single kind of democratic effect marginalizes other effects. Should some kinds of effects become predominant—say, subsidiarity or representations of differences—they can function in antidemocratic ways. Democrats will need to judge whether, in particular ecologies, the overall mix of associations so privileges some effects that others atrophy and die.

Most imbalances can be traced to associations that have powers that enable them to deprive individuals of autonomy, or to bypass accountability to the publics affected by their actions, or to dominate representative institutions. Associational powers are not, as I have suggested, *inherently* antidemocratic. To the contrary, associational powers are necessary for the democratic potentials for subsidiarity and resistance. But these same potentials can work antidemocratically if they are not balanced by countervailing associational powers, state regulations, or public scrutiny. In any market society, for example, for-profit businesses clearly harbor such antidemocratic dangers. In aggregate, they control most productive social resources, and there exist no incentives "natural" to this associational kind to connect to other democratic effects. But within the right associational ecology, these capacities can be checked and balanced: representatives of community groups, consumers, and employees may serve on corporate boards; firms may become worker-owned and -managed; public interest groups may pressure for state regulation of "externalities" of production; unions may seek internal reforms or use their pension funds to link ownership to social responsibilities; and environmental groups may organize boycotts of products that have deleterious ecological consequences. Subject to such checks and balances, a firm may be induced to use its resources in the manner of a "good public citizen" by limiting externalities and attending to uses of resources that complement other interests, even though its core motivations and actions remain oriented toward markets.

Some kinds of associations, especially rent-seeking business groups and other well-organized lobbies, can insinuate themselves into the powers of the state. In the United States, this danger is especially prevalent in the form of a nonpublic corporatism that displaces the powers of representative institutions. In some other cases, associations serve statelike regulatory functions—certifying accountants, for example—in ways that produce a monopoly control over a necessary social resource. In the United States, unions can function as rent-seeking associations. Plumbers' unions, for example, often collude with large city governments to require that plumbing be done by union-certified plumbers, effectively enabling an unaccountable government-backed monopoly over these services. Historically in the United States, many such trade unions have multiplied their antidemocratic effects by also functioning as exclusive identity groups, restricting membership by race, ethnicity, and family relationships.

Antidemocratic dangers are not limited to rent-seeking groups. Nonprofits that operate with government funds can also become powerful and yet remain unaccountable. In the United States, for example, Catholic hospitals have become the sole providers of health care in many locales (often inner cities) and are viable because they are the only places residents can spend Medicaid and Medicare dollars. In the area of reproductive health, however, these hospitals are accountable only to church dogma—not to the communities they serve, to their workers, or to the governments that provide public funding.

In other cases of imbalance, states may sanction and even organize associations as their social representatives. In many countries (Mexico, Colombia, Bolivia, and other Latin American countries, for example), states establish and finance associations as means of social control, a practice that has led to a powerful, privileged, and well-protected layer of secondary associations. These associations link people to the state through their monopolies over union jobs, housing, education, welfare, and social assistance, with the effect that associations serve as means for the state to coopt individual and political autonomy. Clearly, the problem here is not that such associations have high capacities for subsidiarity (which they do), but that these capacities have little or no connection to other democratic effects. Whenever associations "borrow" state authority and resources, they should also be connected by law to other democratic effects, especially through representation and public accountability.

We can even speak of antidemocratic potentials of those associations well placed to mobilize bias. Again, following the idea that potentially democratic capacities can, in some contexts, produce antidemocratic consequences, democrats should be especially wary of associations that pur-

sue cultural strategies that emphasize commonality while also possessing
the powers to decide who counts as one of "us" and who does not. Businesses, unions, realtors' associations, RCAs, and other associations that
have powers over jobs, housing, or other essential resources are dangerous to democracy when they enforce common prejudices and distinctions
by combining them with powers of exclusion.

External versus Internal Connections among Democratic Potentials

Fortunately, these antidemocratic twists on democratic potentials are not
general to associations. The dangers reside within *vested* associations that
lack checks and balances among democratic effects internal to the association. Democrats, in other words, should be attentive to associations with
significant powers—especially as indicated by high capacities for subsidiarity, resistance, and representation—but no inherent incentives that
would link these powers to individual and political autonomy effects. This
is why, for example, firms and business associations stand out as uniquely
problematic: they have high capacities for making collective decisions and
following through on collective actions as well as for representation and
resistance, but they are oriented toward market "accountability" (consumers and owners represented by their buying power and ownership),
not toward the others their actions affect. It is not accidental, then, that
the potentially democratic effects of these kinds of associations are likely
to be actualized only when they are checked and balanced *externally*—
through state regulation, union and citizen activism, socially conscious
investment, and the like.

Many other kinds of associations are *internally* checked and balanced,
so that even when they have significant potential powers, there are few
scenarios under which they could have antidemocratic effects within an
associational ecology. Very often these internal checks stem from combinations of low exit combined with purposes that tend toward internal
democracy and external accountability. Surveying the possibilities detailed in the last chapter suggests that many associational types have these
internally checking combinations of effects: universities, public schools,
civic and environmental groups, rights advocacy groups, unions engaged
in social investing, political parties, public corporatist bodies, the mass
media, self-help economic networks, and other cases as well. Thus, we
should expect societies with more of these kinds of associations to have
a more vigorously democratic associational ecology—one that will be less
dependent upon the more delicate and often problematic strategies of external checking and balancing.

The distinction between external and internal checks and balances also applies to the impact of associations on individuals' democratic capacities and dispositions. What is desirable is that over time individuals have a variety of associational attachments that, in aggregate, provide the full range of developmental effects. Thus, a recreational group may not be very good at cultivating critical skills. But if its members are, say, also members of a university, PTA, or rights advocacy group, then its contributions to civic sensibilities may complement the critical skills gained in these other forums. These would be instances of *external* balancing of developmental effects. Without these balancing effects, we might very well have some citizens whose political skills have no civic or critical elements, so that they act only in cynical, strategically calculating ways. Alternatively, a society might be replete with well-meaning, civically virtuous citizens who lack the political and critical skills necessary to make their virtues effective.

Here again, there are associational types that combine these developmental effects, thus providing checks and balances *internal* to the associational kind. Democrats should be especially interested in these associational kinds, which, if we follow the analyses in the last chapter, include universities, public schools, groups devoted to public knowledge, the mass media, civic and environmental groups, political parties, public corporatist bodies, public interest NGOs, rights advocacy groups, unions engaged in social issues, and families with democratic structures. In contrast, identity-based groups, social clubs, fundamentalist churches and religious schools, firms and business lobbies, parochial schools, and similar associational types may provide one or more developmental experiences but are likely to fail to connect them to critical skills or civic virtues. Their developmental contributions are much more dependent upon complementary experiences from other associational types. In environments lacking these complements, these associations may add little to democracy or may even produce antidemocratic effects. No doubt this is one factor within societies where the key cleavages follow ethnic or religious differences. It is not that these societies lack associations, but that the kinds of associations they have are not by themselves sufficient to form democratic citizens.

A similar logic applies to public sphere effects, especially with respect to the balance between representations of commonality and difference. The greatest dangers here, I think, are groups with incentives to represent commonalties while suppressing differences—for example, the ubiquitous self-appointed civic representatives of small American cities and towns such as the Jaycees. These characteristics reinforce dominant cultures while making it difficult for public agendas to extend to those who most need to be heard. As the analyses in the previous chapter suggested, of those associational types that "go public" in one way or another, most have incentives to represent their interests as common interests. Although rhetorics of difference and multiculturalism are commonly decried as divisive, the far greater danger to democracy is the pervasiveness of associations that speak the language of commonality but fail to attend to the exclusions such language entails. For political autonomy effects to be vigorous, it is important that public spheres be populated with associations that can also represent differences, thus extending the margins of public deliberation and judgment.

In contrast to the many associational kinds that have incentives to represent commonalties while suppressing differences, only one associational kind is imbalanced in representing differences without commonalties—namely, the high-exit, identity-based political kind which includes New Social Movements, religious advocacy groups, some racial and ethnic advocacy groups, and militia movements. To be sure, these groups are often particularly visible and noisy, and sometimes mischievous. Often they must be so in order to be heard. But we should not conclude that their noisiness is symptomatic of a public sphere in which the rhetoric of difference has gotten out of hand (as neoconservatives claim and egalitarian liberals fear). Because these associations often have few resources to deploy, they are left with oppositional publicity as their sole strategy. Indeed, even among the few kinds of groups with incentives to represent differences, this type of association is exceptional. The other associational kinds that represent differences—rights advocacy groups, oppositional media, political process advocacy groups, and environmental advocacy groups, for example—all have incentives to represent commonalities as well. These latter groups are, in other words, subject to internal checks and balances, with incentives to stretch the margins of public discourse while representing and redefining common interests. Owing to their internal checks, groups such as these will reliably and vigorously contribute to public spheres, and thus to a more vigorously democratic associational ecology.

Distributions of Associational Attachments

If associational attachments form democratic citizens, enable their participation in public judgments, and magnify their voices and power within democratic institutions, then democrats need to know who has the kinds of associational ties that enable these advantages. If associational ties provide, perhaps increasingly, the lifeblood of democracy, then joiners have advantages that nonjoiners do not. While it is true in principle that association is a more broadly available resource than money and power, it may also be that associational ties increase money and power, while the economic and power disadvantages of those who are isolated are, as it were, reinforced by their isolation.[1] Thus, even if the mixes of associations in a society are, on balance, democratic, if they are distributed in ways that reinforce other social and economic cleavages, then their aggregate effect may be, as it were, democracy for the few.

There are, of course, many kinds of associational ties we would not expect to be distributed equally—those that are both cause and effect of privilege. Elite social clubs, elite corporatist groups, gated communities, private schools, and the like reinforce (and often have as their purpose to reinforce) inequalities. These associational ties more or less mirror inequalities of money and power, and democrats should seek ways to contain their effects. Of greater (theoretical) concern, however, are disparities in associational ties that are *not* inherently inegalitarian: participation in neighborhood groups, recreational associations, civic groups, and other kinds of associations that generate social capital, as well as participation in political groups, parties, unions, and other organizations that might help to compensate for lack of power and money.

In the United States there is much evidence that these associational ties mirror cleavages of education, income, and race/ethnicity. A study by the Pew Center suggests that associational ties are stratified by income and education, both of which show strong correlations to civic, voluntary, and informal associational activities.[2] The large study by Verba, Schlozman, and Brady provides a somewhat more nuanced picture. Their "civic volunteerism model" explains political participation as an effect of individuals' politically relevant resources—time, money, and civic skills—combined with their levels of political interest and engagement. "Civic skills"—communication and organizational abilities—are, they find, developed by nonpolitical associational participation, especially those of workplaces and churches. Of particular note is their finding that civic skills developed in nonpolitical contexts have an important independent effect upon political participation, especially upon acts that require time rather than money.[3] As they argue, the importance of this finding is that since time is more equally distributed than money, a political system based on time is more egalitarian than one based on money.

However, it is important to know how these effects of association are distributed. Do they mirror the disparities of education and income that also predict political participation (a necessary although not sufficient condition of political influence)? Many of the opportunities to gain civic skills are highly stratified, especially those associated with workplaces and occupations.[4] Managers and professionals have opportunities to develop civic skills in ways that filing clerks, line workers, and janitors do not. Moreover, the United States lacks working-class parties and strong unions that help compensate for these inequalities in many other advanced liberal democracies. Nonetheless, Verba, Schlozman, and Brady find that participation in the associations that foster "civic skills" is less stratified than are education and income. In the United States, what stands out is church membership, which shows more equality of distribution than other associational ties. By "providing opportunities for the practice of politically relevant skills, the American churches—particularly Protestant ones— may partially compensate for the weakness of institutions that ordinarily function to mobilize the disadvantaged."[5]

The Verba, Schlozman, and Brady study is one of the few to seek to describe and explain the complex of factors that cause political activity. It is the only study of which I am aware that, as part of its broader purpose, looks at the impact of the distribution of associational ties on democracy. Unfortunately, the approach of the study is limited by a narrow conception of what the democratic contributions of associations might be. The authors' notion of "civic skills" captures only two of the twelve dimensions I develop here. Thus, while it is significant that the distribution of church membership is the more egalitarian than other associational ties in the United States, it may be hasty to conclude as they do that religious associations can compensate for the lack of class-based parties and strong unions. Both parties and unions provide a variety of democratic effects beyond civic skills. Religious associations, even allowing for the wide variety of forms, produce a very limited number of democratic effects, and in some contexts may function antidemocratically owing to their strong exclusive-identity basis.[6] For example, church membership may increase political skills, but tends to have a negative impact on at least one civic virtue, tolerance.[7] The important exception of the black churches tends to prove the rule: their key democratic functions evolved in a context that denied African Americans any other associational venue for pursuing a variety of nonreligious purposes. Verba, Schlozman, and Brady's emphasis on the importance of workplace experience as a stratified source of civic skills is suggestive in another way, however. Because work is more broadly experienced even than religious association, it suggests that democrats should look anew at the potential effects of workplace democracy—an area that could turn out to be promising in an era of management philosophy that emphasizes the efficiencies of flattened hierarchies and heightened employee responsibilities.

But it is likely that on average, especially in the United States, associational ties reinforce other forms of stratification. Along with many democrats, I suspect, however, that the parallels are neither direct nor exact, leaving associations as key arenas for deepening and extending democracy. Yet, we still know too little to generalize, and so we are left mostly with anecdotes that illustrate democratic hopes and fears.

Association and Democratic Individuality

A final issue concerning the democratic potentials of associational ecology has to do with the ways individuals combine associational attachments within their biographies, an issue I touched on in discussing associational checks and balances. This is the issue prominent in Nancy Rosenblum's investigation of the "personal uses of pluralism," where she rightly insists that a democratic ethos is closely related to experiences of associational pluralism, as well as to experiences of making and breaking associational ties.[8] Experiences of pluralism build on the decisive advance of democratic over ascriptive societies: in a democracy, no person is reducible to a single scale of judgment, nor are their life-chances determined by a single place in the social hierarchy. People may not be the same, but their moral equality is predicated on the fact that there is no one measure that determines their social worth in toto. This aspect of American society so impressed Tocqueville that he credited it with causing the "easy and natural manners" of Americans, even in the company of strangers.[9] The pattern of associational attachments over the course of a person's lifetime—especially their multiplicity and fluidity—is essential to developing and sustaining the initial assumption of equality when individuals meet, as well as for containing the spillover effects of inequalities from one sphere to another.[10]

This point suggests three antidemocratic patterns of associational attachment. The first, emphasized by Rosenblum, concerns the antidemocratic consequences of "greedy" associations: those that encompass the totality of an individual's experiences and relationships. Or, in the terms I used in chapter 2, democrats should be concerned about forms of association that seek to become encompassing communities. In the United States, some forms of religious association seek to organize all facets of life—family, school, work, neighborhood, and even consumer networks—around a community of believers. Clearly, these patterns of attachment replicate homogeneity and reduce the experiences of pluralism in ways that cannot but undermine a democratic ethos.

But democrats should be equally concerned about patterns of self-segregation that replicate similar effects such as those apparent in residential enclaves that select for residents of similar income, race, lifestyle, and political persuasion, and then combine with public or private schools with similar demographics. Work experience is usually more varied, but may be limited by profession and education to people of similar backgrounds;

work life can become increasingly homogeneous as businesses leave cities for suburban ring developments. When cleavages overlap, experiences of pluralism become rarer, which in turn makes it less likely that an ethos of democracy might develop.

There is still a third pattern of associational attachment that is problematic from a democratic perspective. Rosenblum notes that part of the genius of association is that the everyday injuries of social life need not replicate themselves in a pluralistic society. The indignity of having a low-status, low-paying job may be compensated by recognized skill in the gardening club, prowess on the softball team, fraternal recognition in the Elks Lodge, and so on. But not all pluralism is compensatory in this way. The dangers to democratic habits and ethics are especially pronounced within the weightiest and least voluntary of ties—those of family, school, some churches, and workplace. In each of these arenas authoritarianism is common, and it is certainly not uncommon that authoritarian experiences in the family and church generate a psychological comfort with authoritarian schools and workplaces. It is unclear how widespread these patterns are, although it is clear that in the advanced liberal democracies many authoritarian associations are no longer reproduced by tradition as such, but rather—to use Ulrich Beck's term—by countermodern reactions to modern developments.[11]

Agents of Democracy

Even a complex associational ecology is not, then, necessarily a democratic one. What I have hoped to show, however, is that when there are multiple associational types, there are also multiple democratic potentials that might be encouraged. But what might be the agents of encouragement? There is, of course, no purely theoretical answer to this question; ultimately, the issue is a political matter that goes far beyond my topic here. There are, however, some general theoretical points that follow from my analysis that may help to identify and assess political potentials.

State Involvement

Although I have suggested that the most important avenues of democratization may not be through the collective actions of the state, states are deeply and inextricably involved in constituting the associational life of today's societies, not only through regulation, but through devolution of social services to associations, tax incentives, the structuring and devolving of political processes, partnerships, and alterations in the bargaining powers of social actors. In addition, the politics and policies of state intervention on behalf of civil society are in place, for better or for worse. Bodies such as the Agency for International Development (AID) as well as powerful, state-supported NGOs such as the World Bank increasingly intervene in democratizing countries to support "civil society associations" in the name of democracy. For most kinds of association—from the family to the firm, from social clubs to political lobbies—the key questions are not *whether* the state should be involved, but rather *how* it should be involved. If guided by the right principles, state involvement is not only not a bad thing for a democratic ecology of associations, it is necessary to protect and enhance its democratic characteristics. Associational life depends upon the rights, securities, supports, adjustments of social and economic powers, and political processes that only a strong state can provide.

In speaking of "state" involvement, of course, I am not referring to any one agent. In the United States there are, after all, well over eighty-five thousand units of government, each with distinct constituencies. Moreover, in liberal democracies "the state" lacks the unity of a singular agent, certainly in terms of its motivations and purposes. So state "interests" in cultivating a democratic associational ecology are likely to be mixed at best. Representatives in political branches, for example, are more likely to be interested in the support of associational coalitions than they are in democracy as such. Administrators prefer a well-behaved associational landscape that can be governed according to their enabling legislation. But administrators must, unlike representatives, execute the laws and policies *universally*, which increases the potential disruptive powers of associations. In highly politicized areas of policy—national forest management in the western United States, for example—administrators may develop an interest in the democratic mix of associations, if only to increase their legitimacy and thereby minimize potential disruptions of policy.

Although we should not generalize about reasons of state, we can generalize, as I suggested in chapter 5, about the legal-administrative means of influence that governments use to regulate, tax, distribute, coerce, police, and manage. Assuming actors with motivations not inconsistent with democratic effects, we can ask how these state powers might enhance a democratic associational ecology.

In the case of liberal democratic states, there are at least six broad kinds of involvements that affect the nature and quality of associational life. First, the classically liberal involvements are negative and protective: the state recognizes zones of social, economic, and interpersonal freedom, and uses its legal system to underwrite rights that enable associational ties to flourish. Certain kinds of rights—those of speech, conscience, assembly, and privacy—directly protect specific associational purposes and domains, especially those related to public sphere effects. But as many commentators have pointed out, in the U.S. Constitution there is no right of association *as such*. My analysis shows that this is as it should be, at least from the perspective of enhancing democracy. Association is not an unqualified good for democracy (nor even for other liberal purposes), especially when associations become vested in economic and political powers.[12]

The other five kinds of involvements are interventionist in nature—with means ranging from coercions to incentives. The classic coercive intervention is, of course, regulation—usually in the form of administrative laws and rules designed to achieve some social or political good or to avoid potential harms. Although the kinds and purposes of regulation are widely varied and extensive, the point worth making here is that regulations count as democratic when they function as countervailing powers that cause potentially antidemocratic associational powers to function in ways consistent with democracy. The most common examples are economic: regulation of externalities of production (pollution, worker injuries, and the like), of monopoly, and of the potentials for fraud can have the effect of enabling subsidiarity while limiting potentially antidemocratic consequences of economic association for individual development, public spheres, and democratic institutions. Regulation on behalf of democracy should also accompany devolutions of public purposes. When associations administer public monies (as do most health-related nonprofits and many charities) or regulate areas of social or economic activities in quasi-legal ways, then state powers ought to ensure that these devolved public functions capture the benefits of devolution without doing harm to other democratic goods.

A related but distinct strategy devolves regulatory processes to the social actors most directly involved with disputes or damages, a strategy that Günther Teubner has called "reflexive law."[13] In such cases, the state equalizes the bargaining power of otherwise unequal social actors, and then allows them to negotiate over the matters that concern them. The classic example is collective bargaining, in which the state generates the conditions of fair bargaining but does not impose solutions. It leaves monitoring of outcomes up to the parties, involving itself only as the agent of last resort. Superfund legislation (aimed at cleaning up toxic waste dumps in the United States) provides for public hearings as well as structured negotiations between responsible and damaged parties. Innovations in developing and enforcing worker safety regulations in Oregon involve legal requirements that employers form committees of employees to monitor work conditions, suggest improvements, and so on. In these cases, regulation is indirect and amounts to lending the powers of the state to weaker or unorganized social powers in order to produce a democratic political process aimed at collective self-regulation.

Income supports constitute a third means of shaping the associational landscape. Minimum wage legislation, Social Security, unemployment insurance, and welfare programs can—depending upon how generous they are and how they are structured—serve to reduce individuals' vulnerabilities to those who control employment and increase their relative bargaining powers. Depending upon circumstances, increasing the bargaining power of the economically vulnerable can affect associational relations within firms, as well as the capacities of individuals to organize employment-related associations. In some more recent and innovative strategies—for example, recent Medicaid coverage reform in Oregon—governments have provided income supports for associations to hire experts and make presentations in public hearings. In such cases, governments undertake to increase the future legitimacy of policies by increasing the communicative powers of associations. There are, of course, many dangers here: incomes supports, especially in the area of means-tested welfare, are often combined with government control over recipients' lives. Income insurance such as Social Security (as opposed to means-tested welfare) is surely more conducive to the democratic effects of association than income supports administered by social workers charged with policing recipients' behavior.

A fourth strategy involves economic incentives that affect associational purposes and viability. The broadest forms of economic incentives work through tax systems. In the United States, for example, there exist hundreds of thousands of tax-exempt associations, a status that carries with it numerous benefits, including not only exemption from many kinds of taxes, but also the valuable income tax deduction for charitable contributions. In many cases, tax-exempt status makes an association economically viable, thus amounting to a government policy to "grow" associational life in general. Tax-exempt status amounts to an indirect preference for social associations over political associations, since favoring political associations would presumably involve the state in generating its own public support. Nonetheless, the policy does generate a very significant lobby on behalf of maintaining tax privileges, fueled by businesslike nonprofits such as hospitals and private universities.[14] In other respects, the policy does tend to depoliticize the associational terrain, indicated by the fact that only 5% of tax-exempt entities have advocacy as one of their purposes.[15] Nor, of course, does tax-exempt status extend to for-profit organizations. Indeed, since many associations such as hospitals and the YMCA operate as if they were tax-exempt businesses, advocates of free markets often complain that tax-exempt status amounts to unfair competition with for-profit businesses.[16] Other policies provide direct income supports to associations through grants or reimbursements for services. These amount to incentives for associations to serve public functions, especially in the areas of social service and health care delivery, education, research, and economic development.

Finally, governments increasingly form public-private partnerships that themselves take on the qualities of associations. Ideally, these associations serve as public venues for turning private resources to public benefit while limiting the inflexibilities of regulatory approaches. In many cases, firms take on public responsibilities in exchange for publicly granted profit-making opportunities. In other cases, governments can constrain economic powers by becoming actors in the market, forming government corporations in locales or sectors with natural monopolies, or granting monopolies in exchange for close regulation.

Principles of State Involvement

There is no necessity, of course, that these well-known state strategies will work to democratic ends. States are never neutral actors, and their interventions too often reflect powerful social agents hoping to become more powerful by enlisting state powers and resources.[17] But let us assume that if there were supportive political coalitions, these strategies could be used to underwrite a democratic associational ecology. Under this assumption, which strategies should democrats prefer?

Just as there is no one kind of association, there is no one kind of strategy that will maximize democratic results. Appropriate interventions will depend upon the kind of association and its potentials to generate democratic goods. Although this is not the place for a general account, we can pull together some guidelines from the literature as well as from my analysis in chapter 5.

Two qualities of association are especially relevant to the kind and extent of state involvement: ease of exit and the kind of medium within which the association is embedded. With respect to ease of exit, the liberal view has always been that government regulation is less justified when associations are voluntary, since individual autonomy is not compromised if people can leave the association. The (correct) assumption is that high-exit associations are less able to exercise power over individuals and are more likely to be disciplined by the market in associational membership. Nancy Rosenblum, for example, emphasizes the voluntary quality of religious association as a reason for state forbearance. "Government nonintervention rests on the assumption that membership in a religious association is voluntary and based on faith. . . . Voluntarism and religious faith together are the key."[18] In contrast, because it is difficult for individuals to exit (say) a union shop, there is more justification for state regulation to establish democratic procedures within the union.[19] It is important to be clear, however, that even on the liberal account "government nonintervention" does not imply that the state is (or ought to be) merely laissez-faire with regard to voluntary association. Rather, states do (and often should) protect and facilitate associational relations by (for example) enforcing rights and providing tax-exempt status.

The second dimension concerns the kind of medium within which the association is embedded, as implied in Rosenblum's afterthought above. Government nonintervention in religious association is based on "voluntarism and religious faith together." Religious faith is a *social* medium that generates *communicative* power, rather than a medium that generates its force through money or (coercive) legal-administrative means. In contrast, when an association controls means of economic success or borrows legal-administrative powers from the state, then the case for more direct state interventions in associational life is more compelling.

Amy Gutmann makes a similar distinction in discussing *Bob Jones University v. United States*, in which the U.S. Supreme Court upheld the Internal Revenue Service's denial of tax-exempt status to Bob Jones University on the grounds that it practiced racial discrimination.[20] Although Bob Jones University argued that as a religious university it was entitled to the same treatment as other religious associations, the Court held that the government had an overriding interest in overcoming social discrimination in education. Gutmann agrees with the Court's ruling, noting that the state's "overriding interest" was in part predicated on the economic power universities possess as a means to individual economic success:

> Suppose that Bob Jones had been not a university but a church, and Bob Jones Church had claimed the right to forbid miscegenation among its congregants. A primary purpose of a university, by virtue of its being a university, is that it directly serves the social function of contributing to a system of fair educational opportunities in this society in a way that a church need not, by virtue of its being a church. Colleges and universities are educational gatekeepers to the professions and to other scarce and highly valuable social offices that require advanced educational credentials. Churches serve largely social purposes.[21]

It follows that a church's claim to be exempt from state regulation is much stronger than that of a social organization with important economic functions and the powers that attach to these functions. Likewise, Gutmann notes, a church would be on weak grounds were it to claim exemption from nondiscrimination regulations in hiring office staff, in contrast to hiring staff more closely integrated into its religious mission.[22] When associations are able to deploy economic or legal/administrative powers, then the case for state intervention is much greater than when an association is primarily social and deploys communicative power.

TABLE 7.1

Principles of state involvement according to the power and exit characteristics of associations

	Media embeddedness enables:		
Ease of exit	*Communicative power*	*Economic or coercive power*	
Higher	Social clubs	Professional and business associations	Protection, cultivation
Lower	Families, public schools	Firms, unions, quasi-gov't bodies	$\updownarrow$
	Protection, cultivation	$\longleftrightarrow$	Regulation, power balancing

We can generalize these guidelines, as suggested by table 7.1. While there are no neutral stances the state can take toward associations, there are a variety of possible relationships, ranging from less interventionist strategies such as the protection and cultivation of associations to the more interventionist strategies such as including regulation, altering the bargaining powers of social and economic actors, entering the marketplace, and developing partnerships. As suggested in table 7.1, the associational kinds that have the best claim to noninterventionist relations are high-exit social associations—that is, those that are voluntary and deploy only the powers of communication. When we combine the dimensions of exit and medium, however, we can also see that some kinds of social associations such as families and schools have less claim to remain independent of state interventions. In the case of the family, for example, it is because it is difficult for children to exit the state ought to ensure that their parents or guardians see to their welfare. Similarly, because marriages are often difficult to dissolve, states ought to intervene where possible to prevent spousal abuse. And although public schools are also embedded in economic and legal-administrative relations, it is in part because many parents have no other options for their children's education that higher-level government regulation of educational quality is justified. But because of the fragile nature of social relationships and communicative powers, state strategies should be indirect, aimed, for example, at equalizing the economic bargaining power of partners in marriages, limiting the abuses of parenting rather than imposing norms of child raising, equalizing the educational influence of parents by enabling parent-teacher associations, providing information about the performances of schools, equalizing resources, and so on.

It is also possible for associations with easy exit to amass powers by virtue of their embeddedness in economic or legal-administrative media. The fact that the Jaycees is a voluntary association, for example, does not diminish its important role as a gatekeeper to local business networks, as Sandra Day O'Connor noted in her concurring opinion in the Supreme Court's 1984 ruling in *Roberts v. United States Jaycees* that the Jaycees may not exclude women. Similar reasoning ought to apply to schools and universities insofar as they provide skills necessary for economic advancement. Likewise, because they control vast economic resources that are easily converted into political power, business lobbies can and ought to be regulated. Regulation in this case is not—contra recent Supreme Court rulings—a limitation on "speech." Rather, such regulations are necessary to induce such associations to resort to speech by limiting the political uses of economic power.

The cases in which state interventions are most justified are low-exit associations embedded within economic or legal-administrative media. Firms, unions, quasi-governmental bodies, and similar organizations are likely to contribute to a democratic associational ecology only if their considerable powers are regulated and monitored by state powers, or by associations empowered by the state to carry out these functions.

States can and do take up a variety of relations to associational life. Of the many strategies states have available, however, the democratic ecology of associations will be enhanced if the strategy is matched to the kind of the association. High-exit associations that thrive on communicative powers should be protected and cultivated. Low-exit associations embedded within economic and political power relations should be regulated and counterbalanced to limit their antidemocratic potentials.

Cultural Developments

It is more difficult to generalize about cultural agents of a democratic associational ecology—in spite of the ultimate importance of civil society as the location of political autonomy. It does seem to me, however, that many cultural developments in the developed liberal democracies are a net plus. If it is true, as Ronald Inglehart argues, that a postmaterial ethos is taking hold in the wealthy liberal democracies through generational succession, this is good for democracy. Postmaterial individuals place a higher value on self-government, are more likely to expect good government, and are more likely to question authorities than are their mothers and fathers. In addition, as postmaterialists find their material needs satisfied, their preferences shift toward public and social goods.[23] While many traditional forms of association are apparently on the wane in the United States—fraternal associations, for example—new and more informal forms of association are in the making, as are forms of association closely related to functional necessities—day care, school, work, and neighborhood integrity, for example—as well as associations related to recreation and lifestyles.[24] Although these new mixes of associations may have democratic effects that are different in aggregate from older forms (weaker, for example, as means of representation as the older federated forms of association decline, but perhaps stronger in subsidiarity), it is by no means clear that on average there are, or will be, democratic losses. Jeffrey Berry, for example, finds that over the last three decades groups representing the postmaterial concerns of New Social Movements (such as environmental, gender, and consumer issues) have been increasingly successful at placing their issues on the congressional agenda. Importantly for democracy, these groups tend to increase representation of traditionally underrepresented groups.[25] Moreover, postmaterially oriented groups tend, on average, to win their congressional battles. While these groups have not been successful at increasing the visibility of issues having to do with economic equality or their presence on the congressional agenda, neither have they reduced the visibility and presence of these issues—suggesting that postmaterial concerns do not trade off against economic concerns, at least when measured by the attention given to them by Congress.[26] Judging by congressional agendas, there seems to be little warrant for the fear that attention to economic inequalities is being displaced by the postmaterial politics, but neither, apparently, does postmaterialism enhance attention to these inequalities.

It is broadly important that the politicization of society means that it is more difficult for governments to impose global directions, not only because of the limits of global planning in complex and pluralized societies, but also because increases in identity-based "lifestyle" politics make institutionally contained compromises more difficult.[27] But it may also mean that democracy, while more chaotic in nature, can increase its scope. New Social Movements have been challenging the more traditional forms of association and institutions, leading to new kinds of inclusions.[28] The pluralization and internationalization of society may pluralize the experiences of most people, and make parochial ethics and judgments more difficult to sustain. Of course, there is nothing necessary in any of these developments. As William Connolly and Ulrich Beck have argued at length, each of these late-modern/postmodern developments, when combined with new risks or newly perceived risks, can provoke counter modern, antidemocratic reactions.[29]

Economic Developments

It is more difficult to see democratic promise in current economic developments, not just in the United States, but in the increasing hegemony of neoliberal policies in Latin America, the increasing mobility of capital, and the integration of the European bloc with the consequent loss of national control over fiscal and monetary policy. Unions seem increasingly powerless, and many states seem increasingly unwilling to attend to the most vulnerable of their citizens, especially if the cost is to constrain or disrupt markets. Income distributions, especially in the United States but also in Britain and other developed liberal democracies, have become increasingly unequal since the mid-1970s. In the United States, almost all of the incomes gains from the recent economic expansion have been captured by the wealthiest 20% of households. Real wages have stagnated since the mid-1970s, although there has been a very modest improvement in the last few years. Real declines in incomes of the poorest 20% since the mid-1970s seem to have bottomed out, and now show some increases. W. Lance Bennett has argued that insofar as there have been erosions in associational life in the United States, they have been caused by the economic insecurity indicated by these trends. Americans are responding to increasing economic insecurity by placing more emphasis on making money, which represents an opportunity cost for noneconomic forms of association.[30] Disturbingly for democrats, since economic insecurity is borne disproportionately by the poor, increasing economic inequality is likely to produce increasingly unequal distributions of associational attachments. Findings such as these highlight the need for social welfare policies that directly address economic insecurities in ways that enhance associational life.

Are there any economic developments that *are* likely to enhance a democratic ecology of associations? While a general survey is beyond my capabilities, a few developments are worth mention. First, global expansions of markets have led the globalization of information technologies, from the fax and public access cable television to the Internet. These developments enable communication as never before and can underwrite publics that are less easily controlled by the state and the commercial mass media. The new information technologies enable new forms of association that have the potential to dramatically enhance public spheres and communicative power.

Second, global economic integration has provoked, and continues to provoke, global associations devoted to environmental causes, labor conditions, human rights, economic development, and other issues closely related to the externalities of markets, which have tended to increase with market integration. In many cases, the progress of internationally oriented associations is tracking international economic integration. Associations are scaling up political actions to meet global markets, filling in for the failures of political regimes, and—in some cases—seeking to make effective existing political agreements such as the labor and environmental riders to the North American Free Trade Agreement[31] Although the European Union has only the most minimal democratic structure, it is likely that it will be democratized over time by associational pressures both within and beyond national boundaries. Political integration will no doubt follow economic integration, but it will be unlikely to have the technocratic structure and leadership that now exist in the EU.

Third, we can no longer take for granted that the hierarchical-authoritarian structure of firms is the most efficient means of organizing labor. Although each sector has its own requirements, within those that demand more skill, creativity, initiative, and flexibility from workers, hierarchy turns out to be an inefficiency. Hierarchies that are flattened in response to their inefficiencies, can potentially strengthen associational relations within workplaces and can potentially add a dimension to democracy.

To be sure, these are weak forces when compared to the now massively powerful global currency and capital markets. Nonetheless, economic developments never stand alone: they develop and provoke new associational ties even as they corrode older forms.

Democracy, once again in favor, is in need of conceptual renewal. While the traditional concerns of democratic theory with state-centered institutions remain importantly crucial and ethically central, they are increasingly subject to the limitations we should expect when nineteenth-century concepts meet twenty-first -century realities. Democratic theory needs to catch up. By focusing on associational relationships and venues, I have sought to add definition to emerging problems of democracy. My hope is that such added definition will help to identify, evaluate, and configure new forms of democracy while reinvigorating the old. That this is a messy business is, in the end, for the best: it means that a multitude of democratic possibilities exist within our increasingly pluralized and dynamic societies—some partially realized and many not. In contrast to this myriad of democratic possibilities, however, the ethical significance of focusing on associational life remains straightforward. The associational ideal returns us to the perennially radical goal of democracy to integrate self-governance and collective action, a goal that is as rich as ever in ethical meaning.

Notes

Chapter One
Introduction

1. This formula amounts to a rediscovery of the sociology of American plural-ism, as developed by Seymour Martin Lipset, *Political Man: The Social Bases of Politics* (Baltimore: Johns Hopkins University Press, 1981); William Kornhauser, *The Politics of Mass Society* (New York: Free Press, 1959); and others. See David Held, *Models of Democracy*, 2nd ed. (Stanford, CA: Stanford University Press, 1996), chap. 6.

2. Sidney Verba, Kay Lehman Schlozman, and Henry E. Brady, *Voice and Equality: Civic Voluntarism in American Politics* (Cambridge: Harvard University Press, 1995), chap. 10; Jeffrey M. Berry, *The New Liberalism and the Rising Power of Citizen Groups* (Washington, DC: Brookings Institution Press, 1999). This last point is especially relevant in the United States, where politics is too often conducted under the sway of money, and where—because of its system of checks and balances at the federal and state levels (and in many other jurisdictions as well)—the political impact of voting is less clear than in nonfederal parliamentary systems. That associational life is relatively strong in the United States as com-pared to other democracies even as voting has declined suggests that associations may be carrying much of the burden of political life.

3. The best recent case to this effect is John Dryzek, *Democracy in Capitalist Times: Ideals, Limits, and Struggles* (Oxford: Oxford University Press, 1996). This is not to say, of course, that there have not been society-centered theories of democracy, including those of Marx as well as those of the anarchists. Within liberal-democratic theory, J. S. Mill and John Dewey are both notable for their emphases upon the complementary relationship between democratic states and democratic social institutions.

4. Claus Offe, *Modernity and the State: East, West* (Cambridge: MIT Press, 1996), vii–viii.

5. Dryzek, *Democracy in Capitalist Times.*

6. Cf. Gianfranco Poggi's Weberian analysis of the location and limitations of the modern state—in particular, the nature of its "ultimacy"—in *The State: Its Nature, Development, and Prospects* (Oxford: Polity Press, 1990).

7. James C. Scott, *Seeing Like a State: How Certain Schemes to Improve the Human Condition Have Failed* (New Haven: Yale University Press, 1998).

8. Ulrich Beck, *Risk Society: Toward a New Modernity*, trans. Mark Ritter (London: Sage Publications, 1992).

9. Offe, *Modernity and the State*, 9.

10. Ibid., 8.

11. Ulrich Beck, *The Reinvention of Politics: Rethinking Modernity in the Global Social Order*, trans. Mark Ritter (Cambridge: Polity Press, 1997), 107.

12. Cf. William Connolly's analysis in *Identity/Difference: Democratic Negotiations of Political Paradox* (Ithaca: Cornell University Press, 1991); Robert Jay Lifton, *The Protean Self* (New York: Basic Books, 1993); and Beck, *The Reinvention of Politics*, chap. 2.

13. This possibility is best analyzed by Jürgen Habermas, *Moral Consciousness and Communicative Action*, trans. by Christian Lenhardt and Shierry Weber Nicholsen (Cambridge: MIT Press, 1990).

14. Linda Kintz, *Between Jesus and the Market: The Emotions That Matter in Right-Wing America* (Durham, NC: Duke University Press, 1997).

15. Offe, *Modernity and the State*, viii.

16. Compare Ulrich Beck's argument in *The Reinvention of Politics* that society has become "subpoliticized," a discussion that opens a new range of questions that are roughly parallel to the more traditional arenas of political science: As Beck puts it, political science has worked with the categories of *polity* (the institutional constitution of the political community), *policy* (the substance of political programs), and *politics* (the process of political conflict and decision making).

> *Subpolitics* is distinguished from politics in that (a) agents *outside* the political or corporatist system are also allowed to appear on the stage of social design (this group includes professional and occupational groups, the technical intelligentsia in companies, research institutions and management, skilled workers, citizens' initiatives, the public sphere, and so on), and (b) not only social and collective agents, but *individuals* as well compete with the latter and each other for the emerging power to shape politics.
>
> If one transfers the distinction between polity, policy, and politics to subpolitics . . . then the following questions come up:
>
> 1. How is the "*subpolity*" constituted and organized institutionally? What are the sources of its power, its resistance possibilities and its potential for strategic action? What are its switch-points and what are the limits of its influence? How does the scope and power to shape things emerge in the wake of reflexive modernization?
>
> 2. With what goals, content and programs is "*subpolity*" conducted, and in what areas of action (occupations, professions, companies, trade unions, parties, and so on)? How is subpolicy objectified, restricted conducted and implemented into non-policy? Which strategies—for example, "health precautions," "social security" or "technical necessities"—are applied for this purpose, how and by whom?
>
> 3. What organizational forms and forums of "*subpolitics*" are emerging and can be observed? What power positions are opened up, solidified and shifted here, and how? Are there internal conflicts over the policy of an enterprise or a group (labor, technology or product policy)? Are there informal or formalizing coalitions for or against certain strategic options? Are specialist, environmental and feminist circles or working groups separating out inside occupational groups or plant labor circles? What degree and quality of organization do the latter exhibit (informal contacts, discussion meetings, bylaws, special journals, focused publicity work, congresses, codes of ethics or a flag with a special emblem)? (103–4)

17. Cf. Franklin I. Gamwell's reconstruction of Dewey's approach to association in *Beyond Preference: Liberal Theories of Independent Associations* (Chicago: University of Chicago Press, 1984), 144–50. Following Dewey, Gamwell argues that association is a "teleological priority" in democracy, since it is the primary means through which the ethical dimension of human existence is projected into the public domain.

18. Robert N. Bellah, Richard Madsen, William M. Sullivan, Ann Swidler, and Steven M. Tipton, *The Good Society* (New York: Alfred A. Knopf, 1991); Michael Sandel, *Democracy and Its Discontents: America in Search of a Public Philosophy* (Cambridge: Harvard University Press, 1996).

19. Robert Putnam, *Making Democracy Work: Civic Traditions in Modern Italy* (Princeton: Princeton University Press, 1993).

20. Nancy Rosenblum, *Membership and Morals: The Personal Uses of Pluralism in America* (Princeton: Princeton University Press, 1998).

21. Gabriel Almond and Sidney Verba, *The Civic Culture: Political Attitudes and Democracy in Five Nations* (Princeton: Princeton University Press, 1963); Verba, Scholzman, and Brady, *Voice and Equality*.

22. John Rawls, *A Theory of Justice* (Cambridge: Harvard University Press, 1971), 462–72.

23. The U.S. Constitution protects freedom of association through its First Amendment protections of political and religious expression, since association is instrumental to exercising rights of religious expression, freedom of assembly, and freedom to petition the government for redress of grievances, and through the "zone of privacy" doctrine developed out of the due process clause of the Fourteenth Amendment. See Aviam Soifer, *Law and the Company We Keep* (Cambridge: Harvard University Press, 1995). See also George Kateb, "The Value of Association," in *Freedom of Association*, ed. Amy Gutmann (Princeton: Princeton University Press, 1998), 35–63; Kent Greenawalt, "Freedom of Association and Religious Association," in *Freedom of Association*, ed. Amy Gutmann (Princeton: Princeton University Press, 1998), 109–44; Peter de Marneffe, "Rights, Reasons, and Freedom of Association," in *Freedom of Association*, ed. Amy Gutmann (Princeton: Princeton University Press, 1998), 145–73; Yael Tamir, "Revisiting the Civic Sphere," in *Freedom of Association*, ed. Amy Gutmann (Princeton: Princeton University Press, 1998), 214–38; and Sam Fleischacker, "Insignificant Communities," in *Freedom of Association*, ed. Amy Gutmann (Princeton: Princeton University Press, 1998), 273–313.

24. Jürgen Habermas, *Between Facts and Norms: Contributions to a Discourse Theory of Law and Democracy* (Cambridge: MIT Press, 1996); Jürgen Habermas, *The Structural Transformation of the Public Sphere*, trans. Thomas Berger (Cambridge: MIT Press, 1989); Jean Cohen and Andrew Arato, *Civil Society and Political Theory* (Cambridge: MIT Press, 1992); Offe, *Modernity and the State*; Ulrich Preuss, *Constitutional Revolution: The Link between Constitutionalism and Progress*, trans. Deborah Lucas Schneider (Atlantic Highlands, NJ: Humanities Press, 1995); Beck, *Risk Society*; Beck, *The Reinvention of Politics*; cf. Phillipe Schmitter and Wolfgang Streek. "Community, Market, State—and Associations? The Prospective Contributions of Interest Governance to Social Order," *European Sociological Review* 1 (1985): 119–38.

25. Joshua Cohen and Joel Rogers, "Secondary Associations and Democratic Governance," in *Associations and Democracy*, ed. Eric Olin Wright (New York: Routledge), 7–98; Paul Hirst, *Associative Democracy: New Forms of Economic and Social Governance* (Amherst: University of Massachusetts Press, 1994).

26. Virginia Ann Hodgkinson, Murray S. Weitzman, John A. Abrahams, Eric A. Crutchfield, and David R. Stevenson, *Nonprofit Almanac 1996–1997: Dimensions of the Independent Sector* (San Francisco: Jossey-Bass Publishers, 1996), 234.

27. Robert Wuthnow, *Sharing the Journey* (Princeton: Princeton University Press, 1994), 45, 71, 73–74, cited in Rosenblum, *Membership and Morals*, 359–60.

28. Amy Gutmann, "Freedom of Association: An Introductory Essay," in *Freedom of Association*, ed. Amy Gutmann (Princeton: Princeton University Press, 1998), 3–32, at 5.

29. Michael Walzer's account of monopoly and domination in *Spheres of Justice: A Defense of Pluralism and Equality* (New York: Basic Books, 1983) is right on target in this respect.

30. Jon Van Til, *Growing Civil Society: From Nonprofit Sector to Third Space* (Bloomington: Indiana University Press, 2000), 290–91.

31. Rosenblum, *Membership and Morals*, 186.

32. I draw here on an analysis of goods I develop in Mark E. Warren, "Democratic Theory and Self-Transformation," *American Political Science Review* 86 (1992):8–23.

Chapter Two
Approaches to Association

1. Rawls, *A Theory of Justice*, 472.

2. Putnam, *Making Democracy Work*, 89–90.

3. Sandel, *Democracy and Its Discontents*.

4. Iris Marion Young, "Polity and Group Difference: A Critique of the Ideal of Universal Citizenship," *Ethics* 99 (1989): 250–74.

5. Cohen and Rogers, "Secondary Associations and Democratic Governance," 44–46.

6. Hirst, *Associative Democracy*.

7. See, e.g., Gutmann, "Freedom of Association"; and Daniel A. Bell, "Civil Society versus Civic Virtue," both in *Freedom of Association*, ed. Amy Gutmann (Princeton: Princeton University Press, 1998), 239–72.

8. Rosenblum, *Membership and Morals*, 15.

9. Ibid., 26; cf. 285.

10. Ibid., 15–17.

11. Alan Wolfe, Review of Nancy Rosenblum, *Membership and Morals: The Personal Uses of Pluralism in America*, *New Republic*, June 1, 1998: 39, 36–40.

12. Stephen Macedo, "Community, Diversity, and Civic Education: Toward a Liberal Political Science of Group Life," *Social Philosophy and Policy Foundation* 13 (Winter 1996): 240–68.

13. Tamir, "Revisiting the Civic Sphere," 218.

14. Ibid., 218.

15. Ibid., 223–25.

16. Cf. Claus Offe's critique of Cohen and Rogers view that the "artifactuality" of associations also makes them malleable by the state, in "Some Skeptical Considerations on the Malleability of Representative Institutions," in *Associations and Democracy*, ed. Eric Olin Wright (New York: Verso, 1995) 114–32.

17. Tamir, "Revisiting the Civic Sphere," 232–35.

18. Charles Taylor, *Sources of the Self* (Cambridge: Harvard University Press, 1989).

19. Francis Fukuyama, *Trust: The Social Virtues and the Creation of Prosperity* (New York: Free Press, 1995). See also my critique of Fukuyama in "Democratic Theory and Trust," in *Democracy and Trust*, ed. Mark E. Warren (Cambridge: Cambridge University Press, 1999), 310–45, at 318–29.

20. Michael Walzer, "On Involuntary Association," in *Freedom of Association*, ed. Amy Gutmann (Princeton: Princeton University Press, 1998), 64–74.

21. Cf. Macedo, "Community, Diversity, and Civic Education."

22. Michael Walzer, "Michael Sandel's America," delivered at the McDonough Symposium, Georgetown University Law Center, April 25, 1997.

23. Michael Walzer, "The Civil Society Argument," in *Dimensions of Radical Democracy*, ed. Chantal Mouffe (London: Verso, 1992), 89–107.

24. Walzer, *Spheres of Justice*, chaps. 1, 12.

25. Bell, "Civil Society versus Civic Virtue," 239–40.

26. Mark E. Warren, "What Is Political?" *Journal of Theoretical Politics* 11 (April 1999): 207–31.

27. Andrew Szasz, "Progress through Mischief: The Social Movement Alternative to Secondary Associations," in *Associations and Democracy*, ed. Eric Olin Wright (New York: Verso, 1995), 148–56.

28. Soifer, *Law and the Company We Keep*, 82.

29. Ibid., 35.

30. This point is fundamental to Cohen and Arato's approach to associations in *Civil Society and Political Theory*, chaps. 9–10.

31. Rosenblum, *Membership and Morals*, 36–40

32. Ibid., 57.

33. Ibid., chaps. 7–8.

34. Ibid., 55.

35. Rawls, *A Theory of Justice*, 467–72.

36. Rosenblum, *Membership and Morals*, 61.

37. Kateb, "The Value of Association."

38. Stuart White, "Freedom of Association and the Right to Exclude," *Journal of Political Philosophy* 5 (December, 1997), 373–91.

39. Both Gutmann, "An Introductory Essay," and Rosenblum, *Membership and Morals*, make this point.

40. This is the essence of Justice Brennan's majority opinion in *Roberts v. Jaycees*, which compelled the Jaycees to admit women. *Roberts, Acting Commissioner, Minnesota Department of Human Rights, et. al. v. United States Jaycees*, 468 U.S. 609 (1984). Some liberal commentators argue that the case for state intervention becomes stronger as possibilities for exit from association diminish.

See, e.g., Rosenblum, *Membership and Morals*, 45; Stuart White, "Trade Union-ism in a Liberal State," in *Freedom of Association*, ed. Amy Gutmann (Princeton: Princeton University Press, 1998), 330–56.

41. Alexis de Tocqueville, *Democracy in America*. 2 vols., trans. George Law-rence, ed. J. P. Mayer (Garden City, NY: Doubleday, 1969).

42. I take this term from C. B. Macpherson, *The Life and Times of Liberal Democracy* (Oxford: Oxford University Press, 1977).

43. Robert Dahl, *A Preface to Democratic Theory* (Chicago: University of Chicago Press, 1956); cf. David Truman, *The Governmental Process: Political Interests and Public Opinion* (New York: Knopf, 1971). For a short history of the American pluralist view of the political functions of voluntary associa-tions, see John W. Chapman, "Voluntary Association and the Political Theory ofPluralism," in *Voluntary Associations*, NOMOS XI, ed. J. Roland Pennock and John W. Chapman (New York: Atherton Press, 1969), 87–118, esp. 103–6.

44. Almond and Verba, *The Civic Culture*; cf. Edward Shils, *Political Develop-ment in the New States* (The Hague: Mouton, 1965).

45. James Coleman, *Foundations of Social Theory* (Cambridge: Harvard Uni-versity Press, 1990), chap. 5.

46. Putnam, *Making Democracy Work*, 174.

47. Talcott Parsons likewise emphasized the reciprocity inherent in horizontal association, in contrast to traditional vertical hierarchies, as central to democratiz-ing effects. *The System of Modern Societies* (Englewood Cliffs, NJ: Prentice-Hall, 1971), 24–26.

48. These effects are mentioned repeatedly in the literature, although with vari-ations. Nancy Rosenblum, for example, notes the roles associations play in culti-vating political skills and norms of reciprocity. In addition, she is especially inter-ested in "voice," or the capacity of an association to represent the interests and concerns of its members. *Membership and Morals*, 61–65, chap. 6.

49. Here I rely on the distinctions developed by Jürgen Habermas, *The Theory of Communicative Action*, vol. 2, trans. Thomas McCarthy (Boston: Beacon Press, 1987), and refined by Cohen and Arato, *Civil Society and Political Theory*, as well as by Habermas, *Between Facts and Norms*.

50. Held, *Models of Democracy*, chap. 6.

51. This possibility is suggested by the finding that individuals' levels of associ-ational activity are closely related to their race and class. See Henry E. Brady, Kay L. Schlozman, Sidney Verba, and Laurel Elms, "Who Bowls? Class, Race, and Changing Participatory Equality," presented at the Annual Meeting of the American Political Science Association, September 1998; cf. Rosenblum, *Member-ship and Morals*, 63.

52. Cf. Warren, "What Is Political?"

53. Hodgkinson, et. al., *Nonprofit Almanac, 1996–1997*, 234, 257–59.

54. Julian Wolpert, "Civil Society and Governance in a Regional and Commu-nity Context," presented at the Conference on Civil Society in the United States, Georgetown University, June 1999.

55. This kind of market analogy drove Joseph Schumpeter's elite-pluralist conception of democracy in *Capitalism, Socialism, and Democracy* (New York: Harper and Row, 1942), 232–302. Carl Schmitt was the first to note the contradiction between a liberal conception of parliamentary judgment based on discourse and a "democratic," marketlike aggregative mechanism of judgment in *The Crisis of Parliamentary Democracy*, trans. Ellen Kennedy (Cambridge: MIT Press, 1985).

56. Habermas, *Between Facts and Norms*, chap. 8; cf. Offe, *Modernity and the State*, chap. 2.

57. Will Kymlicka, "Ethnic Associations and Democratic Citizenship," in *Freedom of Association*, ed. Amy Gutmann (Princeton: Princeton University Press, 1998), 177–213.

58. Warren, "Democratic Theory and Trust."

59. Szasz, "Progress through Mischief." Cf. Nancy Fraser, "Rethinking the Public Sphere," in *Habermas and the Public Sphere*, ed. Craig Calhoun (Cambridge: MIT Press, 1992) 109–42.

60. Warren, "Democratic Theory and Self-Transformation." In *Making Democracy Work*, Putnam associates these desirable consequences with social capital by definition, a view he has since modified. See Robert D. Putnam, "The Prosperous Community: Social Capital and Public Life," *American Prospect* 13 (Spring 1993): 35–42. The Mafia, for example, generates social capital in the sense that it creates powers of collective action through association. But whatever trust and reciprocity is created by association comes at the expense of trust and reciprocity in the broader society.

61. Rosenblum, *Membership and Morals*, chap. 8.

62. I borrow the distinction from Robert K. Merton, *Theoretical Sociology: Five Essays, Old and New* (New York: The Free Press, 1967), chap. 3. Cf. Rosenblum, Introduction to *Membership and Morals*; and Gutmann, "Freedom of Association."

63. Hannah Arendt, *The Human Condition* (Chicago: University of Chicago Press, 1958).

64. Habermas, *Moral Consciousness and Communicative Action*.

65. Cf. ibid.

66. Habermas, *Between Facts and Norms*, 162–68.

Chapter Three
The Concept of Association

1. The distinction between primary and secondary associations seems to have been introduced by Charles Horton Cooley, *Human Nature and Social Order* (New York: Schocken Books, 1964). Cf. Gutmann, "Freedom of Association," 10.

2. One finds this assumption in Theda Skocpol's recent work, "Associations without Members, *American Prospect* 45 (July–August 1999): 66–73. Still, many of Skocpol's concerns are well taken: she is especially concerned with the skewed class basis of association, combined with a shift away from the democratic ethic

of "doing with" to the implied noblesse oblige of "doing for" (exemplified by Washington, DC–based service and advocacy groups). Although the older forms of national federated membership organizations (such as the Knights of Columbus and the Elks) are clearly diminished in importance, as an empirical matter it remains to be seen whether new forms of association are introducing new forms of "doing with."

3. Ferdinand Tönnies, *Community and Association* (1887; reprint, London: Routledge and Kegan Paul, 1955).

4. John Locke, *Political Writings of John Locke*, ed. David Wootton (New York: Penguin Books, 1993), 186–210.

5. Ibid., 209–10.

6. Ibid., 202.

7. John Locke, *Two Treatises of Government* (Cambridge: Cambridge University Press, 1963).

8. Adam Seligman, *The Idea of Civil Society* (Princeton: Princeton University Press, 1992): 23–25.

9. Adam Ferguson, *An Essay on the History of Civil Society* (Cambridge: Cambridge University Press, 1995).

10. Tocqueville, *Democracy in America* 2: 562, 564.

11. Ibid. 1:14–15.

12. Emile Durkheim, *Professional Ethics and Civic Morals* (London: Routledge and Kegan Paul, 1957).

13. G. D. H. Cole, *Social Theory* (New York: Frederick A. Stokes, 1920), 37.

14. Ibid., 26; cf. Rosenblum, *Membership and Morals*, 341.

15. Cf. Cris Shore, "Community," in *The Blackwell Dictionary of Social Thought*, ed. William Outhwaite and Tom Bottomore (Oxford: Basil Blackwell, 1994), 98–99.

16. Hirst, *Associative Democracy*, 49–56.

17. Cohen and Rogers, "Association and Democracy." Cf. Claus Offe's criticisms in "Some Skeptical Considerations on the Malleability of Representative Institutions."

18. Soifer, *Law and the Company We Keep*. Cf. Kateb, "The Value of Association."

19. S. N. Eisenstadt and L. Roniger, *Patrons, Clients, and Friends: Interpersonal Relations and the Structure of Trust in Society* (Cambridge: Cambridge University Press, 1984).

20. Cole, *Social Theory*, 49.

21. Ibid., 54–55. See Hirst's criticisms of Cole's functionalism in *Associative Democracy*, 45–49.

22. Parsons, *The System of Modern Societies*, 22–26. In earlier work Parsons does not distinguish associational relations at this level of generality. In *The Social System* (New York: Free Press, 1951), 100, for example, he defines association simply as an organization in which "expressive interests have primacy" and which has achieved a rule-based level of formal organization. That is, association is not a generic type of social organization but is only another kind of rule-based organization. The notion that modern societies are distinguished from premodern socie-

ties by the differentiation of these three types of organization has become central to much contemporary social theory. Parsons's approach in particular has been retrieved by Niklas Luhmann, *The Differentiation of Society*, trans. Stephen Holmes (New York: Columbia University Press, 1982); and Habermas, *The Theory of Communicative Action*, vol. 2.

23. Parsons, *The System of Modern Societies*, 22.

24. Habermas, *The Theory of Communicative Action*, vol. 2.

25. Parsons, *The System of Modern Societies*, 24.

26. Cf. Cohen and Arato, *Civil Society and Political Theory*, 461–62.

27. Cf. Amitai Etzioni's distinctions in *The Active Society: A Theory of Societal and Political Process* (New York: Free Press, 1968):

> There are three basic analytic ways in which social atoms may be built into social molecules: A relationship may be normative, utilitarian, or coercive. A normative relationship entails shared values and norms; the relating actors treat each other as goals, and their mutual commitments are non-rational. Utilitarian relations entail a complementary interest; the actions treat each other as means, and commitments are rational. Coercion entails the use, or threatened use, of means of violence by one actor against one or more other actors. Actors treat each other as objects, and the commitment may be either rational or non-rational. (96)

Etzioni's distinctions parallel Parsons's and—with the exception of his equation between rationality and instrumental reason—anticipate Habermas's.

28. Parsons, *The System of Modern Societies*, 92.

29. Ibid., 24.

30. Ibid., 94–98.

31. The most visible exception to this trend, Parsons notes, is in the high degree of coincidence of race and class for African Americans. So while the "structural outline of 'citizenship' in the new societal community is complete," it is not yet fully "institutionalized," "the present salience of which is an index of the importance of the new structures: race and poverty." Ibid., 93–94, 115.

32. Ibid., 24.

33. Cf. Sandel, *Democracy and Its Discontents*. Walzer, "On Involuntary Association," misunderstands this point as well.

34. Parsons, *The System of Modern Societies*, 14.

35. Ibid., 25.

36. This point is essential to Habermas's analysis of the normative bases of constitutional procedures in *Between Facts and Norms*, esp. chap. 7.

37. Benjamin Barber, *The Conquest of Politics: Liberal Philosophy in Democratic Times* (Princeton: Princeton University Press, 1988).

38. Parsons, *The System of Modern Societies*, 25–26, 105, 116.

39. Habermas, *The Theory of Communicative Action*, vol. 2.

40. Cohen and Arato, *Civil Society and Political Theory*, 471–87.

41. Ibid., chap. 9.

42. Cf. Jean Cohen's construction in "Interpreting the Notion of Civil Society," in *Toward a Global Civil Society*, ed. Michael Walzer (Providence, RI, and Oxford: Berghahn Books), 35–40.

Chapter Four
The Democratic Effects of Association

1. These two ideals are broadly shared features of most democratic theories—although some are more likely to emphasize power mechanisms (as in those theories in the tradition of Bentham, James Mill, and Schumpeter), whereas others give pride of place to communicative processes of collective judgment (as do theories in the tradition of Kant, John Stuart Mill, Dewey, and Habermas). Although most democratic theories differentiate between problems of power and problems of collective judgment and decision, they differ on (*a*) the extent to which ideals of equality ought to be mitigated by other goods, such as liberty and economic welfare; (*b*) the question of who is included in the political unit to which ideals of equality apply; (*c*) the extent to which the ideal of equal participation in political judgment is mitigated by unequal capacities of citizens, problems of scale, and limits of knowledge, time, and other political resources; (*d*) the extent to which participation is an inherent rather than an instrumental good; and (*e*) the question of what domains of decision ought to be organized by democratic means. While these differences are crucial to the meaning of democracy, it is sufficient for purposes of this chapter to focus on the broadly shared view that democracy entails equal distributions of power of one sort or another as well as inclusion in collective judgment. On the other hand, theories that fail to include both dimensions in democracy—specifically, the view that democracy is simply a mechanism for aggregating individual preferences by means of the vote—are simply uninteresting. See, for example, William H. Riker, *Liberalism against Populism* (San Francisco: Freeman, 1982), 5: "Voting . . . is the central act of democracy." Such a conception excludes collective judgment from democracy by definition, while taking individual preferences as given. It thus excludes by definition questions of the potential impact of association on the dispositions of individuals, as well as in constituting public spheres of judgment.

2. With the development of deliberative theories of democracy, treating autonomy as the fundamental norm of democracy is becoming more common. See Habermas, *Between Facts and Norms*; David Held, *Models of Democracy*, chap. 9; Robert Dahl, *Democracy and Its Critics* (New Haven: Yale University Press, 1989), chap. 7; Jennifer Nedelsky, "Reconceiving Rights as Relationship," *Review of Constitutional Studies* 1 (1993): 1–16. For development, see Mark E. Warren, "What Should We Expect from More Democracy? Radically Democratic Responses to Politics," *Political Theory* 24 (1996): 241–70; Warren, "What Is Political?"; and Mark E. Warren, "The Self in Discursive Democracy," in *The Cambridge Companion to Habermas*, ed. Stephen K. White (Cambridge: Cambridge University Press, 1995), 167–200.

3. For analysis, see Warren, "What Is Political?"

4. The following description borrows from Warren, "The Self in Discursive Democracy," which reconstructs Habermas's conception of individual autonomy.

5. Habermas, *The Theory of Communicative Action* 2:98–99, 102–5.

6. Jürgen Habermas, *Postmetaphysical Thinking*, trans. William Mark Hohengarten (Cambridge: MIT Press, 1992), 182.

7. Habermas, *The Theory of Communicative Action* 2:98–99; cf. Arendt, *The Human Condition*, p. 5.

8. Habermas, *Moral Consciousness and Communicative Action*, 199.

9. Habermas, *Postmetaphysical Thinking*, 190–91.

10. Ibid., 189–191.

11. John Dryzek, *Democracy in Capitalist Times* lists authenticity together with scope and domain as the three dimensions in which democracy can be expanded. Dahl, *Democracy and Its Critics* is exemplary of the approaches that list conditions of democracy. Among these are adequate education and information, combined with rights protections. Both are contributions to the authenticity of individuals' votes, expressions, and other political activities. See chap. 7.

12. Habermas uses the terms *political autonomy* as well as *public autonomy* in *Between Facts and Norms*. Here I use the term *political autonomy* because I mean to refer to *political* publics rather than other kinds of publics—literary, artistic, religious, and so on. Although Habermas is the first democratic theorist to develop the concept of political autonomy systematically, the concept has a long history within democratic theory, making its first appearance in Rousseau's *Social Contract*, which introduced the idea that individual autonomy is completed by the General Will. Kant, in his essay "What Is Called Enlightenment?" in Immanuel Kant, *Kant's Political Writings*, ed. Hans Reiss (Cambridge: Cambridge University Press, 1970), makes the case for freedom of public argumentation on the grounds that no single individual has access to all the reasons and evidence required of public judgments. The skeptical epistemology that underwrites John Stuart Mill's defense of liberty of conscience and speech in *On Liberty* (London: J. W. Parker, 1859) includes the notion that political judgments have no correlates in individual wisdom or expertise. Hannah Arendt provides an intriguing reading of Kant's *Critique of Judgment* in *Lectures on Kant's Political Philosophy* (Chicago: University of Chicago Press, 1982). Here she notes the inherent limitations of individual perspective in judging objects (political decisions) that are themselves effects of interactions. See also Barber, *The Conquest of Politics*; and Ronald Beiner, *Political Judgment* (Chicago: University of Chicago Press, 1983) for similar conceptions. For an analysis, see Mark E. Warren, "Nonfoundationalism and Democratic Judgment," *Current Perspectives in Social Theory* 14 (1994): 151–82.

13. This is why, as Habermas puts it, the "idea of self-legislation by citizens . . . should not be reduced to the *moral* self-legislation of *individual* persons." *Between Facts and Norms*, 121.

14. The following paragraphs are adapted from Warren, "Nonfoundationalism and Democratic Judgment."

15. Hannah Arendt, *Between Past and Future* (New York: Viking, 1968), 246.

16. Ibid., 239.

17. Ibid., 242.

18. Idid., 241.

19. Showing this is, of course, Habermas's project in *The Theory of Communicative Action*.

20. For analysis of the failings of epistemological models of political authority, see Mark E. Warren, "Deliberative Democracy and Authority," *American Political Science Review* 90 (1996): 46–60.

21. Habermas, *Between Facts and Norms*, 364.

22. Cf. Axel Honneth, *The Struggle for Recognition* (Cambridge: MIT Press, 1995).

23. Cf. Cohen and Arato, *Civil Society and Political Theory*, chap. 9.

24. This case is nicely developed by Michael Schudson, *The Good Citizen: A History of American Civic Life* (New York: Free Press, 1998), 287–92.

25. Habermas, *Between Facts and Norms*, 103–4. Cf. Tocqueville's view that the right to association is constitutive of freedoms of speech and assembly, which are in turn constitutive of association. *Democracy in America* 1:189–90.

26. Habermas, *Between Facts and Norms*, 89. The "principle of democracy," on Habermas's construction, is constituted by the close relationship between communicative power and the laws that define rights. In his terms, the

> key idea is that the principle of democracy derives from the interpenetration of the discourse principle and the legal form. I understand this interpenetration as a *logical genesis of rights*, which one can reconstruct in a stepwise fashion. One begins by applying the discourse principle to the general right to liberties—a right constitutive for the legal form as such—and ends by legally institutionalizing the conditions for a discursive exercise of political autonomy. By means of this political autonomy, the private autonomy that was at first abstractly posited can retroactively assume an elaborated legal shape. Hence the principle of democracy can only appear as the heart of a *system* of rights. (121)

27. Tocqueville, *Democracy in America* 1:14.

28. Ibid. 2:517.

29. Ibid. 2:511.

30. Ibid. 1:14.

31. See, for example, Verba, Schlozman, and Brady, *Voice and Equality*, chap. 5; Carole Pateman, *Participation and Democratic Theory* (Cambridge: Cambridge University Press, 1970); Cohen and Rogers, "Secondary Associations and Democratic Governance," 43.

32. Cohen and Rogers, "Secondary Associations and Democratic Governance," 42–43; Hirst, *Associative Democracy*, 34–40; James Bohman, "Democracy as Inquiry, Inquiry as Democratic: Pragmatism, Social Science, and the Cognitive Division of Labor," *American Journal of Political Science* 43 (1999): 590–607. Cf. Warren, "Deliberative Democracy and Authority."

33. Verba, Schlozman, and Brady, *Voice and Equality*, 17–18, 325–33, 366; Rosenblum, *Membership and Morals*, 206.

34. Cole, *Social Theory*, 34–35, 77; Cohen and Rogers, "Secondary Associations and Democratic Governance," 43.

35. Benjamin Barber, *Strong Democracy* (Berkeley: University of California Press, 1984); Pateman, *Participation and Democratic Theory*.

36. Habermas, *Between Facts and Norms*; Jane Mansbridge, "A Deliberative Perspective on Neocorporatism," in *Associations and Democracy*, ed. Erik Olin Wright (London: Verso, 1995), 133–47.

37. Sandel, *Democracy and Its Discontents*; Bellah et al., *The Good Society*.

38. William Galston lists many of these as civic virtues in *Liberal Purposes* (Cambridge: Cambridge University Press, 1991), 221–24.

39. Rosenblum, *Membership and Morals*, 60.

40. Verba, Schlozman, and Brady, *Voice and Equality*, chap. 17; cf. Skocpol, "Associations without Members."

41. Verba, Schlozman, and Brady, *Voice and Equality*, 514.

42. Gutmann, "Freedom of Association," 25.

43. Cohen and Rogers, "Secondary Associations and Democratic Governance," 43–44. This cluster of virtues is sometimes associated with the claim that democracy requires tolerance. The claim is useful, however, only if we distinguish two meanings of tolerance, since one is necessary for democracy and the other is not. What democracy requires is that individuals recognize the claims of others— that is, recognition *as claims* within democratic processes and discourses. This notion all too often (especially in neoconservative rhetoric) spills over into a strong notion of tolerance: that to tolerate the substance of another position is a sign of moral indifference, and amounts to a substantive commitment to the "good" of moral pluralism. Democracy does not require tolerance in this sense, but rather the "process tolerance" that enables disagreements to be mediated by democratic means. These issues are confused in a widely cited article in which Kuklinski et al. report on experiments in which they find that deliberation and tolerance trade off against one another: more deliberation reduces tolerance. What they measure as "tolerance," however, is substantive agreement, which diminishes as individuals find out more about others' positions. The trade-off is a threat to democracy, however, *only* if it diminishes "process tolerance"—that is, the willingness of individuals to recognize the rights of others to speak and defend their positions even when they disagree, and then to resolve disputes through democratic means. In any case, the experiment described in this article is flawed from the perspective of deliberative democracy, since the authors use a questionnaire that provokes respondents to think about issues, but does not have them actually deliberate with those who hold positions contrary to their own. The experiment thus fails to measure the transformative dimensions of deliberation expected by deliberative theories of democracy. See James H. Kuklinski, Ellen Riggle, Victor Ottati, Norbert Schwarz, and Robert S. Wyer, Jr, "The Cognitive and Affective Bases of Political Tolerance Judgments," *American Journal of Political Science* 35 (1991): 1–27.

44. Rosenblum, *Membership and Morals*, 59.

45. Ibid., 59, quoting from Mark Granovetter, "Economic Action and Social Structure: The Problem of Embeddedness," *American Journal of Sociology* 91 (1985): 492, 481–510.

46. Rosenblum, *Membership and Morals*, 61.

47. Putnam, *Making Democracy Work*, chap. 6.

48. Orlando Patterson, "Liberty against the Democratic State: On the Historical and Contemporary Sources of American Distrust," in *Democracy and Trust*. ed. Mark E. Warren (Cambridge: Cambridge University Press, 1999), pp. 151–207.

49. Rosenblum, *Membership and Morals*, 61–62.

50. Cohen and Rogers, "Secondary Associations and Democratic Governance," 43–44.

51. The specificity of conditions that enable deliberative resolutions of political conflict within interest groups is noted by Mansbridge in arguing for the deliberative potentials of neocorporatist arrangements in "A Deliberative Perspective on Neocorporatism," 144: "Today, few interest associations in the United States or Europe institutionalize any formal deliberative processes among their membership, let alone deliberative processes designed to promote identification with the public good." Unfortunately, Mansbridge notes, "no political scientist has empirically investigated the deliberative functions of the system of interest representation, including groups outside, under, and partially under a state umbrella."

52. Cf. ibid.

53. Parsons, *The System of Modern Societies*, 25.

54. Joshua Cohen, "Procedure and Substance in Deliberative Democracy," in *Democracy and Difference: Contesting the Boundaries of the Political*, ed. Seyla Benhabib (Princeton: Princeton University Press, 1996), 95–119, at 112–13.

55. Gutmann, "Freedom of Association," 25.

56. Habermas, *The Structural Transformation of the Public Sphere* and *Between Facts and Norms*; Cohen and Arato, *Civil Society and Political Theory*; Arendt, *Lectures on Kant's Political Philosophy*.

57. John Dewey, *The Political Writings*, eds. Debra Morris and Ian Shapiro (Indianapolis, IN: Hackett Publishing, 1993), 244; cf. Durkheim, *Professional Ethics and Civic Morals*; Hirst, *Associative Democracy*, 34–40.

58. Habermas, *Between Facts and Norms*, 360.

59. Thus Seyla Benhabib notes that the reason that deliberative models of democracy do not, and need not, operate with the fiction of a general deliberative assembly is that they privilege

> a *plurality of modes of association* in which all affected can have the right to articulate their point of view. These can range from political parties to citizens' initiatives, to social movements, to voluntary associations, to consciousness-raising groups, and the like. *It is through the interlocking net of these multiple forms of associations, networks, and organizations that an anonymous "public conversation" results. It is central to the model of deliberative democracy that it privileges such a public sphere of mutually interlocking and overlapping networks and associations of deliberation, contestation, and argumentation.*

"Toward a Deliberative Model of Democratic Legitimacy," in *Democracy and Difference: Contesting the Boundaries of the Political*, ed. Seyla Benhabib (Princeton: Princeton University Press, 1996), 67–94, at 73–74.

60. Cohen and Arato, *Civil Society and Political Theory*, 530–31.

61. Cf. Habermas, *Between Facts and Norms*, 359.

62. Cf. Cohen and Rogers, "Secondary Associations and Democratic Governance," 42–43.

63. Habermas, *Between Facts and Norms*, 359.

64. Ibid., 360.

65. As Habermas puts it, "Those actors who are the carriers of the public sphere put forward 'texts' that always reveal the same subtext, which refers to the critical function of the public sphere in general. Whatever the manifest content of

their public utterances, the performative meaning of such public discourse at the same time actualizes the function of an undistorted political public sphere as such." Ibid., 369.

66. Rosenblum, *Membership and Morals*, 205–11.

67. Ibid., 208.

68. Ibid., 206.

69. Fraser, "Rethinking the Public Sphere," 109–42, at 123–24.

70. As Habermas rightly notes, in "the course of the nineteenth and twentieth centuries, the universalist discourses of the bourgeois public sphere could no longer immunize themselves against a critique from within. The labor movement and feminism, for example, were able to join these discourses in order to shatter the structures that had initially constituted them as 'the other' of a bourgeois public sphere." *Between Facts and Norms*, 374.

71. The pluralist framework is dominant in Verba, Schlozman, and Brady, *Voice and Equality*, which focuses on the impact of participation in voluntary associations on representation—who is represented, in what proportion, on what issues, and with what intensity.

72. Cohen and Rogers "Secondary Associations and Democratic Governance," 43.

73. Verba, Schlozman, and Brady, *Voice and Equality*, chap. 10.

74. Cohen and Rogers "Secondary Associations and Democratic Governance," 43.

75. Skocpol, "Associations without Members."

76. Verba, Schlozman, and Brady, *Voice and Equality*, chap. 16; cf. Patterson, "Liberty against the Democratic State."

77. In "Associations without Members," Theda Skocpol argues that over the course of the twentieth century the associational landscape of America has transformed from large-scale, national membership associations to advocacy associations. The former linked local projects and communities to national levels of organization, and thus cut across classes. Advocacy associations, however, rely on anonymous attachments organized by professionals; they draw their membership from a wealthier, more educated strata. While there are more small groups devoted to local projects than ever before, Skocpol argues that the organizational linkages to national levels are missing, reflecting a new parochialism as well as a lowered capacity for political leverage among the less educated, less wealthy. In my view, however, the jury is not in. It is quite clear—as Skocpol's work shows—that the older forms of national association such as the Masons, the Elks, the American Legion, and the Knights of Columbus are in decline and are being replaced by a multitude of local groups. This transformation increases parochialism, however, only if these groups are parochially based—that is, devoted only to local issues. It decreases political leverage among the less educated and less wealthy only if local groups fail to include or develop coalitions with groups that represent less educated and less wealthy people. At least on the face of it, neither condition describes the current American associational landscape relative to a more egalitarian past.

78. Max Weber, "Classes, Status Groups, and Parties," in *Selections From Max Weber*, ed. W. G. Runciman, trans. Eric Matthews (Cambridge: Cambridge University Press, 1978), 57–61.

79. Rosenblum, *Membership and Morals*, 341.

80. Tocqueville, *Democracy in America* 2:692.

81. Ibid., 516.

82. Ibid., 696.

83. Hodgkinson et al., *Nonprofit Almanac 1996–1997*.

84. Rosenblum, *Membership and Morals*, 35.

85. Hirst, *Associative Democracy*, 20, 167; Cohen and Rogers, "Secondary Associations and Democratic Governance," 45; Schmitter and Streek, "Community, Market, State—and Associations?"; Offe, *Modernity and the State*; Dryzek, *Democracy in Capitalist Times*; Cohen and Arato, *Civil Society and Political Theory*; cf. Cole, *Social Theory*.

86. Warren, "Democratic Theory and Trust."

87. Cf. Cohen and Rogers "Secondary Associations and Democratic Governance"; Phillipe Schmitter, "The Irony of Modern Democracy and the Viability of Efforts to Reform Its Practice," in *Associations and Democracy*, ed. Eric Olin Wright (New York: Verso, 1995), 167–83; Offe, "Some Skeptical Considerations."

88. Hirst, *Associative Democracy*, 75.

89. The problem, as Claus Offe puts it, "consists precisely in that solutions of such coordination problems are merely (ex post) given as systemic *conditions of continued existence*, not as (ex ante) *motives for action*; that is to say, there is no agency that could produce such motives for coordinative action in both legitimate and reliable fashion or otherwise assume responsibility for solving this task." *Modernity and the State*, 10.

90. Günther Teubner, "Substantive and Reflexive Elements in Modern Law," *Law and Society Review* 17 (1983): 272, 239–85.

91. Habermas, *Between Facts and Norms*, 355.

92. Cohen and Rogers "Secondary Associations and Democratic Governance," 44.

93. Cohen and Arato, *Civil Society and Political Theory*, 482.

94. Jürgen Habermas, *Law and Morality*, vol. 8 of The Tanner Lectures on Human Values, (Salt Lake City: University of Utah Press, 1988), 231.

95. Cf. Tamir, "Revisiting the Civic Sphere," 224.

96. Verba, Schlozman, and Brady, *Voice and Equality*, 115, 517–18.

97. Cf. Walzer, *Spheres of Justice*.

98. Teubner, "Substantive and Reflexive Elements in Modern Law," 275.

99. Cf. Offe, *Modernity and the State*, chap. 2; Jürgen Habermas, *Legitimation Crisis*, trans. Thomas McCarthy (Boston: Beacon Press, 1975).

Chapter Five
The Associational Terrain: Distinctions That Make a Difference

1. The most interesting challenge, Albert O. Hirschman's important *Exit, Voice, and Loyalty: Responses to Decline in Firms, Organizations, and States* (Cambridge: Harvard University Press, 1970), has come from outside of democratic theory. Hirschman's account makes a partial appearance in Samuel Bowles and Herbert Gintis, *Democracy and Capitalism: Property, Community, and the Con-*

traditions of Modern Social Thought (New York: Basic Books, 1986), which argues that markets ought to be eliminated because they allow problems to be solved through exit from collective decisions rather than voice, thus undermining a "vibrant democratic culture." Bowles and Gintis in this way link nonvoluntary association to democratic participation. Without dealing directly with the relationship between democracy and associations, Michael Walzer in "On Involuntary Association" points out that many forms of associations that are nonvoluntary—family, culture and ethnicity, associations formed on the basis of moral obligations, and state membership, for example—are nonetheless central to democracy.

2. The compulsory qualities of states exist even though most states maintain a formal right of exit, since there are no equivalent rights of entrance into other states. The difficulties of establishing legal residence in another state combine with the high costs for most people of leaving family and friends, culture, language, and other securities. Of course, the costs of exit are relative, and will look better under the all-too-common circumstances of desperate impoverishment or physical threat in one's home country.

3. Because I am interested in the structural consequences of voluntary association for democracy, I avoid those motivation-based conceptions that view voluntary association as the vehicle for volunteerism. See, e.g., David Horton Smith, "Altruism, Volunteers, and Volunteerism," *Journal of Voluntary Action Research* 10 (1981): 21–36. Cf. discussion by Jon Van Til, *Mapping the Third Sector: Volunteerism in a Changing Social Economy* (New York: Foundation Center, 1988), p. 1.

4. Walzer, "On Involuntary Association."

5. Ibid., 67.

6. Rosenblum, *Membership and Morals*, 84.

7. 486 U.S. 609 (1984).

8. Rosenblum, *Membership and Morals*, 158

9. Rosenblum mentions the issue of the Jaycee's possible monopoly over business opportunities, but simply denies that it exists. Ibid., 169. While the Jaycees' monopoly does not exist in metropolitan areas in the United States, the Jaycees remain an almost obligatory association for young men seeking business opportunities in smaller cities and towns.

10. Thus, Rosenblum objects to government regulation that would "curtail the voices" of corporations as an incoherent, selective silencing. Ibid., 224–29. She dismisses the common fear that accumulations of capital undermine self-government, although she does give it enough credence to suggest that whatever imbalances exist should be remedied not by limiting corporate voices but by increasing the voices of others. While on the face of it, the solution seems reasonable—a market solution to political voice—it overlooks the fact that corporations are uniquely privileged in a free market economy because they benefit directly from the flow of productive resources. This location not only provides resources for voice, but also the blackmail power of exiting with socially necessary resources. No other kind of association enjoys these advantages. A deliberative arena in which economic powers are not counterbalanced by political powers will lead not to a diverse pluralism of voices, but to a political marketplace saturated by corporate resources.

11. Ibid., 332.

12. Hirschman, *Exit, Voice, and Loyalty*, 34. In Hirschman's view, voluntary associations represent the optimal mix of voice and exit, for the reason that members are often loyal to the association, and if faced with conflicts will carry the burdens of voice. See 77, 120–21. Hirschman, I think, has an overly optimistic view of voluntary associations that he has based (presumably) on exemplary cases.

13. Warren, "What Should We Expect from More Democracy?"

14. Cf. Rosenblum, *Membership and Morals*, 356–59.

15. Hirschman, *Exit, Voice, and Loyalty*, 43.

16. Ibid., 37.

17. Ibid., 33.

18. Ibid., 47.

19. While radical democrats have always viewed authoritarian institutions within civil society and the economy as targets of democracy, on this formulation it is not their authoritarian nature per se that makes them targets, but rather their *compulsory* nature (and the implied power relations that attend compulsion). Still, authoritarian associations even with possibilities for exit do not provide promising or important opportunities for democracy. Nonetheless, the fact that voice and exit can trade off as means for disciplining and organizing suggests the possibility that markets might, after all, have a generic place in a radically democratic theory.

20. Warren, "What Is Political?"

21. Robert Michels, *Political Parties; A Sociological Study of the Oligarchical Tendencies of Modern Democracy*, trans. Eden Paul and Cedar Paul (New York: Collier Books, 1962).

22. Cf. Parsons, *The System of Modern Societies*, 25.

23. Hirschman, *Exit, Voice, and Loyalty*, 70. Hirschman fails to consider that people may exit political parties altogether, faced with two alternatives that are equally disagreeable. The cost, of course, is often little or no voice whatsoever—at least within party politics. There is no necessity that two parties can represent the range of political interests in the United States, nor have the parties demonstrated that their internal and informal brokerage of political differences is superior to more formal and institutionalized political mechanisms, such as exist in a multiparty parliamentary system.

24. Cf. Cole, *Social Theory*; Robert Dahl, *A Preface to Economic Democracy* (Berkeley and Los Angeles: University of California Press, 1985). Gutmann, "An Introductory Essay," 7, notes that legal regulation is justified if an association controls resources that people need—that is, if an association can, by virtue of its power, introduce elements of nonvoluntary association. Similarly, liberals have long argued that democracy internal to associations is not important as long as opportunities for exit exist. Cf. White, "Trade Unionism in a Liberal State," 349.

25. Seymour Martin Lipset, Martin A. Trow, and James S. Coleman argued in *Union Democracy: The Internal Politics of the International Typographical Union* (Glencoe, IL: Free Press, 1956) that increasing internal democracy also makes members more loyal to the organization, for the reasons that democracy allows leadership to be separated from the organizational process and identity, while it also allows members to experience a higher degree of ownership of union

policies and positions. As Hirschman might have predicted, internal democracy strengthens rather than weakens unions.

26. Hirschman, *Exit, Voice, and Loyalty*, 74.

27. Cf. my analysis of the inherent tensions between trust and politics: Warren, "Democratic Theory and Trust." In a very interesting and careful study of the relationship between group characteristics and the development of trust in Germany, Sweden, and the United States, Dietlind Stolle finds that in the homogeneous cultures of Germany and Sweden, homogeneous groups produce in-group trust rather than generalized trust. In the more diverse culture of the United States, in contrast, homogeneous groups tend to produce in-group trust that then extends to generalized trust. In addition, she finds that the "conversational breadth" of an association—that is, their communication about personal concerns, professional issues, neighborhood issues, and the like—is positively correlated with generalized trust. More narrowly focused groups—hobby groups, for example—tend to foster in-group trust. "Making Associations Work: Group Characteristics, Membership, and Generalized Trust," presented at the American Political Science Association Annual Meeting, 1998. Stolle's findings suggest that the contributions of associations to precivic virtues cannot be predicted on the basis of homogeneity alone, but are likely to be the effect of a combination of exit, functional location, and purpose. Her finding that the homogeneity of the surrounding culture affects the impact of association on in-group trust is highly suggestive: in diverse cultures, homogeneity may serve as a crucible of reciprocity and generalized trust by enabling a background of shared norms that could not otherwise be taken for granted. In homogeneous cultures, homogeneous associations may select for a status-insecure membership seeking the securities of in-group trust against the broader culture.

28. Rosenblum, *Membership and Morals*, 151.

29. Cohen, "Procedure and Substance in Deliberative Democracy," 111–13.

30. Although the revisions are not important for the uses I shall make of these distinctions in the present chapter, Habermas criticizes Parsons for overemphasizing the role of culture in social integration as well as for providing an account of modern societies that is overly harmonious and fails to account for "pathological patterns of development." See *The Theory of Communicative Action* 2:202–03.

31. I say "usually" because the state does not always have a monopoly over violence. Thus, gangs, organized crime, militias, and terrorist organizations can also make use of coercion to hold their associations together.

32. This is the central argument in Habermas's *Between Facts and Norms*.

33. Russell Jacoby, "Can We Talk? We'd Better—Or Else Multicultural America Is in Big Trouble," *Washington Post*, Sunday, June 26, 1994, C1–2.

34. Diego Gambetta, in " 'Claro!' An Essay on Discursive Machismo," in *Deliberative Democracy*, ed. Jon Elster (Cambridge: Cambridge University Press, 1998), 19–43, provides an interesting analysis of differences between cultures that value analytic knowledge (mostly Anglo-American cultures) and those that value "indexical knowledge" (mostly Mediterranean cultures, in which one responds to an assertion with "claro!"—that is, "of course I already knew that"). In an analytic culture, the fact that a person knows things in one area does not qualify him as an expert in other areas. In indexical cultures, knowledge in one area signi-

fies knowledge in all areas. Deliberation is especially difficult in indexical cultures because every assertion is a challenge to the entire person and personality of a partner in conversation. Admitting ignorance is tantamount to losing face. The result, ironically, is that people are talkative in private (in families, for example) because social orders are already established, but silent in more public arenas owing to the risks attending the uncertainties of status and the volatilities of public conversations. See esp. 31–37. Although Gambetta sees analytic cultures as more favorable to discourse, he may overlook a different kind of social barrier, namely, that agreement is itself a manifestation of solidarity that it is impolite to disrupt.

35. Habermas, *Between Facts and Norms*, 375.

36. Ibid., 374.

37. Ibid., 361.

38. The term is from Diego Gambetta, " 'Claro!' An Essay on Discursive Machismo."

39. Habermas, *Between Facts and Norms*, 361.

40. Cf. ibid., 375–76; Cole, *Social Theory*, 66.

41. This argument is developed by Dennis Thompson, "Mediated Corruption: The Case of the Keating Five," *American Political Science Review* 87 (1993), 369–81; and by Amy Gutmann and Dennis Thompson, *Democracy and Disagreement* (Cambridge: Harvard University Press), chap. 3.

42. Habermas, *Between Facts and Norms*, 375.

43. Habermas describes the dual possibilities of power distributions as follows:

> The principle of separation of state and society requires a civil society, that is, a network of voluntary associations and a political culture that are sufficiently detached from class structures. In this regard, the relation between social power and democracy is problematic. . . . Civil society is expected to absorb and neutralize the unequal distribution of social positions and the power differentials resulting from them, so that social power comes into play only insofar as it *facilitates* the exercise of civic autonomy and does not *restrict* it. I use the term "social power" as a measure for the possibilities that an actor has in his social relationships to assert his own will and interests, even against the opposition of others. Social power can both facilitate and restrict the formation of communicative power. As facilitative, the disposition over social resources means that the necessary material conditions for an autonomous exercise of equal liberties and communicative freedoms are satisfied. In political bargaining, for example, the involved parties must be able to make their threats or promises credible in light of their social power. As restrictive, the disposition over social power provides some parties with a privileged opportunity to influence the political process in such a way that their interests acquire a priority not in accord with equal civil rights. (Ibid., 175)

44. Following an analysis by Bernard Peters, Habermas notes that "for different policy fields, complex networks have arisen among public agencies and private organizations, business associations, labor unions, interest groups, and so on; these networks fulfill certain coordination functions in more or less opaque social sectors." But these groups, in part because they are limited by their coordination functions and the entanglements these bring, are also unlikely to contribute much to public sphere effects or representation. Thus, Habermas argues, we

should distinguish this type of clientele bargaining from the "supplier" groups, associations, and organizations that, before parliaments and through the courts, give voice to social problems, make broad demands, articulate public interests or needs, and thus attempt to influence the political process more from a normative point of view than from the standpoint of particular interests. The spectrum extends from organizations representing clearly defined group interests; through associations (with goals recognizably defined by party politics) and cultural establishments (such as academies, writers' associations, and "radical professionals"); up to "public-interest groups" (with public concerns, such as the protection of the environment, the testing of products, and the protection of animals) and churches or charitable organizations. These opinion-forming associations, which specialize in issues and contributions and are generally designed to generate public influence, belong to the civil-social infrastructure of a public sphere dominated by the mass media. With its informal, highly differentiated and cross-linked channels of communication, this public sphere forms the real periphery. (Ibid., 355–56)

45. Jane Mansbridge, *Why We Lost the ERA* (Chicago: University of Chicago Press, 1986).

46. Verba, Schlozman, and Brady, *Voice and Equality,* chap. 12.

47. The following analysis is taken, with revisions, from Warren, "Democratic Theory and Self-Transformation."

48. Carmen Sirianni, "Production and Power in a Classless Society: A Critical Analysis of the Utopian Dimensions of Marxist Theory," *Socialist Review* 59 (1981): 33–82; Warren, "Deliberative Democracy and Authority."

49. Robert E. Lane, *The Market Experience* (Cambridge: Cambridge University Press. 1991).

50. Hirschman, *Exit, Voice, and Loyalty,* 101–2. See also E. S. Savas's discussion of the logic of providing public material goods: *Privatization: The Key to Better Government* (Chatham, NJ: Chatham House Publishers, 1987), chap. 3.

51. Cf. Cole, *Social Theory,* 32–38.

52. Status goods include what Fred Hirsch termed "positional goods" in *Social Limits to Growth* (Cambridge: Harvard University Press. 1976). A positional good is a material good whose supply is fixed and is degraded by demand—a beach, for example, or space on a public highway. Status attaches to positional goods when one's relative income allows one to avoid the degradation of the good—as when one has access to a private beach.

53. This is the key point in Nancy Rosenblum's critique of identity-based associations in *Membership and Morals,* chap. 9.

Chapter Six
The Democratic Effects of Associational Types

1. Clyde Wilcox, "The Christian Right in Virginia: A Mixed Blessing," presented at the Conference on Civil Society in the United States, Georgetown University, June 1999.

2. Albert Camus, "The Just Assassins," in *"Caligula" and Three Other Plays* (New York: Knopf, 1958).

3. Verba, Schlozman, and Brady, *Voice and Equality*, chap. 6.

4. Cf. ibid., 503–6.

5. Cf. Nancy Rosenblum's nuanced of account of the "fusion republicanism" that characterizes the ideology of many such groups. *Membership and Morals*, chap. 8.

6. Carmen Sirianni, "Civic Environmentalism as Community Problem Solving and Public Policy for Democracy," presented at the Conference on Civil Society in the United States, Georgetown University, June 1999.

7. Hirschman, *Exit, Voice, and Loyalty*, 49.

8. Cf. Warren, "Democratic Theory and Trust."

9. These speculations are supported in part by Kuklinski et al., "The Cognitive and Affective Bases of Political Tolerance Judgments." Kuklinski and his colleagues found that in experimental settings, considered deliberation and tolerance trade off against each other. Stolle's findings that in the United States relatively homogeneous groups can have an independent effect in cultivating the generalized trust that extends beyond the group are also suggestive in this regard. See "Making Associations Work."

10. Verba, Schlozman, and Brady, *Voice and Equality*, 505, find that in the United States membership in a religious congregation has a small negative effect on tolerance. Since these effects aggregate a large number of denominations, they should not be generalized to all denominations. Indeed, some may have precisely the opposite effect. Quakers and Unitarians, for example, specialize in horizontal organization and count an inclusive civicness as part of their ethos.

11. Wilcox, "The Christian Right in Virginia"; Clyde Wilcox and Ted G. Jelen, "Evangelicals and Political Tolerance," *American Politics Quarterly* 18 (1990): 25–46.

12. Robert Putnam, in *Making Democracy Work*, 107, argues that in Italy organized religion is "an alternative to civic community, not part of it." In the case of the Catholic Church, as Putnam suggests, lack of civicness probably has less to do with identity than with the ways vertical relations displace horizontal relations, leaving no room for reciprocity and the civic virtues that follow from it. Putnam's suggestions are generalized by Ronald Inglehart, "Trust, Well-Being and Democracy," in *Democracy and Trust*, ed. Mark E. Warren (Cambridge: Cambridge University Press, 1999), 88–120; Inglehart finds that people in historically Catholic countries score markedly lower in social trust than do people in other countries. It may be that the historical effects of Protestantism, especially when compared to those of Catholicism and today's fundamentalist Protestant sects, tend toward civic cultures. Historically, Protestantism emphasized an inclusive equality, which may have contributed to an ethos attuned to cooperative forms of collective action.

13. Consistent with this hypothesis, Carmen Sirianni finds these effects generated by community-based environmental groups. See "Civic Environmentalism as Community Problem Solving and Public Policy for Democracy."

14. Eric Uslaner, "Democracy and Social Capital," in *Democracy and Trust*, ed. Mark E. Warren (Cambridge: Cambridge University Press, 1999), 121–50.

15. Cf. my analysis of these effects in "The Self in Discursive Democracy."

16. In his extensive study of associations that provide services to the handicapped, for example, Ralph Kramer notes that it is not feasible to expect social service providers to engage in political advocacy, "since most of the public support for voluntary agencies and most of their influence are derived from their legitimacy, credibility, and expertise as service providers." *Voluntary Agencies in the Welfare State* (Berkeley and Los Angeles: University of California Press, 1984), 261–62.

17. Cited by Van Til, *Growing Civil Society*, 224.

18. The reliance on communicative power by "citizen groups" that have "postmaterial" goals is documented by Berry, *The New Liberalism*, 24–25. The credibility of and trust in such citizen groups is much higher than for other politically oriented groups. See 130–37. This effect may follow from the public nature of these groups (they have nothing to hide), combined with the public and social qualities of the goods they seek (they are not "special interests").

19. Cf. Szasz, "Progress through Mischief."

20. Nancy Rosenblum emphasizes the limits of ascriptive identity groups with respect to representation, which follow from the fact that spokespersons are self-selected and not accountable to members. This is a specific instance of a more general problem: unless they are very carefully structured so as to encourage and take account of members' voices, associations with constrained exit will be unable to speak legitimately for their members. *Membership and Morals*, 339–43.

21. Cf. Charles E. Lindblom's elegant statement of the problem in "The Market as Prison," *Journal of Politics* 44 (1982): 324–36.

22. Kramer, *Voluntary Agencies in the Welfare State*, 263.

23. Ibid., 265–67.

24. Cf. Gutmann and Thompson, *Democracy and Disagreement*, chap. 3. In some cases there are reasons to shelter some deliberative processes from broad public exposure, at least initially. Sometimes foreign policy decisions require strategic secrecy; sometimes scientific discourses are conducted in languages that are unsuited to public discourse. In both cases, however, the results ought to be publicly justifiable. Knowing that results will eventually be subject to public scrutiny should place on notice those engaging in sheltered discourses. Cf. Warren, "Deliberative Democracy and Authority."

25. Carmen Sirianni, "Civic Environmentalism as Community Problem Solving and Public Policy for Democracy."

26. Habermas, *Legitimation Crisis*, 70, italics removed.

Chapter Seven
Conclusion: Democratic Associational Ecologies

1. These are the key arguments in Francis Fukuyama, *Trust*, and Putnam, *Making Democracy Work*.

2. The Pew Research Center for the People and the Press, *Trust and Citizen Engagement in Metropolitan Philadelphia: A Case Study* (Washington, DC: Pew Research Center, 1997), 72–77. Cf. Skocpol, "Associations without Members."

3. Verba, Schlozman, and Brady, *Voice and Equality*, chap. 12, esp. 363.

4. Ibid., 332–33.

5. Ibid., 333.

6. It is peculiar to Protestant universalism, however, that exclusion is unstable: because of Protestanism's missionary element, its members seek to involve others. In some social contexts, these elements can produce a dogmatic emphasis on tolerance, understanding, and love.

7. Verba, Schlozman, and Brady, *Voice and Equality*, 505.

8. Rosenblum, *Membership and Morals*. Cf. my discussion of Rosenblum, chap. 2 above.

9. Tocqueville, *Democracy in America* 2:565–67.

10. Cf. Michael Walzer's conception of "complex equality" in *Spheres of Justice*.

11. Beck, *The Reinvention of Politics*, chap. 3. Cf. Ronald Inglehart's argument that a "postmodern" (antiauthoritarian) ethic is gaining ground on a generational replacement basis. *Culture Shift in Advanced Industrial Society* (Princeton: Princeton University Press, 1990).

12. Cf. Gutmann, "Freedom of Association," 7. Contrast Soifer, *Law and the Company We Keep*.

13. Teubner, "Substantive and Reflexive Elements in Modern Law."

14. Van Til, *Mapping the Third Sector*, 118–20.

15. Van Til, *Growing Civil Society*, 224.

16. Van Til, in *Mapping the Third Sector*, 114–20, provides an illuminating account of the pervasive "boundary wars" between these "third sector" associations, for-profit organizations, and government.

17. Cf. Offe, "Some Skeptical Considerations on the Malleability of Representative Institutions," 128–30.

18. Rosenblum, *Membership and Morals*, 84.

19. Cf. Stuart White, "Trade Unionism in a Liberal State," 349.

20. Gutmann, "Freedom of Association," 6.

21. Ibid., 7.

22. Ibid., 8.

23. Inglehart, *Culture Shift*.

24. The thesis that civic America is in decline is argued by Robert Putnam, "Bowling Alone: America's Declining Social Capital." *Journal of Democracy* 6 (January 1995): 65–78. See also Skocpol, "Associations without Members." The Putnam-Skocpol thesis has been criticized for focusing on more traditional forms of association rather than emerging forms. See Everett Carll Ladd, *The Ladd Report* (New York: Free Press, 1999); and W. Lance Bennett, "The Uncivic Culture: Communication, Identity, and the Rise of Lifestyle Politics," *PS: Political Science and Politics* 31 (December 1998): 741–61.

25. Berry, *The New Liberalism*, chap. 3.

26. Ibid., 55–59. These findings are corroborated by Julian Wolpert's findings that associations within regions and communities are more effective at addressing cultural issues than structural economic inequalities. "Civil Society and Governance in a Regional and Community Context."

27. Bennett, "The Uncivic Culture," 749; Offe, *Modernity and the State*, chap. 1; Beck, *The Reinvention of Politics*.

28. Cf. Jean Cohen's analysis of the "decline of social capital" thesis, "Trust, Voluntary Association, and Workable Democracy: The Contemporary American Discourse of Civil Society," in *Democracy and Trust*, ed. Mark E. Warren (Cambridge: Cambridge University Press, 1999), 208–48.

29. Connolly, *Identity/Difference*; Beck, *The Reinvention of Politics*.

30. Bennett, "The Uncivic Culture," 551–53.

31. Cf. Dryzek, *Democracy in Capitalist Times*, chap. 4; David Held, *Democracy and the Global Order: From the Modern State to Cosmopolitan Governance* (Stanford, CA: Stanford University Press, 1995).

Bibliography

Almond, Gabriel, and Sidney Verba. *The Civic Culture: Political Attitudes and Democracy in Five Nations*. Princeton: Princeton University Press, 1963.

Arendt, Hannah. *Between Past and Future*. New York: Viking, 1968.

———. *The Human Condition*. Chicago: University of Chicago Press, 1958.

———. *Lectures on Kant's Political Philosophy*. Chicago: University of Chicago Press, 1982.

Barber, Benjamin. *The Conquest of Politics: Liberal Philosophy in Democratic Times*. Princeton: Princeton University Press, 1988.

———. *Strong Democracy*. Berkeley and Los Angeles: University of California Press, 1984.

Beck, Ulrich. *The Reinvention of Politics: Rethinking Modernity in the Global Social Order*. Translated by Mark Ritter. Cambridge: Polity Press, 1997.

———. *Risk Society: Toward a New Modernity*. Translated by Mark Ritter. London: Sage Publications, 1992.

Beiner, Ronald. *Political Judgment*. Chicago: University of Chicago Press, 1983.

Bell, Daniel A. "Civil Society versus Civic Virtue." In *Freedom of Association*, ed. Amy Gutmann, 239–72. Princeton: Princeton University Press, 1998.

Bellah, Robert N., Richard Madsen, William M. Sullivan, Ann Swidler, and Steven M. Tipton. *The Good Society*. New York: Alfred A. Knopf, 1991.

Benhabib, Seyla. "Toward a Deliberative Model of Democratic Legitimacy," In *Democracy and Difference: Contesting the Boundaries of the Political*, ed. Seyla Benhabib, 67–94. Princeton: Princeton University Press, 1996.

Bennett, W. Lance. "The Uncivic Culture: Communication, Identity, and the Rise of Lifestyle Politics." *PS: Political Science and Politics* 31 (December 1998): 741–61.

Berry, Jeffrey M. *The New Liberalism and the Rising Power of Citizen Groups*. Washington, DC: Brookings Institution Press, 1999.

Bohman, James. "Democracy as Inquiry, Inquiry as Democratic: Pragmatism, Social Science, and the Cognitive Division of Labor." *American Journal of Political Science* 43 (1999): 590–607.

Bowles, Samuel, and Herbert Gintis. *Democracy and Capitalism: Property, Community, and the Contradictions of Modern Social Thought*. New York: Basic Books, 1986.

Brady, Henry E., Kay L. Schlozman, Sidney Verba, and Laurel Elms. "Who Bowls? Class, Race, and Changing Participatory Equality." Presented at the Annual Meeting of the American Political Science Association, September 1998.

Camus, Albert. "*Caligula*" *and Three Other Plays*. New York: Knopf, 1958.

Chapman, John W. "Voluntary Association and the Political Theory of Pluralism." In *Voluntary Associations*, NOMOS XI. Ed. J. Roland Pennock and John W. Chapman, 87–118. New York: Atherton Press, 1969.

Cohen, Jean. "Interpreting the Notion of Civil Society." In *Toward a Global Civil Society*, ed. Michael Walzer, 35–40. Providence, RI, and Oxford: Berghahn Books, 1995.

Cohen, Jean. "Trust, Voluntary Association and Workable Democracy: The Contemporary American Discourse of Civil Society." In *Democracy and Trust*, ed. Mark E. Warren, 208–48. Cambridge: Cambridge University Press, 1999.

Cohen, Jean, and Andrew Arato. *Civil Society and Political Theory.* Cambridge: MIT Press, 1992.

Cohen, Joshua. "Procedure and Substance in Deliberative Democracy." In *Democracy and Difference: Contesting the Boundaries of the Political*, ed. Seyla Benhabib, 95–119. Princeton: Princeton University Press, 1996.

Cohen, Joshua, and Joel Rogers. "Secondary Associations and Democratic Governance." In *Associations and Democracy*, ed. Eric Olin Wright, 7–98. New York: Verso, 1995.

Cole, G. D. H. *Social Theory.* New York: Frederick A. Stokes, 1920.

Coleman, James S. *Foundations of Social Theory.* Cambridge: Harvard University Press, 1990.

Connolly, William. *Identity/ Difference: Democratic Negotiations of Political Paradox.* Ithaca: Cornell University Press, 1991.

Cooley, Charles Horton. *Human Nature and Social Order.* New York: Schocken Books, 1964.

Dahl, Robert. *Democracy and Its Critics.* New Haven: Yale University Press, 1989.

———. *A Preface to Democratic Theory.* Chicago: Chicago University Press, 1956.

———. *A Preface to Economic Democracy.* Berkeley and Los Angeles: University of California Press, 1985.

de Marneffe, Peter. "Rights, Reasons, and Freedom of Association." In *Freedom of Association*, ed. Amy Gutmann, 145–76. Princeton: Princeton University Press, 1998.

Dewey, John. *The Political Writings.* Edited by Debra Morris and Ian Shapiro. Indianapolis, IN: Hackett Publishing, 1993.

Dryzek, John. *Democracy in Capitalist Times: Ideals, Limits, and Struggles.* Oxford: Oxford University Press, 1996.

Durkheim, Emile. *Professional Ethics and Civic Morals.* London: Routledge and Kegan Paul, 1957.

Eisenstadt, S. N., and L. Roniger. *Patrons, Clients, and Friends: Interpersonal Relations and the Structure of Trust in Society*, Cambridge: Cambridge University Press, 1984.

Etzioni, Amitai. *The Active Society: A Theory of Societal and Political Process.* New York: Free Press, 1968.

Ferguson, Adam. *An Essay on the History of Civil Society.* Cambridge: Cambridge University Press, 1995.

Fleischacker, Sam. "Insignificant Communities." In *Freedom of Association*, ed. Amy Gutmann, 273–313. Princeton: Princeton University Press, 1998.

Fraser, Nancy. "Rethinking the Public Sphere." In *Habermas and the Public Sphere*, ed. Craig Calhoun, 109–42. Cambridge: MIT Press, 1992.

Fukuyama, Francis. *Trust: The Social Virtues and the Creation of Prosperity*, New York: Free Press, 1995.

Galston, William. *Liberal Purposes*. Cambridge: Cambridge University Press, 1991.

Gambetta, Diego. " 'Claro!' An Essay on Discursive Machismo." In *Deliberative Democracy*, ed. Jon Elster, 19–43. Cambridge: Cambridge University Press, 1998.

Gamwell, Franklin I. *Beyond Preference: Liberal Theories of Independent Associations*. Chicago: University of Chicago Press, 1984.

Granovetter, Mark. 1985. "Economic Action and Social Structure: The Problem of Embeddedness." *American Journal of Sociology* 91:481–510.

Greenawalt, Kent. 1998. "Freedom of Association and Religious Association." In *Freedom of Association*, ed. Amy Gutmann, 3–32. Princeton: Princeton University Press, 1998.

Gutmann, Amy. "Freedom of Association: An Introductory Essay." In *Freedom of Association*, ed. Amy Gutmann, 3–32. Princeton: Princeton University Press, 1998.

Gutmann, Amy, and Dennis Thompson. *Democracy and Disagreement*. Cambridge: Harvard University Press. 1996.

Habermas, Jürgen. *Between Facts and Norms: Contributions to a Discourse Theory of Law and Democracy*. Cambridge: MIT Press, 1996.

———. *Law and Morality*. The Tanner Lectures on Human Values. Vol 8. Salt Lake City: University of Utah Press, 1988.

———. *Legitimation Crisis*. Translated by Thomas McCarthy. Boston: Beacon Press. 1975

———. *Moral Consciousness and Communicative Action*. Translated by Christian Lenhardt and Shierry Weber Nicholsen. Cambridge: MIT Press, 1990.

———. *Postmetaphysical Thinking*. Translated by William Mark Hohengarten. Cambridge: MIT Press, 1992.

———. *The Structural Transformation of the Public Sphere*. Translated by Thomas Berger. Cambridge: MIT Press, 1989.

———. *The Theory of Communicative Action*. Vol. 2. Translated by Thomas McCarthy. Boston: Beacon Press, 1987.

Held, David. *Democracy and the Global Order: From the Modern State to Cosmopolitan Governance*. Stanford, CA: Stanford University Press, 1995.

———. *Models of Democracy*, 2d ed. Stanford, CA: Stanford University Press, 1996.

Hirsch, Fred. *Social Limits to Growth*. Cambridge: Harvard University Press, 1976.

Hirschman, Albert O. *Exit, Voice, and Loyalty: Responses to Decline in Firms, Organizations, and States*. Cambridge: Harvard University Press, 1970.

Hirst, Paul. *Associative Democracy: New Forms of Economic and Social Governance*. Amherst: University of Massachusetts Press, 1994.

———, ed. 1989. *The Pluralist Theory of the State: Selected Writings of G. D. H. Cole, J. N. Figgis, and H. J. Laski*. New York: Routledge.

Hodgkinson, Virginia Ann, Murray S. Weitzman, John A. Abrahams, Eric A. Crutchfield, and David R. Stevenson. *Nonprofit Almanac, 1996–1997: Dimensions of the Independent Sector*. San Francisco: Jossey-Bass Publishers, 1996.

Honneth, Axel. *The Struggle for Recognition*. Cambridge: MIT Press, 1995.

Inglehart, Ronald. *Culture Shift in Advanced Industrial Society*. Princeton: Princeton University Press, 1990.

———. "Trust, Well-Being, and Democracy." In *Democracy and Trust*, ed. Mark E. Warren, 88–120. Cambridge: Cambridge University Press, 1999.

Kant, Immanuel. *Kant's Political Writings*. Edited by Hans Reiss. Cambridge: Cambridge University Press, 1970.

Kateb, George. "The Value of Association." In *Freedom of Association*, ed. Amy Gutmann, 35–63. Princeton: Princeton University Press, 1998.

Kintz, Linda. *Between Jesus and the Market: The Emotions That Matter in Right-Wing America*. Durham, NC: Duke University Press, 1997.

Kornhauser, William. *The Politics of Mass Society*. New York: Free Press, 1959.

Kramer, Ralph. *Voluntary Agencies in the Welfare State*. Berkeley and Los Angeles: University of California Press, 1984.

Kuklinski, James H., Ellen Riggle, Victor Ottati, Norbert Schwarz, and Robert S. Wyer, Jr. "The Cognitive and Affective Bases of Political Tolerance Judgments." *American Journal of Political Science* 35 (1991): 1–27.

Kymlicka, Will. "Ethnic Associations and Democratic Citizenship." In *Freedom of Association*, ed. Amy Gutmann, 177–213. Princeton: Princeton University Press, 1998.

Ladd, Everett Carll. *The Ladd Report*. New York: Free Press, 1999.

Lane, Robert E. *The Market Experience*. Cambridge: Cambridge University Press, 1991.

Lifton, Robert Jay. *The Protean Self*. New York: Basic Books, 1993.

Lindblom, Charles E. "The Market as Prison." *Journal of Politics* 44 (1982): 324–36.

Lipset, Seymour Martin. *Political Man: The Social Bases of Politics*. Baltimore: John Hopkins University Press, 1981.

Lipset, Seymour Martin, Martin A. Trow, and James S. Coleman. *Union Democracy: The Internal Politics of the International Typographical Union*. Glencoe, IL: Free Press, 1956.

Locke, John. *Political Writings of John Locke*. Edited by David Wootton. New York: Penguin Books, 1993.

———. *Two Treatises of Government*. Cambridge: Cambridge University Press, 1963.

Luhmann, Niklas. *The Differentiation of Society*. Translated by Stephen Holmes. New York: Columbia University Press, 1982.

Macedo, Stephen. "Community, Diversity, and Civic Education: Toward a Liberal Political Science of Group Life." *Social Philosophy and Policy Foundation* 13 (Winter 1996): 240–68.

Macpherson, C. B. *The Life and Times of Liberal Democracy*. Oxford: Oxford University Press, 1977.

Mansbridge, Jane. "A Deliberative Perspective on Neocorporatism." In *Associations and Democracy*, ed. Erik Olin Wright, 133–47. London: Verso, 1995.

———. *Why We Lost the ERA*. Chicago: University of Chicago Press, 1986.

Merton, Robert K. *Theoretical Sociology: Five Essays, Old and New*. New York: Free Press, 1967.

Michels, Robert. *Political Parties; A Sociological Study of the Oligarchical Tendencies of Modern Democracy.* Translated by Eden Paul and Cedar Paul. New York: Collier Books, 1962.

Mill, John Stuart. *On Liberty.* London: J. W. Parker, 1859.

Nedelsky, Jennifer. "Reconceiving Rights as Relationship." *Review of Constitutional Studies* 1 (1993): 1–16.

Offe, Claus. *Modernity and the State: East, West.* Cambridge: MIT Press, 1996.

———. "Some Skeptical Considerations on the Malleability of Representative Institutions." In *Associations and Democracy,* ed. Eric Olin Wright, 114–32. New York: Verso, 1995.

Parsons, Talcott. *The Social System.* New York: Free Press, 1951.

———. *The System of Modern Societies.* Englewood Cliffs, NJ: Prentice-Hall, 1971.

Pateman, Carole. *Participation and Democratic Theory.* Cambridge: Cambridge University Press, 1970.

Patterson, Orlando. "Liberty against the Democratic State: On the Historical and Contemporary Sources of American Distrust." In *Democracy and Trust,* ed. Mark E. Warren, 151–207. Cambridge: Cambridge University Press, 1999.

The Pew Research Center for the People and the Press. *Trust and Citizen Engagement in Metropolitan Philadelphia: A Case Study.* Washington, DC: Pew Research Center, 1997.

Poggi, Gianfranco. *The State: Its Nature, Development, and Prospects.* Oxford: Polity Press, 1990.

Preuss, Ulrich. *Constitutional Revolution: The Link between Constitutionalism and Progress.* Translated by Deborah Lucas Schneider. Atlantic Highlands, NJ: Humanities Press, 1995.

Putnam, Robert D. "Bowling Alone: America's Declining Social Capital." *Journal of Democracy* 6 (January 1995): 65–78.

———. *Making Democracy Work: Civic Traditions in Modern Italy.* Princeton: Princeton University Press, 1993.

———. "The Prosperous Community: Social Capital and Public Life." *American Prospect* 13 (Spring 1993): 35–42.

Rawls, John. *A Theory of Justice.* Cambridge: Harvard University Press, 1971.

Riker, William H. *Liberalism against Populism.* San Francisco: Freeman, 1982.

Rosenblum, Nancy L. *Membership and Morals: The Personal Uses of Pluralism in America.* Princeton: Princeton University Press, 1998.

Sandel, Michael. *Democracy and Its Discontents: America in Search of a Public Philosophy.* Cambridge: Harvard University Press, 1996.

Savas, E. S. *Privatization: The Key to Better Government.* Chatham, NJ: Chatham House Publishers, 1987.

Schmitt, Carl. *The Crisis of Parliamentary Democracy.* Translated by Ellen Kennedy. Cambridge: MIT Press, 1985.

Schmitter, Phillipe. "The Irony of Modern Democracy and the Viability of Efforts to Reform Its Practice." In *Associations and Democracy,* ed. Eric Olin Wright, 167–83. New York: Verso, 1995.

Schmitter, Phillipe, and Wolfgang Streek. "Community, Market, State—and Associations? The Prospective Contributions of Interest Governance to Social Order." *European Sociological Review* 1 (1985): 119–38.

Schudson, Michael. *The Good Citizen: A History of American Civic Life*. New York: Free Press, 1998.

Schumpeter, Joseph. *Capitalism, Socialism, and Democracy*. New York: Harper and Row, 1942.

Scott, James C. *Seeing Like a State: How Certain Schemes to Improve the Human Condition Have Failed*. New Haven: Yale University Press, 1998.

Seligman, Adam. *The Idea of Civil Society*. Princeton: Princeton University Press, 1992.

Shils, Edward. *Political Development in the New States*. The Hague: Mouton, 1965.

Shore, Cris. "Community." In *The Blackwell Dictionary of Social Thought*, ed. William Outhwaite and Tom Bottomore, 98–99. Oxford: Basil Blackwell, 1994.

Sirianni, Carmen. "Civic Environmentalism as Community Problem Solving and Public Policy for Democracy." Presented at the Conference on Civil Society in the United States, Georgetown University, June 1999.

———. "Production and Power in a Classless Society: A Critical Analysis of the Utopian Dimensions of Marxist Theory." *Socialist Review* 59 (1981): 33–82.

Skocpol, Theda. "Associations without Members." *American Prospect* 45 (July–August 1999): 66–73.

Smith, David Horton. "Altruism, Volunteers, and Volunteerism." *Journal of Voluntary Action Research* 10 (1981): 21–36.

Soifer, Aviam. *Law and the Company We Keep*. Cambridge: Harvard University Press, 1995.

Stolle, Dietlind. "Making Associations Work: Group Characteristics, Membership, and Generalized Trust." Presented at the American Political Science Association Annual Meeting, 1998.

Szasz, Andrew. "Progress through Mischief: The Social Movement Alternative to Secondary Associations." In *Associations and Democracy*, ed. Eric Olin Wright, 148–56. New York: Verso, 1995.

Tamir, Yael. "Revisiting the Civic Sphere." In *Freedom of Association*, ed. Amy Gutmann, 214–38. Princeton: Princeton University Press, 1998.

Taylor, Charles. *Sources of the Self*. Cambridge: Harvard University Press, 1989.

Teubner, Günther. "Substantive and Reflexive Elements in Modern Law." *Law and Society Review* 17 (1983): 239–85.

Thompson, Dennis. "Mediated Corruption: The Case of the Keating Five." *American Political Science Review* 87 (1993): 369–81.

Tocqueville, Alexis de. *Democracy in America*. 2 vols. Translated by George Lawrence, edited by J. P. Mayer. Garden City, NY: Doubleday, 1969.

Tönnies, Ferdinand. *Community and Association*. 1887. Reprint, London: Routledge and Kegan Paul, 1955.

Truman, David. *The Governmental Process: Political Interests and Public Opinion*. New York: Knopf, 1971.

Uslaner, Eric. "Democracy and Social Capital." In *Democracy and Trust,* ed. Mark E. Warren, 121–50. Cambridge: Cambridge University Press, 1999.

Van Til, Jon. *Growing Civil Society: From Nonprofit Sector to Third Space.* Bloomington: Indiana University Press, 2000.

————. *Mapping the Third Sector: Volunteerism in a Changing Social Economy.* New York: Foundation Center, 1988.

Verba, Sidney, Kay Lehman Schlozman, and Henry E. Brady. *Voice and Equality: Civic Voluntarism in American Politics.* Cambridge: Harvard University Press. 1995.

Walzer, Michael. "The Civil Society Argument." In *Dimensions of Radical Democracy,* ed. Chantal Mouffe, 89–107. London: Verso, 1992.

————. "Michael Sandel's America." Delivered at the McDonough Symposium, Georgetown University Law Center, April 25, 1997.

————. "On Involuntary Association." In *Freedom of Association,* ed. Amy Gutmann, 64–74. Princeton: Princeton University Press, 1998.

————. *Spheres of Justice: A Defense of Pluralism and Equality.* New York: Basic Books, 1983.

Warren, Mark E. "Deliberative Democracy and Authority." *American Political Science Review* 90 (1996): 46–60.

————. "Democratic Theory and Self-Transformation." *American Political Science Review* 86 (1992): 8–23.

————. "Democratic Theory and Trust." In *Democracy and Trust,* ed. Mark E. Warren, 310–45. Cambridge: Cambridge University Press, 1999.

————. "Nonfoundationalism and Democratic Judgment." *Current Perspectives in Social Theory* 14 (1994): 151–82.

————. "The Self in Discursive Democracy." In *The Cambridge Companion to Habermas,* ed. Stephen K. White, 167–200. Cambridge: Cambridge University Press, 1995.

————. "What Is Political?" *Journal of Theoretical Politics* 11 (1999): 207–31.

————. "What Should We Expect from More Democracy? Radically Democratic Responses to Politics." *Political Theory* 24 (1996): 241–70.

Weber, Max. "Classes, Status Groups, and Parties." In *Selections from Max Weber,* ed. W. G. Runciman, trans. Eric Matthews, 57–61. Cambridge: Cambridge University Press, 1978.

White, Stuart. "Freedom of Association and the Right to Exclude." *Journal of Political Philosophy* 5 (1997): 373–91.

————. "Trade Unionism in a Liberal State." In *Freedom of Association,* ed. Amy Gutmann, 330–56. Princeton: Princeton University Press, 1998.

Wilcox, Clyde. "The Christian Right in Virginia: A Mixed Blessing." Presented at the Conference on Civil Society in the United States, Georgetown University, June 1999.

Wilcox, Clyde, and Ted G. Jelen. "Evangelicals and Political Tolerance." *American Politics Quarterly* 18 (1990): 25–46.

Wolfe, Alan. Review of Nancy Rosenblum, *Membership and Morals: The Personal Uses of Pluralism in America. New Republic* (June 1, 1998): 36–40.

Wolpert, Julian. "Civil Society and Governance in a Regional and Community Context." Presented at the Conference on Civil Society in the United States, Georgetown University, June 1999.

Robert Wuthnow. *Sharing the Journey.* Princeton: Princeton University Press, 1994.

Young, Iris Marion. "Polity and Group Difference: A Critique of the Ideal of Universal Citizenship." *Ethics* 99 (1989): 250–74.

Index